Knowledge, ideology and discourse

The traditional problems of the sociology of knowledge – the roles of power and knowledge, the status of relational knowledge, and the empirical analysis of knowledge – are here tackled from a new perspective. Tim Dant argues that, looked at from a sociological viewpoint, knowledge, ideology and discourse are different aspects of the same phenomenon. He draws on recent developments in social theory, such as discourse analysis, to reassert the central thesis of the sociology of knowledge that knowledge *is* socially determined.

In developing the argument, Dr Dant examines the major contribution of Karl Mannheim to the sociology of knowledge, traces the development of the theory of ideology in a Marxist tradition, and shows how discourse has become the central focus in structuralist analysis. Pointing out the link between the theoretical framework of the sociology of knowledge and the structuralist analysis of discourse, he also looks at recent work in the sociology of science, critical linguistics and the analysis of women's knowledge.

The book brings together a wide range of theoretical issues, but is always oriented to practical and empirical problems. Its lucid and accessible approach will appeal to students of the sociology of knowledge and to all who are interested in knowledge and its cultural context.

Tim Dant is Senior Lecturer in Sociology at Manchester Polytechnic.

Knowledge, ideology and discourse

A sociological perspective

Tim Dant

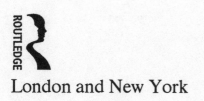

London and New York

First published in 1991
by Routledge
11 New Fetter Lane, London EC4P 4EE

Simultaneously published in the USA and Canada by
Routledge
a division of Routledge, Chapman and Hall Inc.
29 West 35th Street, New York, NY 10001

© 1991 Tim Dant

Typeset in Times by
NWL Editorial Services, Langport, Somerset

Printed and bound in Great Britain by
Mackays of Chatham PLC, Chatham, Kent

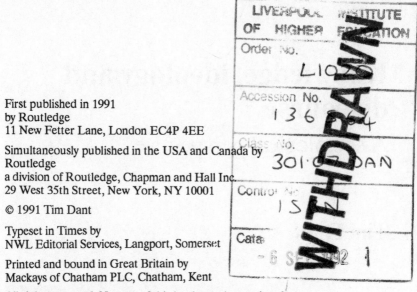

British Library Cataloguing in Publication Data
Dant, Tim
   Knowledge, ideology and discourse: a sociological
   perspective.
   1. Knowledge – Sociological perspectives
   I. Title
   306.42

Library of Congress Cataloging in Publication Data
Dant, Tim 1951–
   Knowledge, ideology and discourse: a sociological
   perspective / Tim Dant
   p.   cm.
   Includes bibliographical references and index.
   1. Sociology–Methodology.   2. Sociology–Philosophy.
   3. Knowledge, Sociology of.   4. Ideology.   5. Discourse
   analysis.
   I. Title.
   HM24.D35   1991   90–24337
   301'.01–dc20   CIP

ISBN 0–415–04786–2
     0–415–06458–9 (pbk)

To Olive and Doug

Contents

Acknowledgements

This book was derived from a doctoral dissertation, work that was supported by a studentship from the Social Science Research Council. I would like to thank Andy Tudor, who supervised my thesis and patiently read and commented on various drafts. Michael Mulkay, Jonathan Potter, Barry Sandywell and Janet Wolff also read and commented on various parts of the doctoral dissertation. With their comments in mind and with the aim of making a more readable statement, I derived this book from the dissertation. I am grateful for their interest and their comments – all errors, omissions, elisions, oversights and slips are of course mine.

Without Mollie's support, encouragement and critical reading I would never have managed to write it. And then write it again but smaller. Without Jo to remind me what life is really all about it would not have seemed worth it.

1 Introduction

Knowledge is a key feature of societies. It is part of what binds individuals and groups of humans into that larger group which we call society. It is a link between each of us and everyone else who shares our society and its culture. But it is also a key feature of the fragmentation between social groups. Differences in what people share as knowledge, not only in terms of their beliefs but also in terms of that unspoken knowledge hidden within social practices and customs, mark the differences between social groups. Knowledge is both part of what joins people in groups and what divides groups; it is a dimension of human life that involves agreement and disagreement, debate and negotiation. And yet, we tend to live as if knowledge could be settled, as if there is only one true knowledge which we are striving for and which we, each of us, is getting closer to. Together with those who share our perspective we agree on something which we might call 'truth'. But the knowledge of those with whom we disagree we treat as ideological, as being mere ideas, as not knowledge in the sense of something consistent with our lived reality.

As we negotiate with those who share our views and dispute with those who disagree, we do it through language. We talk, we write, we argue, we communicate – we even represent ideas in pictures, music, dance and movement, in material forms including sculptures, architecture and tools. All of these forms of cultural communication can be treated as discourse in the sense that they involve human beings exchanging meanings about the world in which they live.

Since the mid-1960s sociology has become increasingly concerned with knowledge. As the interpretative nature of systematic approaches to discovering social facts has been clarified and the presuppositions underlying scientist methodologies have been opened up to question, so attention has been turned towards social actors' own accounts of their social world. Methods of social research have been developed which attempt to use actors' knowledge of their own experience and of the world they live in. These methods are no longer exclusive to methodological clubs ('symbolic interactionism', 'ethnomethodology', 'phenomenological sociology') but have become part of a plurality of methods available to social researchers.

During the same period, the study of culture has also enjoyed great attention but with a shift of emphasis from the study of elite culture and its aesthetics towards the mainstream culture of newspapers, magazines, films and television. The studies of these mass media have addressed the various social processes surrounding the production of culture – the organizations and institutions which manage and control these organs of culture. But cultural studies have increasingly paid attention to the interpretation of the *meaning* of cultural products. These meanings which are consumed by so many members of the society are treated as a significant representation of the culture as a whole – they are taken to embody the values and concerns of society, or at least identifiable sub-sections of it. Whether it is because society is seen as determining of or determined by the media, its cultural products are treated as a summation of the common knowledge: knowledge which is potentially available to everyone in the society.

The period has also seen a shift of emphasis in social theory away from the attempt to sum up the whole of society, towards an explanatory framework into which any empirical data of different types would fit and towards an interest in philosophy and language. Since the mid-1960s social theory has been influenced less by sociologists and more than ever before by linguists, anthropologists, historians and philosophers. Of particular importance have been writers in the European critical theory and structuralist traditions and some of their work will be the focus of later chapters.

And yet there has been little synthesis of these three trends: the methodological shift towards qualitative methods, the increasing significance of mainstream culture, the piecemeal borrowing of social theory. While all these trends have been deeply concerned with knowledge (the knowledge of social actors, the embodiment of knowledge in cultural products, the presuppositions of knowledge about the social world) the sociology of knowledge has been increasingly neglected as an arcane and unproductive area.

The chapters of this book will progressively introduce theoretical issues from different approaches – the sociology of knowledge, the theory of ideology, structuralism, discourse and cultural analysis. As these different approaches are introduced some of the connections and common ground will be marked and some of the ways the different perspectives compliment each other will be suggested. As a whole, the book is intended as a sustained argument that the sociology of knowledge has a renewed relevance in contemporary sociology and can be developed in the light of theoretical and methodological advances relating to the critique of ideology and the structure of meaning.

The theme of the book is that knowledge, ideology and discourse are social processes that are inextricably linked; a sociological perspective of one necessitates consideration of the other two. But the aim of the book is more optimistic than just pointing to the links between these three processes. The real aim is to show that sociological analysis of knowledge and ideology is possible through the empirical analysis of discourse. This aim is not so grand as it sounds – much contemporary work is already doing this, although often not under the heading of the sociology of knowledge, and some of it will be referred to in Chapters 8 and 9. By situating certain types of discourse analysis in relation to the sociology of knowledge and the theory of ideology, those analyses can be established as contributions to sociology, and so to the critique and development of society.

The aims of the book are largely theoretical, drawing out the links between different types of existing work to establish bridges between what are often, at the moment, separate areas of inquiry. Once these bridges have been established however the attention will turn in the final chapters of the book to the practicalities of undertaking empirical analyses within the sociology of knowledge, taking into account the impact of the theory of ideology and utilizing techniques of discourse analysis.

KNOWLEDGE

The sociology of knowledge is both an important starting point and an appropriate topic to conclude with. It is the sociology of knowledge that gives the approach being developed its sociological perspective in contrast to much of the work that will be referred to in the sections on the theory of ideology (with its origins in political analysis) and on discourse (with its origins in linguistic and cultural analysis). The sociology of knowledge is a perspective which emphasizes the social character of knowledge. What we treat as knowledge is created by people in groups. It is the sociological features of the group that in large measure determine the content of knowledge and in even larger measure determine its form. Knowledge is produced as the people who make up society, work out their lives together. What is generated as knowledge and what is taken as knowledge reflects the values and the sociological features of the society.

This perspective that lies at the heart of the sociology of knowledge exists in tension with at least two opposing versions of the determinants of knowledge. In one version the origins of knowledge are located beyond human control, in an omniscient force – god. In this version god makes available knowledge to human beings through a variety of means: visions, the teachings of emissaries and prophets, religious writings, interpretations of these texts by holy men and the rulings of religious leaders. In the other version, the origins of knowledge are located within human beings. Knowledge is made available directly through particular actions of their own. In this second version, by following rules and procedures, those of 'science', the workings of the world are revealed to the minds of women and men.

In the religious version it is god who controls the revelation of knowledge and in the science version it is particular human activities that control the process (although there are always constraints: nature itself, lack of resources for following scientific activity, the limits of existing knowledge to pose questions and understand answers). But to put things so starkly is to imply a simple state of affairs; that 'versions' of the process of knowledge exist independently and in contrast. There is no practical reason why these two versions should not co-exist and even intermingle. All societies and most people seem to subscribe to both the religious and scientific versions of knowledge to some extent. These two versions may even be drawn on simultaneously although there are points of contradiction that are difficult to reconcile – the account of the origin of species for example.

The sociology of knowledge is a relatively new version of the process of knowledge which, in Mannheim's account, emerged at a certain point in the breakup of the unitary world-view provided by religion. This breakup is the consequence of the scientific version of knowledge (for Mannheim, rationalist thought) being successful in challenging the unified and all-encompassing power of the religious version. The sociology of knowledge emerges by explaining its own origins sociologically without recourse to the dogmatic formulae of either religion or science. This ability of the sociology of knowledge to consider not only knowledge in general; but also the knowledge produced by its own practice, involves a reflexivity that is both a strength and a weakness in the sociology of knowledge perspective. The spectre of relativism that accompanies reflexivity is often seen as a weakness but the ability to treat itself in the same way as the knowledge it studies means that the sociology of knowledge can never merely be an excuse for judging the merits and value of different types of knowledge.

It will help if I offer definitions of the categories of knowledge, ideology and discourse that I am using. By knowledge I mean the *construal of relations between abstract entities that are taken to represent the world of human experience, that can be shared by humans through communication and that can be used by them both to understand their experience of the world and to guide their actions.* The origins of the sociology of knowledge in the work of Karl Mannheim will be the focus of Chapter 2 and will be developed in Chapter 3 with a brief account of how those origins were responded to.

IDEOLOGY

The mode of description utilized by the early sociology of knowledge was characterized not only by a disarming, sometimes crippling, reflexivity but also by a form of critique that is characteristic of describing false knowledge: the analysis of ideology. By analysing the social situatedness of all world-views on the same basis using what he called the 'total conception of ideology', Mannheim was not aiming to dismiss or disregard that ideology as knowledge. He understood that what he called the 'particular conception of ideology' was effective as a political strategy because it pointed to the social situatedness of opponents' views (their basis not in 'truth' but in class or self interest). The same strategy for discounting opposing views has been found in scientists' strategies for accounting for others' errors (see Chapter 8). But analysis using the 'particular conception of ideology' always speaks from a position of superiority, assuming that its own perspective is not socially situated. Mannheim's 'total conception of ideology' incorporated the recognition that *all* perspectives were ideological and socially situated. To point to the social contingency of a particular knowledge claim is a traditional way of devaluing it; it is a discursive strategy. Yet the aim of the sociology of knowledge is precisely to focus attention on the social contingency of all knowledge. However, in contrast to the critic of particular ideology or scientists' errors, the sociology of knowledge does not need to contest the validity of knowledge because the perspective is agnostic as to truth or falsehood.

The development of the theory of ideology has moved away from the criticism of the particular conception of ideology – but it has not lost its potency as critique. The contemporary theory of ideology describes a process of socially contingent values, interpretations and taken-for-granted knowledge that is necessary for the operation of society. In this formulation, ideology is cast not as the bogey of false knowledge to contrast with the purity of science as truth, but as a process that is intertwined with all other social processes including science. The analysis of ideology demonstrates that cultural forms which obscure the concrete relations between human beings do not do so wilfully by following the conscious intentions of particular humans. Although some early accounts treated ideology as obscuring a 'true' version of circumstances which waited to appear once the ideological cloud was lifted, recent accounts take a more complex view.

A modern analysis of ideology recognizes that the repair and concealment of contradictions in the concrete form of human relations is necessary if those relations are to be lived. The acceptance of ideology as a characteristic of social being does not preclude transformation either of the lived or the imaginary relations of existence. But the achievement of liberation from domination does not follow from a neat epistemological solution or even from a transformation of the level of consciousness. What the modern theory of ideology does suggest is that through a critique of the process of ideology, the process can, at least partially, be made accessible to the will of human beings rather than contingent on the extant conditions of existence.

What I mean by ideology, then, is *the general determinative relationship between the social and material conditions of existence and the abstract relations construed in knowledge.* The generality of this relationship refers to the necessary form for the production of abstract relations, in particular the reduction from complex relations to more simple ones and the concealment of contradictions. Chapters 4 and 5 will look at the development of the theory of ideology in a Marxist tradition and at the problems of attempting to distinguish ideology and science or truth in a political account of society.

DISCOURSE

As the aims and perspective of the theory of ideology merge with those of the sociology of knowledge, techniques of reflexivity and critique can be refined to guard against the tendencies to dogma and mechanism present in the religious and science based versions of the process of knowledge. But a problem remains – how shall substantive analysis of knowledge/ideology proceed? What will be the object of study and what techniques shall be utilized? Mannheim took 'thought' as his object of study; sometimes 'modes of thought', or 'world-views'. As an object of empirical study 'thought' is difficult to pin down because it does not have a material form that can be located in time and space prior to summation and interpretation by the analyst. Mannheim's insights on conservatism, the intelligentsia, utopianism and the tension between generations seem to be arrived at despite any clear or convincing articulation of where another analyst should look for the 'thought'. In the early sociology of science, the most successful development from Mannheimian sociology of knowledge, analytical attention was focused on the social origins of knowledge rather than on the contents of knowledge. The contents of knowledge (scientific knowledge) were largely taken for granted; the problem was to find out how such knowledge was produced.

'Discourse' emerges as an appropriate object of study in a number of places at more or less the same time. Within the tradition that is concerned with the critique of ideology, attention was turned towards hermeneutics and the pragmatics of communication. Another branch of the same tradition is enmeshed with an approach that derives from structural linguistics. In structuralism and 'post-structuralism' a variety of techniques for the analysis of discourse are explored. The object of study ranges from the single utterance, to the text, to the episteme but all are related to each other as constituting 'discourse'. In characterizing the linguistic production of human beings as 'discourse', the structuralist approach takes seriously both the form and content of language. The various contents of discourse are related according to their form. The consistency of structural features of discourse is also related to social features of the context of utterance: the processes of power, the presuppositions that underlie discourse, the connotative references to other discourses and other social processes obscured by taken-for-granted participation in discourse.

By discourse then, I mean *the material content of utterances exchanged in social contexts that are imbued with meaning by the intention of utterers and treated as meaningful by other participants*. Intentionality marks the exchange as meaningful but, although it may contribute to it, does not constitute the meaning of discourse. Meaning is a property of the structural features (both synchronic and diachronic) of discourse. Chapters 6 and 7 will look at the development of structuralism which both delivers a particular way of understanding knowledge and within which a number of ways of studying discourse emerge.

While the philosophical rumblings of critical theory and structuralism generated an object of study in 'discourse', the empirical and academic traditions of linguistics and the sociology of science developed techniques of inquiry that are appropriate for the analysis of the interactive features of everyday speech or major debates at the frontiers of knowledge. Language, including non-linguistic modes of communicating meaning, is shown to mean more than just what utterers say. Interpretation of discourse by looking beyond just the content, draws on three contextual settings which contribute to the construal of meaning:

1   the structural context (the way language is used to convey meaning)
2   the wider discursive context (what is uttered before and after and in other discourses)
3   the social context (the power relations embodied in and realized by the discourse)

The way that the sociology of science has moved towards the analysis of discourse as a strategy for studying knowledge will be looked at in Chapter 8 as will different work that has begun to explore the ways in which language has ideological effects. Chapter 9 will look at some broader cultural views of the construction of understanding and ideology and refer to some of the issues in understanding perspectives brought out by feminism.

Social knowledge, as it is shared by people, exists as discourse. Knowledge becomes and is available for sharing when it is uttered; either spoken or written down. Certain formalized types of knowledge may reside within people (the teacher, the technician, the skilled worker) but they acquire or transfer their knowledge through discourse. The social practices surrounding the generation, dissemination, acquisition, review and criticism of knowledge all take place as discourse. Discourse is then an appropriate object for study by the sociology of knowledge. While analysis need not debate the truth or falsity of knowledge, it can provide a critique of it by analysing its origins in structural, wider discursive and social contexts. In Chapter 10 the implications of the different approaches will be drawn together and some sociological issues relating to power and social agency will be discussed. In Chapter 11 the idea of analysing discourse as the process of exchanging meaning will be explored with some examples. The final chapter, Chapter 12 will draw some conclusions and begin to own up to some omissions.

2 Mannheim's sociology of knowledge

The most influential figure in the tradition of the sociology of knowledge is Karl Mannheim. His work, especially that in *Ideology and Utopia*, covers a set of issues that characterize subsequent discussions of the sociology of knowledge. In this chapter I will attempt to present these issues in terms of Mannheim's own work and in the following chapter I will look at criticisms and developments of Mannheim's comments by subsequent writers. Of course the social role of knowledge played a part in the study of social forms long before the contribution of Karl Mannheim. Perhaps of most importance in the sociological tradition is Durkheim's account of the interconnections between religious and scientific forms of knowledge with particular forms of social life (see Hamilton 1974: 103–19). There is also a continuing tradition of anthropological work which addresses the links between types of knowledge or thought and social forms (e.g. Horton and Finnegan 1973). This book will, however, concentrate on a Mannheimian tradition in the sociology of knowledge with its particular interests in the social process of ideology and the empirical analysis of knowledge – both of which remain of contemporary concern within the sociological perspective.

The sociology of knowledge is an unusual field within sociology. It cannot be understood merely as the application of a sociological approach to the understanding of a particular aspect of social life. The field of inquiry that Mannheim presents under the rubric of 'sociology of knowledge' involves a reflection on the possibilities of sociological understanding in general. This means that at the centre of Mannheim's proposals for the sociology of knowledge, there are epistemological issues that are important to the whole of sociology. In this sense it is not so much a subdivision of sociology as an approach in its own right that establishes a particular relationship to history, philosophy, sociology, politics and social psychology. The sociology of knowledge might best be understood then as a 'perspective' that bears on topics also dealt with by these different disciplines. Mannheim developed the perspective of the sociology of knowledge in the context of political strife in central Europe. He later went on to attempt to utilize the perspective as a basis for suggestions about how society may be organized in a peaceful, systematic and relatively harmonious way (Mannheim 1940; 1943).

In the political debates of the 1920s in Europe, Mannheim saw that the different political positions were coherent as 'world-views' that expressed the social and historical situations of particular social groups. These world-views were 'rational' within the historical context and interests of the particular groups that held them. The Marxist concept of 'ideology' seemed useful in pointing to the relationship between world-view and the practical experiences and interests of a group. But for Mannheim the Marxist account of ideology was limited; firstly, by its reduction of the determination of ideology to class groups and political-economic interests and, secondly, by not being able to reflect on Marxism itself as an ideology. He proposed the sociology of knowledge as a perspective that could understand the various world-views as contingent on the experience and interests of particular groups. By treating all such views as ideological (that is, at least partly socially determined) the sociology of knowledge would be able to bridge the competing political perspectives. This totalizing perspective of the sociology of knowledge, unattached to any particular class or social interest group, would then be available as the basis for a 'science of politics'. Mannheim believed that with a sound understanding of which political positions were merely reflective of group interests (ideologies) and which were an attempt to transform society (utopias), political science would be able to bridge the stagnating conflict of open political debate.

At the beginning of the 1990s this grand project seems hopelessly naive – although I have somewhat misrepresented the depth and sincerity of Mannheim's work by summing it up in this way. But I have done so to point up the hopelessness of his project if it is taken as a whole and to show why I will be extracting the sociology of knowledge from his overall project of a science of politics. I will bring out certain themes in his account of the sociology of knowledge that I wish to argue can be the basis of a much more prosaic project. I do not intend to discuss Mannheim's later work on social planning, social psychology, culture or education or to attempt any sort of intellectual history. Neither will I attempt to situate Mannheim's work intellectually or politically in the period in which it was produced.

What I will discuss in relation to Mannheim's work are the proposals in it for understanding 'knowledge' as a phenomenon that is contingent, both in its content and in its form, on social processes. I shall argue in Chapter 10 that these 'social processes' are the discursive practices that produce what is treated as knowledge. The principal theme that I will concentrate on in these early chapters is the idea that the sociology of knowledge is not dependent on reducing 'knowledge' to any epistemological criteria. For Mannheim this meant respecting and attempting to understand differing knowledges or world-views. The attempt is made by interpreting them in terms of a 'totality' that might be seen as an incorporation of differing knowledges. For the sociology of knowledge that I wish to draw out of Mannheim's work, its dependence on a form of relativism is most important. In so far as the sociology of knowledge resists evaluation on epistemological criteria, it also raises epistemological questions about its own status as knowledge. This characteristic reflexivity of the sociology of knowledge was an issue confronted by Mannheim as an integral component of analysis; it is important that the sociological theory of knowledge is not seen as operating from a superordinate epistemological position.

The programme for the sociology of knowledge that I do intend to abstract from Mannheim's work can be summarized:

1 knowledge can be understood sociologically as (partially) determined by the social configuration in which it emerges
2 the content and form of knowledge can therefore be analysed in relation to its social context without recourse to an evaluation according to epistemological criteria
3 sociological knowledge can claim no epistemological privilege and has, therefore, to reflect on its own knowledge products as relative to the context of their production.

This programme is embedded in Mannheim's essays on the sociology of knowledge and is part and parcel of his understanding of historicism, of world-views and of the interpretative methods of cultural analysis. In particular I will attempt to draw out Mannheim's conception of 'social being' and his conception of 'knowledge' as the socially derived meanings effective as a world-view for a social group.

THE SOCIOLOGY OF KNOWLEDGE

Mannheim describes what he takes to be the field of the sociology of knowledge in this way:

On the one hand, it aims at discovering workable criteria for determining the interrelations between thought and action. On the other hand, by thinking this problem out from beginning to end in a radical, unprejudiced manner, it hopes to develop a theory, appropriate to the contemporary situation, concerning the significance of the non-theoretical conditioning factors in knowledge.

(Mannheim 1936: 237)

The sociology of knowledge is then an inquiry into the relationship between thought and action. In this it is distinct from a philosophical or a psychological approach concerned with the immanent development of knowledge or thought. The study of the history of ideas with reference only to the theoretical factors conditioning thought, would ignore the effect of 'non-theoretical factors' that influence ideas through their basis in a social context. Simmonds (1978) argues forcefully against Mannheim's critics that there is no textual evidence to suggest that his theory proposed any simple causal relation in which the content of knowledge is completely determined by its social situation. Simmonds suggests that Mannheim, rather than having a causal model of determination, is interested in 'social connectedness' as a means to a further understanding of knowledge (Simmonds 1978: 26–9). There are two features of the context in which Mannheim sought a 'further understanding of knowledge' which are important in grasping why he proposed the sociology of knowledge in the way that he did.

Firstly, he saw that there was a breakdown in the unity of thought. This was due to the failure of the church to retain an intellectual monopoly on the way people thought of the world in which they lived. The breakdown of unity in thought was accompanied by the development of differing intellectual positions:

From a sociological point of view the decisive fact of modern times, in contrast with the situation during the Middle Ages, is that this monopoly of the ecclesiastical interpretation of the world which was held by the priestly caste is broken, and in the place of a closed stratum of intellectuals, a free intelligentsia has arisen.

(Mannheim 1936: 10)

This development of a multiplicity of ways of interpreting the world both made the sociology of knowledge possible and created a need for it. While Mannheim was not attempting to find a new basis for a unitary world-view, he felt the need for grasping different perspectives in such a way that each could understand the other. Importantly, he does not specify a cause for the breakdown but points to the continuity between changes in social forms and changes in the contents of thought. The breakdown is signalled by an 'organisational disintegration of the unitary church' (Mannheim 1936: 11) and at the level of thought, the same process is signalled by the emergence of 'those fundamentally new modes of thought and investigation, the epistemological, the psychological, and the sociological' (Mannheim 1936: 11) from the disintegration of a unified religious mode.

The second contextual feature that facilitated the emergence of the sociology of knowledge was the extensive debate in German academic circles about the methods of social research. This series of academic disputes or *Streiten* began within economics but extended into philosophy and the other social sciences in Germany, during the last two decades of the nineteenth century and the first few of the twentieth (Bryant 1985: chapters 3 and 4). Of particular relevance was the *Methodenstreit*, a long-running dispute over the role of positivism in the human sciences and the *Werturteilsstreit*, or value-judgements dispute. These disputes marked an absence of unity or agreement about the legitimate foundations of knowledge. Reconstructing 'sides' in the disputes or tracing a continuity in the contributions of Dilthey, Windelband, Rickert and Weber amongst others is not easy. But what is clear is that the intellectual environment to which Mannheim contributed was not characterized by a single perspective on the origins of knowledge. His sociology of knowledge incorporated a method which treated the historical actor as both the subject and object of analysis and focused on the very plurality of thought demonstrated by the *Streiten*. In reflecting on this context of plural thought from which the sociology of knowledge emerged, Mannheim was practising the sociology of knowledge by recognizing and incorporating a range of perspectives.

HISTORICISM

Mannheim was committed to a form of historicism that in a simple way locates his work as not positivistic, that is as not based on a reduction to empirical facts. His version of historicism is not 'full blown' because he does not embrace a Hegelian, absolute spirit as the motor of history. But he does see the process of history as a dynamic one, irreducible to specific forces. The adoption of historicism is an attempt to grasp the flow of history in its complexity and its totality; it is a mode of understanding rather than of explanation:

> Historicist theory fulfils its own essence only by managing to derive
> an ordering principle from this seeming anarchy of change – only by

managing to penetrate the innermost structure of this all-pervading change.

(Mannheim 1952: 86)

To achieve an historicist understanding, events have to be seen in terms of their antecedents. Change can be understood in terms of the limits and possibilities present in the situation prior to change so that in retrospect a law of development or evolution can be recognized. It is not an immutable law or one that can be grasped prior to the process and it is in this sense that Mannheim's historicism is an analytical tool rather than a teleology.

Even in the absence of a religious account of the historical process, history does not become meaningless. The historicist approach seizes on the power of human thought to recognize change as meaningful and not incoherent, and attempts to systematize it. By weaving together the causal significances recognized in the antecedents of specific phenomena, a grasp of the overall pattern or 'gestalt' of history is possible:

> As we integrate the element in question (the historical fact) into a totality, indeed a dynamic totality, and thence assess its meaning, our question becomes philosophical and the special science of history as well as the contemplation of life once again becomes philosophical. Whereas in the past it was a religious framework into which the various particular experiences were inserted so as to acquire a philosophical meaning, so now it is an historico philosophical vision, which increasingly refined and made more concrete in research, provides, with the help of the unifying principle of historicism, a philosophical interpretation for our world experience.
>
> (Mannheim 1952: 88)

Historicism, then, is an intellectual labour that provides a worldly basis for grasping the nature of social being in the absence of the religious view. While historical process has created the conditions for an historicist perspective it has not completely determined the contents of philosophy.

EPISTEMOLOGY

For Mannheim the way that differences in perspective can be grasped, without engaging in conflict, is by seeing the different positions as contingent on their particular histories. Intellectual history is not simply the history of ideas, but also the social history of the context in which ideas emerge. So for Mannheim historicism is intertwined with a particular theory of knowledge that questions the ability of epistemology to evaluate knowledge. He challenges the 'autonomy of theory' and accepts that in doing so the historicist becomes 'more or less an "irrationalist"' (Mannheim 1952: 94). But he claims that historicism is superior to an exclusively epistemological perspective:

> it can conceive the contrast not only in the antithesis of the theoretical systems, but can illustrate this contrast in terms of contrasting modes of behaviour.
>
> (Mannheim 1952: 93)

The interconnection between historicism and a theory of the social basis of knowledge is central to Mannheim's work. The very possibility of the sociology of knowledge is dependent on an ontology that formulates knowledge and social being and their relationship in a particular way. There is, for example, a limit to the possible degree of validity of knowledge claims. Mannheim casts this limit in contradistinction to an absolutism implied by an epistemological position that reduces the validity of knowledge to a systematic distinction between what is 'true' and what is 'false'. For Mannheim, epistemology is based on the category of the knowing subject explored in relation to a world of knowable objects. It has two polar extremes. One, an empiricist mode in which the knowledge of the subject is determined by objective factors (Mannheim 1936: 12). The other extreme is where the subject itself is explored for knowledge about the world and this mode is at the centre of the tradition of rationalist philosophy, exemplified in the Cartesian recursion to the knowing self (Mannheim 1936: 18).

Mannheim's historicist theory of knowledge attempts to cut across the subject/object polarity by situating the subject in history rather than reducing subjectivity to a psychologistic account of the operation of the knowing subject. In historicism, the repository of knowledge is located in the 'dynamic totality' of history rather than in either the knowing subject or a realm of objective factors. This means that absolute knowledge is impossible. The knowing subject cannot transcend the total process of history but can only attempt to grasp it.

RELATIVISM AND RELATIONISM

It is at this point that the vulnerability of an historicist theory of knowledge to the charge of relativism becomes clear. Mannheim was fully aware of the dangers of relativism: the collapse of any agreed basis for knowledge. His historicist theory of knowledge is an attempt to resist an absolutist position, dependent on a rigid ontological and epistemological orientation, that would lead to conflicting accounts of truth. At the same time he is trying to avoid the nihilism of an unconditional relativism which flows from the argument:

> that the assertion of relativity itself claims absolute validity and hence by its very form presupposes a principle which its manifest content rejects.
>
> (Mannheim 1952: 130)

Mannheim's solution is to argue that knowledge is 'perspectival' or 'positionally determined':

> That a view of history is 'positionally determined' means that it is formed by a subject occupying a distinct position in the 'historical stream', all parts of which – those occupied by us as well as those occupied by the object we examine – are constantly in transition and motion.
>
> (Mannheim 1952: 120)

In rejecting an absolutist form of knowledge, dependent on the logic of epistemology, Mannheim has to accept that all knowledge, including his own propositions, are not transcendent of the context of their emergence. That is, they will not necessarily endure over time since they are dependent on an historically specific quality:

> Thus it appears that the 'psychic-cultural' element is that component of history which cannot be interpreted 'progressively'; each epoch must re-interpret it anew from its own psychic centre.
>
> (Mannheim 1952: 122)

However, the possibility of knowledge is not completely restricted by its position in history. Firstly, if an historicist theory of knowledge is adopted, then knowledge from another epoch can be understood in terms of its own historical situation. Secondly, rational knowledge, 'civilization', can be understood by reason as being progressive and developmental. That is to say certain types of knowledge (exemplified by the natural sciences) will progress within an inner structure that remains static during changes between epochs. It is only 'cultural' types of knowledge (exemplified by philosophy, history and art) that are determined by the 'psychic' centre of an epoch and therefore have to be studied anew. The historicist theory of knowledge can study the one in the light of the other.

The term Mannheim used to distinguish his historicist approach to knowledge from absolutism and relativism is 'relationism'. In rejecting an epistemological evaluation of knowledge a non-evaluative approach is adopted:

> Relationism signifies merely that all of the elements of meaning in a given situation have reference to one another and derive their significance from this reciprocal interrelationship in a given frame of thought. Such a system of meanings is possible and valid only in a given type of historical existence, to which, for a time, it furnishes appropriate expression.
>
> (Mannheim 1936: 76)

Whereas absolutism evaluates according to the truth/falsity of the contents of knowledge, and relativism merely recognizes the impossibility of such an evaluation because of the multiplicity of truths, relationism eschews an evaluative approach in favour of understanding knowledge in its social context. The relationist position claims that knowledge is by no means illusory but is real and effective in guiding the business of actual life. The elements of meaning in any given situation derive their meaning from their reciprocal interrelationship in a given frame of thought and it is in this sense that knowledge is relational. The frame of thought and the web of interrelating meanings are situationally and historically specific however so that meanings and knowledge can be analysed only with reference to the context in which they occur.

KNOWLEDGE

The category of knowledge is tied to the practice of thinking or cognition for Mannheim, but he tries to avoid a psychologistic reduction to individual thought. It is then a 'style of thought' (Mannheim 1936: 3) that the individual learns from her group that Mannheim is treating as a mode of knowledge that has a social basis. He describes the individual as finding herself:

> in an inherited situation with patterns of thought which are appropriate to this situation and [she] attempts to elaborate further the inherited modes of response or to substitute others for them in order to deal more adequately with the new challenges which have arisen out of the shifts and changes in [her] situation.
>
> (Mannheim 1936: 3)

Knowledge then is social in two ways; it is present in the society into which the individual is socialized (Mannheim uses the analogy of learning a language) and it is also a resource shared by members of the society. Knowledge is given to the knowing subject through his social group, but what is 'inherited' is not the full content of knowledge or an exhaustion of the possibilities of thought for the individual. It is only the 'style' or 'pattern' of thought that is given. It is clear that 'knowledge' is not a category that is determined by its contents or by any specific structure. The notion of 'world-view' (*Weltanschauung*) is more nearly what Mannheim is talking about. The social basis of knowledge lies in the categories of meaning used to think or perceive or understand the world rather than in the full contents of cognition.

Mannheim's ontic realm of knowledge has then two components: the presuppositions pre-given to cognition and the contents of cognition. But the distinction is an analytic one and is not straightforwardly translatable into empirical categories. Rational, conscious thought that is organized and systematized (for example philosophy) may appear to be predominantly the product of cognition. But Mannheim's critique of epistemology claims that even this thought is based on presuppositions (see Mannheim 1952: 94). Irrational thought (for example art) is more clearly a-theoretical and therefore more easily recognizable as based on presuppositions.

It is a feature of Mannheim's category of knowledge that one level of distinction between types of knowledge is to do with the realm of reality taken to be the content of the knowledge. Put simply, knowledge of the natural world is taken to be less subject to ontological presuppositions than knowledge of the social world:

> Whereas in mathematics and natural science, progress seems to be determined to a large extent by immanent factors, one question leading up to another with a purely logical necessity, with interruptions due only to difficulties not yet solved, the history of cultural sciences shows such an 'immanent' progress only for limited stretches.
>
> (Mannheim 1952: 135)

This is an acceptance of some form of naturalism; the content of scientific forms of knowledge is determined by their own history because of the constancy of the natural phenomena they study. While it would be very difficult to accept this proposition today with developments in the philosophy and sociology of science, its importance here is as a component of Mannheim's category of knowledge. Knowledge is subdivided by its structure as thought (presuppositions/cognition) and by its topic as content (social/abstract).

If the production of knowledge is seen as a set of social practices rather than as merely cognitive ones then the issue of 'thought' can be put to one side. By social practice I mean that knowledge is not produced by one individual but by a community working more or less together.

Knowledge as a social product is not a resource over which an individual has exclusive control (though groups may have). It is interesting to note that Mannheim does not use the term 'consciousness' as equivalent to knowledge. In so far as the presuppositions given to the members of a group are existentially determining of knowledge, they are not conscious for that individual. The practice of the sociology of knowledge is designed to bring the unconsciously held presuppositions into consciousness but it is the sociologist with the totalizing perspective that engages in the reflection, not necessarily the members of the group holding the presuppositions.

SOCIAL BEING

Mannheim does not use a category of social practice but he does relate knowledge to social action:

> Men living in groups do not merely coexist physically as discrete individuals. They do not confront the objects of the world from the abstract levels of a contemplating mind as such, nor do they do so exclusively as solitary beings. On the contrary they act with and against one another in diversely organized groups, and while doing so they think with and against one another. These persons, bound together into groups, strive in accordance with the character and position of the groups to which they belong to change the surrounding world of nature and society or attempt to maintain it in a given condition.
>
> (Mannheim 1936: 3)

The social situation is for Mannheim based on collective action and a collective will to act in a particular way. The volition of the individual is, at least to some degree, subsumed under a group will that is not necessarily established by the conscious agreement of all participants. The individual does have some autonomy to think freely and creatively but this freedom operates within constraints that result from being a member of the social group. The analogy between presuppositions of thought and the learning of language that Mannheim uses is helpful in understanding his conception of social being:

> Only in a quite limited sense does the single individual create out of himself the mode of speech and thought we attribute to him; he thinks in the manner in which his group thinks. He finds at his disposal only certain words and their meanings. These not only determine to a large extent the avenues of approach to the surrounding world, but also show at the same time from which angle

and in which context of activity objects have hitherto been perceptible and accessible to the group or the individual.

(Mannheim 1936: 52)

The continuity between the categories of thought and speech that emerges in the category of meaning here is not an issue Mannheim pursues at the level of social practice. But he is clearly describing the individual as a social being for whom some contents of consciousness are given by being a member of a group. Importantly these contents of consciousness are equated with the cohesion of the group as a language community and not as an economic community. Although Mannheim frequently uses the Marxist category of class, especially when referring to political world-views or ideologies, he does not refer to a prime category of social group that shares a perspective, such as 'class' or 'nation state' or 'tribal family':

> If one were to trace in detail, in each individual case, the origin and the radius of diffusion of a certain thought-model, one would discover the peculiar affinity to the social position of given groups and their manner of interpreting the world. By these groups we mean not merely classes, as a dogmatic type of Marxism would have it, but also generations, status groups, sects, occupational groups, schools, etc.
>
> (Mannheim 1936: 247–8)

Indeed Mannheim resists the category of class as a political economic grouping by subsuming the politico-economic under the category of 'competition' which might be either an innate force or an approach learnt through the group. 'Competition' not only controls economic activity but also is the basis of interpretations of the world generated by conflicting groups struggling for power (Mannheim 1936: 241).

Mannheim's conception of social being is of a collectivity of individuals living in a group from which they inherit a language and a way of interpreting the world. This conception concentrates on the individual's experience in common with the social group; the language and presuppositions of the group are functional to the everyday activities of its members. The power of social being to determine thought is based on the continuity of presuppositions as they are passed on from member to member without conscious reflection. The functionality of the presuppositions to the collective experience explains their durability: why they are not questioned and why they are passed on. Frisby makes a similar point and quotes from an unpublished essay by Mannheim on the sociology of culture. For individuals:

> A large part of their total experiences are shared with other

individuals. These experiences which are, as it were, at hand and which are the experiences of individuals within the same society and community must, however, be structurally related to one another in the same way as in the case of the strands of experience within an individual stream of experience.

(Mannheim 1922 – quoted in Frisby 1983: 121)

For Mannheim then it is not the truth or falsity of presuppositions but their functionality for the group that makes them significant. For the individual member of the group these presuppositions are effective as meanings that enable experience to be shared and action to be collective. The individual will experience the presuppositions as meaningful only because it is for the group that they are functional:

> We belong to a group not only because we are born into it, nor merely because we profess to belong to it, nor finally because we give it our loyalty and allegiance, but primarily because we see the world and certain things in the world the way it does (i.e. in terms of the meanings of the group in question).

(Mannheim 1936: 19)

EXISTENTIAL DETERMINATION

The categories of knowledge and social being are tied together and mutually defining in Mannheim's ontology. Individuals exist together as a group on the basis of shared knowledge in the form of shared presuppositions that both enable the individual to experience the world and to act in it. In turn it is the capacity to share meanings, to engage in cognition with shared presuppositions, that constitutes the collectivity of action and will characterizing the social group.

It is important to remember that cognition is not totally determined by socially given presuppositions and that the individual can think creatively and reflectively on their experience and that of the group. For Mannheim this form of cognition is most dominant in rational thought that involves reflection on its own processes as knowledge (e.g. science and history). Even here, presuppositions are to some degree determinant of the content and form of cognition but the degree of determination varies with the sociality of the object of knowledge. Thus knowledge of the natural world is less governed by presuppositions than is knowledge of the social world. Presuppositions always lie behind the process of knowledge unless it is abstract in the sense of not having any given meaning in the social world, as is the case, for example (for Mannheim at least), with mathematics.

What Mannheim means by the existential determination of knowledge is that knowledge is, in part, determined by the experience of the knowing subject. This experience, in so far as it is to be considered determinative of knowledge, is not individual but shared with a social group; the 'existence' that is determinative then is that which constitutes the sociality of the group of which the knowing subject is a member. Existence cannot be reduced to a specific individual because the commonality of the group is not something contained within anyone but is the set of shared meanings that are potentially available to any individual member.

> Every individual participates only in certain fragments of this thought-system, the totality of which is not in the least a mere sum of these fragmentary individual experiences. As a totality the thought-system is integrated systematically, and is no mere casual jumble of fragmentary experiences of discrete members of the group.
>
> (Mannheim 1936: 52)

Mannheim's critique of epistemology attacks the reduction to the relation between the knowing subject and the object of knowledge that is involved in epistemology. His relationism is intended to supersede epistemology (for some purposes) and displace the knowing subject by establishing the relation between knowledge and social context. In that the 'style of thought', the presuppositions determinative of knowledge, are given to the individual as an 'inheritance' and unconsciously, the individual is unable to reflect on the extent that their thought is determined. And here is the radicalness of the sociology of knowledge; it challenges the idea that the knowing subject is constituted by its own cognition or reflection. Instead, the sociology of knowledge proposes that both the individual knowing subject and some of the contents of thought are determined by the specific social and historical existence of the individual. Mannheim leaves intact the immanent process of thought to the extent that knowledge is determined by 'theoretical' (i.e. cognitive) antecedence. His claim is merely that other 'non-theoretical' (i.e. existential) factors 'influence' the process of thought. Thus:

> The existential determination of thought may be regarded as a demonstrated fact in those realms of thought in which we can show ... that the process of knowing does not actually develop historically in accordance with immanent laws, that it does not follow only from the 'nature of things' or from 'pure logical possibilities', and that it is not driven by an 'inner dialectic'. On the contrary, the emergence and

the crystallization of actual thought is influenced in many decisive points by extra-theoretical factors of the most diverse sort. These may be called, in contradistinction to purely theoretical factors, existential factors.

(Mannheim 1936: 239-40)

While the sovereignty of the knowing subject is displaced by the existential determination hypothesis, it is not replaced by any other category of 'subject', such as a group mind (which Mannheim specifically rejects) or a transcendental historical subject. Mannheim is grounding knowledge in a concrete social basis while leaving some, relative, autonomy to the cognitive processes of the individual. Society does not totally determine the individual but influences the thought of the individual in a way which is not immediately available to her consciousness.

MEANING

We have seen that 'meaning' for Mannheim is shared by individuals in the sense that they share a set of presuppositions or a world-view. Mannheim was interested in the sociology of culture before he was interested in the project of the sociology of knowledge and in a way the interests are continuous; the sociology of knowledge is a particular form of the sociology of culture. In considering both culture and knowledge he was anxious to retain the creative quality of meaning and its interpretation is an integral part of the methods he proposed for the sociology of knowledge. The contents of meaningful forms cannot be reduced to components or decoded but have to be understood by a method of interpretation that recovers as much as possible in terms of the situation in which they are produced, for example, with reference to the historical context and relations to other similar meanings as in a genre or an art form.

Mannheim makes a distinction between 'objective' meaning, 'expressive' meaning and what he calls 'documentary' meaning. Objective meaning is that which is immediately given in an object:

If we look at a 'natural object', we shall see at the first glance that which characterizes it, and the modern scientific attitude appropriate to its study is the fact that it is taken as nothing but itself and is fully cognizable without being transcended or rounded out.

(Mannheim 1952: 44)

In contrast to 'natural' objects, 'cultural' objects are 'invariably vehicles of meaning' (Mannheim 1952: 44). Cultural objects do have objective meanings (the statue is a particular piece of marble) but also have 'expressive' meaning (the statue is beautiful) and 'documentary' meaning (the statue as an art form). The method of cultural analysis that Mannheim proposes involves interpreting cultural objects by progressing through their objective, expressive and documentary meanings to situate the meaning of the object in its social context.

Simmonds (1975; 1978), who is keen to explore Mannheim's sociology of knowledge as a hermeneutic method, suggests that Mannheim's theory of interpretation links meaning to specific intentions in a specific subject; the 'author' (Simmonds 1978: 65). But Mannheim says of 'cultural' meanings that they are:

> not integrally located either in the spatio-temporal world ... or within the psychic acts of the individuals who create or experience them.
>
> (Mannheim 1952: 44)

They are, as it were, in both of these worlds and the role of intentionality is to render a material form meaningful, to make it a cultural object. This provides only a starting point for interpretation and is quite clearly no basis for an interpretative method. Susan Hekman (1986) is, like Simmonds, keen to establish a link between hermeneutics and Mannheim's programme for the sociology of knowledge. However, she disputes Simmonds's account of the intentionality of the subject as the basis of Mannheim's method of interpreting meaning (Hekman 1986: 85), claiming instead that like Gadamer, Mannheim reflexively incorporates the role of the interpreter into the construal of meaning.

Mannheim's third level of interpretation, that of 'documentary' meaning, is specifically dissociated from the intentions of authors of acts:

> Nothing will be interpreted in terms of consciously intended meaning, or in terms of objective performance; rather, every behavioural datum will serve to illustrate my synoptical appraisal of his personality as a whole; and this appraisal need not be limited to his moral character – it may take his global orientation as a whole into its purview.
>
> (Mannheim 1952: 47)

The level of documentary meaning is difficult to grasp simply because meaning is so often related to authorial intent as in the everyday question 'What do you mean [by what you said]?' Mannheim even comments on the difficulty of interpreting documentary meaning self-reflexively (i.e. in regard to our own acts) because it is predicated on social being which does not reside in the individual knowing subject but in the world-view or set of presuppositions available to the individual actor through her membership of the group. In the analysis of documentary meaning, acts (or texts) are interpreted with reference to the potentially available meanings that provide the social context in which the act takes place (or the text is uttered).

Without dispensing completely with authorial intention as an interpretative resource, Mannheim is describing an interpretative method that refers to the context of meanings that surround the emergence of cultural objects. The intention of the actor is important in that it 'actualizes' the cultural object, that is, endows it as meaningful, as a social act that can be understood in the context of presuppositions available to that milieu. The interpretation of 'documentary' meaning, related as it is to the social context of meaning, is seen by Mannheim as a significant innovation and as a departure not to be confused with objective or expressive meaning.

AN OBJECT FOR ANALYSIS

Although Mannheim does not discuss at length the method of interpretation specific to the sociology of knowledge, he makes it clear that interpretation is central to the programme of the sociology of knowledge (Mannheim 1936: 272–3). The implication of interpretation being applied in the sociology of knowledge is that it will be applied to 'knowledge'. But Mannheim does not offer a straightforward account of what counts as 'knowledge' for empirical inquiry although he does suggest that words, as a repository of the meanings that constitute the presuppositions of social being, are a significant object for study:

> The slightest nuance in the total system of thought reverberates in the individual word and the shades of meaning it carries. The word binds us to the whole of past history and, at the same time, mirrors the totality of the present.
>
> (Mannheim 1936: 74)

I will argue in this book that it is not mere 'words' but the process of language as a social practice – discourse – that constitutes the most pertinent empirical object of study for the sociology of knowledge. In so far as Mannheim's method of interpreting documentary meaning dispenses with the knowing subject/intending actor as the reference for meaning and replaces it with the social context of meanings given to social practice, I will accord with his proposals for an interpretative method as the basis of the sociology of knowledge. But the documentary method implies a stability of meaning that lies behind the object; the cultural object is the document of its meaning. This is an untenable position within the relationism of the sociology of knowledge which draws attention to the limits imposed on interpretation by the socio-historical situation of the interpreter. Mannheim's notion of 'objective' meaning also seems to sit badly with his ontological position. The perception of any level of meaning in an object would seem to depend on the presuppositions available to social being and would therefore be prone to determination by existential factors. Indeed Mannheim virtually concedes this:

> although objective interpretation is concerned only with objective meaning and has nothing to do with empathic probing of subjective processes, it still is far from presupposing some unique and universally valid 'visual universe'.
>
> (Mannheim 1952: 51)

His point is that for the visual perception of cultural objects there is a level of meaning involving identifying physical form (its size, shape, bulk, texture, colour, etc.) that is less determined by the socio-historical specificity necessary for documentary meaning (what the object represents or signifies, what observers might take it to mean as a document of the world). Even so, I would argue that Mannheim's tendency to naturalism leads him to posit a more stable and consistent universe of natural objects than can be maintained once the relationist perspective of the sociology of knowledge has been adopted. The perception of physical form is not 'pure' in that what can be recognized is immediately related to other perceptions (as big as a house, as red as lips) even if no documentary meaning can be perceived.

IDEOLOGY

'Knowledge' is not an easily identifiable empirical category in Mannheim's account of the sociology of knowledge. He does however use the term 'ideology' to refer to a particular type of knowledge available for empirical analysis. It is particular in the sense that it refers to a political perspective and is associated with classes or political strata. 'Ideology' does not exhaust the possibilities of Mannheim's category of knowledge which does not refer exclusively to political presuppositions or the world-views of political groups. However, Mannheim's most explicit empirical analyses are about political knowledge and utilize the concepts of ideology and utopia.

Mannheim distinguishes three ways of using the concept of ideology. Firstly, in common language it often refers to lies or falsehoods in a pejorative way that makes no reference to the social basis of the content of the ideology. Mannheim rejects this usage in sociology because of its psychologistic basis; it refers to cognitive failure in the individual. The second usage he terms the 'particular' meaning of the concept of ideology which is a development of the common usage and refers to ideas at the level held by the group but still reduces them to the psychology of the individual. When in debate 'ideology' is used to characterize an opponent's position:

> it is still assumed that it is possible to refute lies and eradicate sources of error by referring to accepted criteria of objective validity common to both parties.
>
> (Mannheim 1936: 50-1)

The third meaning of ideology is in its 'total' conception – the one relevant to the sociology of knowledge. It calls into question:

> the opponent's total *Weltanschauung* (including his conceptual apparatus), and attempts to understand these concepts as an outgrowth of the collective life of which he takes part.
>
> (Mannheim 1936: 50)

Whereas the particular concept may grasp ideology in terms of the 'interests' of the individual, the total conception attempts to recover the outlook of the whole group with reference to its socio-historical setting.

The history of both the particular and total conceptions is, for Mannheim, the history of political ontology in which there is debate about the true form of reality; the opponent's position is ideological in that it is an incorrect account of reality (Mannheim 1936: 65). Mannheim recognizes the Marxist analysis with its total conception of ideology as being the most advanced in its account of the socio-historical context of ideology. However, a residue of the psychologistic reduction involved in the partial conception remains, as evidenced by the use of the concept of false consciousness. The Marxist use of the term ideology remains particular and political until it can be used reflexively; that is until Marxism can be recognized as ideology. This is what Mannheim calls the 'general formulation of the total conception of ideology' and is the conception necessary for the sociology of knowledge:

> What was once the intellectual armament of a party is transformed into a method of research in social and intellectual history generally.
>
> (Mannheim 1936: 69)

It is when all political accounts of reality are recognized as ideology that the concept becomes relevant for the sociology of knowledge. The diversity of political perspectives including the sociologist's own have to be recognized in their own socio-historical context of presuppositions. This sociological approach is no longer evaluative of the cognition of the holders of ideology since ideology is seen not as a function of a failure in consciousness but as a characteristic of the presuppositions contingent on a social context.

Mannheim's conception of ideology is informed by Marxism but is significantly different in that he attempts to break with the Hegelianism he see as dominating the Marxist perspective:

> The sphere of ultimate reality rested in the economic sphere and social sphere for it was to this that Marxism in the last analysis, related all ideas and values; it was still historically and intellectually differentiated, i.e. it still contained some fragment of historical perspective (due largely to its Hegelian derivation). Historical materialism was materialist only in name; the economic sphere was, in the last analysis, in spite of occasional denial of this fact, a structural interrelationship of mental attitudes. The extant economic system was precisely a 'system', i.e. something which arises in the sphere of the mind (the objective mind as Hegel understood it).
>
> (Mannheim 1936: 229)

The Hegelian tendency in Marxist thought meant that there was a resistance to recognizing the account of ideology as applicable to all political thought. It prevented the raising of the question of whether it was knowledge as such that was bound up with socio-historical location. For Mannheim, Marxism resisted the sociological generalization partly because of its position in a political debate. But the relationism of the sociology of knowledge would have fitted strangely with either the economic reductionist or more Hegelian versions of Marxism.

I will argue in Chapter 5 that the development of the Marxist theory of ideology confronts exactly this issue. The limits of a Hegelian account of ideology in the writings of Marx and especially Lukács, as well as the limits of a reductionist account, were the starting points for both Habermas and Althusser in their investigations of ideology. Both of these thinkers disengage with the concept of ideology as mere illusion, as a category of false knowledge, and develop ways of understanding ideology as consequent on socio-historical setting. They develop the Marxist account of total ideology that Mannheim saw as so valuable (Mannheim 1936: 115–16) and also develop an understanding of the relationship between ideology and social formation.

THE SOCIOLOGY OF KNOWLEDGE AND EPISTEMOLOGY

The lack of reflexivity that Mannheim saw as the limit of the total conception of ideology in Marxist thought is in a way the basis of the sociology of knowledge. Not only is knowledge recognized as having a basis in social context, but also this is recognized as a feature of all knowledge with the consequent loss of any interpretative frame except the relationist one; knowledge can be understood only in its relation to its socio-historical location. Mannheim does not reject the possibility of evaluative approaches to knowledge (e.g. those from an epistemological or political perspective) but does point out the limits of such approaches in understanding the social process of knowledge.

While he presents the sociology of knowledge as an empirical and interpretive study. Mannheim recognizes that it has epistemological consequences which he regards as within its proper domain. As the sociology of knowledge cannot help but 'particularize' knowledge (i.e. establish it as relational to a particular social context) it undermines the epistemological basis of such knowledge. Furthermore it undermines the project of epistemology as such:

> The theory of knowledge [i.e. epistemology] takes over from the concrete conditions of knowledge of a period (and thereby of a society) not merely its ideal of what factual knowledge should be, but also the utopian construction of a sphere of 'truth as such'.
>
> (Mannheim 1936: 261)

These comments are almost a pre-echo of Althusser's critique of epistemology (see Chapter 5) and Foucault's conception of the 'will to truth' (see Chapter 7). Mannheim does not however propose the abandonment of epistemology or its supersession by the sociology of knowledge. Instead he suggests that epistemology can be modified by the sociology of knowledge reflecting on the epistemological consequences of its findings. Mannheim suggests that the effect of this will be that epistemology will have to incorporate the idea that the genesis of a proposition has a bearing on its validity. The antecedents of an idea, which Mannheim suggests are relevant to its epistemological foundation, are to be revealed by an investigation of its 'meaningful genesis' (Mannheim 1936: 264). Again, this task sounds similar to that attempted by Foucault's genealogical method (see Chapter 7) although Mannheim gives insufficient detail for any serious comparison.

A further consequence for epistemology of recognizing the significance of the social basis of thought will be, Mannheim suggests, the investigation of knowledge in relation to action rather than knowledge as pure ideas. Mannheim is thinking of purposive action (that is action intended to achieve certain ends) and the fact that knowledge is not merely applied to action but is also generated in such action. This is an important development of Mannheim's conception of knowledge as presuppositions and provides the beginnings of a theory of the production of knowledge (Mannheim 1936: 265).

THE METHOD OF IMPUTATION

The reflective and epistemological aspects of the sociology of knowledge are dependent on its empirical project which involves the investigation of the social determination of substantive knowledge. This is in many respects the weakest area of Mannheim's proposals. I have suggested that the empirical category of knowledge is not clearly enough articulated but this is not the only problem. Mannheim proposes a method that he refers to as 'imputation'. The 'products of thought' – presumably articulated ideas – are to be imputed to the 'currents of thought' or *Weltanschauung* from which they emerged. The 'currents of thought', the perspective of the group, are in turn to be imputed to their origins in a set of 'social forces' (Mannheim 1936).

Mannheim's vagueness about the empirical form of these categories means that it is difficult to imagine how the method would work in practice. The process of imputation seems to involve ascribing particular ideas to particular social groups which, as we shall see, is an enduring problem for the sociology of knowledge. The sociological method of imputation also involves relating knowledge to social process; to changes in the social structure and the relations between social groups (Mannheim 1936: 278). But again, it is not clear what will count as evidence of links between knowledge and other social processes.

As part of Mannheim's method of imputation, the sociology of knowledge has to grasp whether the perspective is in accord with its social context. For example it must assess whether it is ideological (i.e. when it 'fails to take account of the new realities applying to a situation, and when it attempts to conceal them by thinking of them in categories which are inappropriate' – Mannheim 1936: 86) or utopian (i.e. when it 'seems to be unrealizable only from the point of view of a given social order which is already in existence' – Mannheim 1936: 177). This task goes beyond merely understanding knowledge in terms of its social context and involves a form of evaluation. Mannheim has proposed the sociology of knowledge as non-evaluative in respect of the truth or falsity of knowledge but the assessment of congruence to a social context is an evaluation of sorts.

Mannheim's account of the method and techniques of the empirical sociology of knowledge is brief and vague. It reintroduces the problem of evaluation and does not clarify what will count for empirical purposes as 'knowledge' or 'social being'. By not specifying what empirical data will constitute 'knowledge' for research, the problem of imputation to specific social contexts seems insurmountable. I will argue in Chapter 10 that if discourse is treated as the empirically recognizable process of knowledge production and use, then empirical instances are located historically and socially since discursive practice involves social action that can be identified in time and place.

THE INTELLIGENTSIA

The situation of the sociologist of knowledge is important because Mannheim has included in his method, the evaluation of the congruence of knowledge to its social context. He suggested that the social location of intellectuals was significant in achieving the perspective of the sociology of knowledge. While traditionally, Mannheim accepted, the intelligentsia were identified with the bourgeoisie or middle classes, he suggested that they could not be homogeneously identified with any one class. He argued that a 'relatively classless stratum' (Mannheim 1936: 137) of intellectuals emerged as the institutional hold of the church over intellectual activity broke down. While as a stratum, the intelligentsia do have interests, Mannheim claims that as a group:

it subsumes in itself all those interests with which social life is permeated. With the increase in the number and variety of the classes and strata from which the individual groups of intellectuals are recruited, there comes greater multiformity and contrast in the tendencies operating on the intellectual level which ties them to one another. The individual, then, more or less takes a part in the mass of mutually conflicting tendencies.

(Mannheim 1936: 140)

With hindsight this account of the intelligentsia seems a vain hope rather than an empirically supportable description. Mannheim's discussion of the intelligentsia as a classless stratum occurs in his essay on the 'Prospects of Scientific Politics' (1936: 97–171) – as I have suggested, Mannheim's hopes of a scientific politics seem to have been in general misguided. Because he associated the increasing freedom of the intelligentsia from institutional and class domination with the emergence of the sociology of knowledge, it does not mean that such an intelligentsia is a necessary prerequisite for maintaining the sociology of knowledge perspective. The point of the perspective is that it is impossible to escape from situational determination but it is not impossible to recognize some of the effects of situational determination. The sociology of knowledge does not attempt to transcend social context (though Mannheim's account of its methods may imply this) but it does aim to grasp knowledge in relation to its context. The reflexivity of the sociology of knowledge is a component of its method but does not guarantee its validity. The result is that different interpretations can be achieved using the same methodology and methods within the sociology of knowledge, and this is likely if interpretation is undertaken at different times or from different social locations.

This chapter has attempted to draw out the main themes in Mannheim's programme for the sociology of knowledge. At the end of Chapter 3 on the post-Mannheimian developments, I will draw together the features of the sociology of knowledge that will be developed in the rest of this book.

3 The inheritors of Mannheim's legacy

Mannheim had set out a project for the sociology of knowledge that opened up a potentially stimulating area of sociological inquiry. But those who read his work, and might potentially have taken up the challenges it provoked, generally modified the project in ways that made it unrecognizable. In this chapter I will look at some of the literature that addresses itself to Mannheim's sociology of knowledge – these writers are the inheritors of his work in the sense that they have read and responded to his ideas. There is no straightforward coherence in this literature except in the use of the phrase 'sociology of knowledge' and in the reference to Mannheim's work as a formative influence.

There is a potentially much broader field of work which could be construed as the sociology of knowledge. Many sociologists have addressed the relationship between ideas or beliefs and social structure and process but I shall not attempt to consider theories that more or less imply a sociology of knowledge perspective. To do so would be to broaden the potential range of literature to most of sociology and much philosophy and history besides. The aim here is to consider the traces of a Mannheimian tradition which responded to his particular account of the relation between knowledge and society.

From sociology there are attempts to adopt and adapt Mannheim's perspective and attempts to more or less 'begin again'. From philosophy concern has focused on the philosophical underpinnings of the sociology of knowledge as well as its implications for philosophical study. As a scholar Mannheim has attracted considerable attention both from commentators interested in the structure of his ideas and from those moved by the possibility of such a bold project as the sociology of knowledge. This interest has kept the Mannheimian tradition alive if not exactly thriving and it seems as if every few years there is a revival of interest. In 1984 for example, Stehr and Meja suggested that there was something of a renaissance of the sociology of knowledge (Stehr and Meja 1984: 4). Whether that renaissance ever really occurred seems very doubtful a few years on – the issues at the centre of Mannheim's sociology of knowledge continue to be debated but usually with little reference to his work. I shall comment firstly on those who dealt with the sociology of knowledge from a philosophical perspective and then consider the responses from sociology. I will go on to look at some developments of the Mannheimian legacy, in particular the work of the social constructionists and at the end of the chapter I shall comment on some aspects of Mannheim's project affected by this series of responses to his work.

Much of the work of those who inherited Mannheim's legacy lost sight of the project of the sociology of knowledge he proposed. The broad reasons for this were the difficulties in adopting his ontology of social being and knowledge and his espousal of 'relationism'. In most of the work I shall discuss here a central position is maintained for the knowing subject as the intending actor who enters social situations. Tied to this is a faith in the competence of epistemology to evaluate different forms of knowledge such that the 'scientific' and 'rational' can be distinguished and privileged as superior forms of knowledge to the 'ideological'.

THE PHILOSOPHICAL RESPONSE

As we shall see, much of the early response from sociology wanted to off-load the epistemological 'freight' that the sociology of knowledge appeared to be carrying. Most of the responses from philosophers were not interested in simply repossessing the epistemological freight, they were keen to stop the whole project in its tracks. The philosophical critique, in varying ways, attempted to undermine the project of the sociology of knowledge by pointing to its at best doubtful, at worst vacuous, epistemological basis.

For philosophers, Mannheim's project was somewhat threatening. It not only dared to enter the domain of philosophy by offering a critique of epistemology but also brought with it the heresy of relativism. Worst of all, the sociology of knowledge challenged the special field of philosophy as a purely cognitive activity in which the application of logical thought could generate knowledge true in all contexts. The task of philosophy itself became somewhat downgraded if, like all other knowledge, it was socially determined.

Grunwald, for example, writing originally in Germany in 1934, argued that the sociology of knowledge was founded not in a secure epistemology but in a metaphysical assertion of the relationship between knowledge and social being. This he derisively referred to as 'sociologism' and distinguished it from the true activity of sociology, the study of social action. Grunwald argued that since the foundation of the sociology of knowledge was 'axiological' rather than a science with an epistemology, it could not engage in empirical research. In a way this was not such a radically different view from Mannheim's because the sociology of knowledge was sociologism in the sense that it held that truth was only 'true "for" certain groups of men' (Grunwald 1970: 238). The sociology of knowledge was not founded on an epistemology but this meant only that its empirical analyses could not be interpreted according to a pre-established system.

Relativism is not an attractive proposition to anyone, least of all philosophers, because everything becomes so uncertain and transitory. A recent commentator, Martin Hollis, even fears that it leads to the 'social destruction of reality' (Hollis 1982: 83). His argument with relativism is much the same as was Grunwald's:

> Relativism asserts the view that everything given – this word being taken in the widest possible sense – can be grasped only in perspectives; but this proposition itself is supposed to be valid absolutely, not just for one perspective. In each proposition it advances, relationism is thus obliged to contradict its own thesis.
>
> (Grunwald 1970: 239)

Grunwald claims that relationism 'turns out to be an illusion' while Hollis claims it is 'just for the birds'. Both find that life, and of course the activity of philosophy, is untenable without some standards of absolute truth, the canon of 'reason', which can generate knowledge that can be held to be true regardless of perspective or context.

The strategy adopted for the defence of absolutism and reason is firstly to protect philosophy from the intrusion of the sociology of knowledge and secondly to assert that there is simply no other way than having the absolute standards of reason. Grunwald wrote of the 'unwarranted pretension' of the sociology of knowledge (1970: 241) and Hinshaw of its 'definite encroachment' into the realms of epistemology (1973: 233). But there is no super-ordinate epistemology which demonstrates the existence of reason; its foundation is, of course, axiological too. Even with the benefit of centuries of debate Hollis can think of no better way to support reason than a grand axiological claim:

> The other way, then, is to place an a priori constraint on what a rational man can believe about his world.
>
> (Hollis 1982: 83)

In trying to limit the domain of the sociology of knowledge, to keep it from intruding into philosophy and from making unjustifiable empirical claims, Hinshaw's review suggests that its real concern is with pragmatics, 'the relationships of signs to their users' (Hinshaw 1973: 237). Hinshaw makes a distinction between the 'cognitive' and 'evocative' contents of knowledge suggesting that the 'truth', at the semantic and syntactic levels, can be considered in isolation from the social basis of knowledge in so far as it can be shown to be cognitive rather than evocative. While Mannheim's programme is concerned with the relationships of signs to their users it is however based on the idea that the cognitive, because of its presuppositions, is rooted in the evocative. It is for this reason that the sociology of knowledge is effective as a critique of epistemology which purports to be a purely cognitive activity.

A more substantial rejection of the sociology of knowledge came from Karl Popper. He has approached it as an example of a much more general position in the debate about the possibilities of knowledge which he called 'historicism' characterized by a presumption about the nature of history:

> it denies that the regularities detectable in social life have the character of the immutable regularities of the physical world.
>
> (Popper 1957: 5)

The historicist position, Popper tells us, insists that any regularities of social life are dependent on historical changes in cultural life. He locates the origins of the sociology of knowledge in the work of Hegel and Marx, whom he regarded as the philosophers most prominent and influential in the historicist tradition. Popper has two arguments against the sociology of knowledge. The first, and political argument, is that historicism 'desires' not only to predict change but also to control it by centralized large-scale planning. In this the sociology of knowledge follows what he calls a 'reactionary prejudice' of Hegel and Engels that asserted that freedom could be gained by knowledge about the determinants affecting social being (Popper 1966: 223). The second, and methodological, argument against historicism was that it was not 'rational', or at least that it fostered irrationalism and mysticism (Popper 1966: 216). The problem with the sociology of knowledge is that:

> It overlooks the fact that it is the public character of science and of its institutions which imposes a mental discipline upon the individual scientist, and which preserves the objectivity of science and its tradition of critically discussing new ideas.
>
> (Popper 1957: 156)

Popper argued that a non-relative form of knowledge was available through scientific method which was rational and not determined by the history of culture. The scientific approach to knowledge involved the free criticism by scientists of each other's work, combined with a basis of information through observation and experiment. The public character of scientific knowledge depended on the interpersonal and critical debate between scientists. Critical rationality could not be a property of individuals; it was a product of a certain set of social relations. Political power could create the institutional framework necessary for free criticism, including things like laboratories, periodicals and congresses.

In other words the limits on the knowing subject's cognition are such that it has to be mediated in a social and discursive context for anything like truth to be achieved:

> In short, the rationalist attitude ... is very similar to the scientific attitude, to the belief that in the search for truth we need co-operation, and that, with the help of argument, we can in time attain something like objectivity.
>
> (Popper 1966: 225)

The claim for the public character of science as a mode for generating critical rational thought was an argument against the need for the sociology of knowledge; with a certain social and political context, the non-cognitive effects on knowledge could be eradicated. But the public character of science is more complicated and less benign than Popper's theory hoped (see Chapters 7 and 8).

The lack of an epistemological foundation for the sociology of knowledge did not seem to all philosophers to signal its failure. Arthur Child wrote a series of articles between 1941 and 1947 on various philosophical aspects of the sociology of knowledge (Child 1941a; 1941b; 1942; 1944; 1947). He attempted to find an alternative grounding for the project in a theory of mind because without it he argued that the 'postulational scepticism' of Grunwald and others was an effective criticism.

To accept the empirical demonstration of the social determination of knowledge one first has to accept the postulate that knowledge is socially determined. Child's solution is to propose a prior social theory of mind similar to that proposed by Mead:

> If mind itself has a social origin – if, that is, it arises through the process of communication – and if thinking consists at bottom in the manipulation of generalized attitudes taken over from the social

group as a whole, then there can be no question of the social determination, in some sense, of knowledge and thought.

(Child 1941b: 416)

This task of completing the sociology of knowledge with a social theory of mind is taken up by Goff (1980), who draws together features of Marx's and Mead's work. Goff sees the problem in terms of the ontological and epistemological assumptions involved in approaches to sociology. While sociology, and the sociology of knowledge in particular, are rooted in a social conception of man, the critique has come from positivism which is rooted in an individualistic, asocial, conception of man. Goff points to the contradiction that ensues when sociology attempts to take on the methodology sanctified by positivism for use in the natural sciences:

a contradiction that is entailed in their uncritical importation of a methodology developed in relation to another subject matter entirely.

(Goff 1980: 111)

Child and Goff are persuasive. However, I have argued that Mannheim's sociology of knowledge is based on a social conception of human being; he is extremely careful not to reduce thought to individual minds and not to conceive of a group 'mind' based on the prior conception of individual mind (Mannheim 1936: 2, 44). The effect of this is to decentre the subject by locating social being in the social practices of groups. The danger in utilizing a theory of 'mind' to solve the problem of grounding the sociology of knowledge is that it depends on concepts that relate to individual and inaccessible behaviour – 'thought', 'consciousness', etc. These concepts require self-reflection for their meaning to be grasped, which necessarily leads to an ontology privileging the individual as a knowing subject. I wish to argue that the insertion of a concept of social practice into Mannheim's account of social being can in effect provide a 'social theory of mind' without reasserting the primacy of the individual.

Child was unusual amongst philosophers proffering a critique of the sociology of knowledge in accepting limits to philosophical analysis that the sociology of knowledge has attempted to overcome:

The sociologists of knowledge ... may well have come to erroneous conclusions; but they have at least attempted in some measure, to solve the philosophical problem that results from the existence of competitive social-world [theoretical] systems.

(Child 1947: 28)

Other commentators (Hartung 1952; De Gré 1970 [though written in 1941]; Horowitz 1961) tended to the position we have already seen adhered to by Grunwald and Hinshaw; that the sociology of knowledge was illegitimate when it refused to recognize the primacy of epistemology in dealing with validity and competition between knowledge systems. Child was of course accepting a degree of relativism which was usually an anathema to philosophers.

Perhaps the most important issue raised by Child was the methodological problem of imputation (Child 1941a; Child 1944 – see also Hartung 1952). Simply put, the sociology of knowledge, to proceed with empirical description, must impute specific 'knowledge' to specific groups. How, given Mannheim's refusal to reduce knowledge to the specific ideas of an individual or to use a category of 'group mind', can this be done? Child's solution was to suggest that ideology can be imputed when it is 'affiliational', that is when members join a group which is organized around the content of an ideology (Child 1944). But Mannheim was referring more to the form of knowledge – the meanings out of which ideas could be constructed and understood – than to the substance of particular ideologies. Since these presuppositions that are the basis of knowledge are not normally recognized at the conscious level, an individual does not normally 'affiliate' to them with a conscious and intentional act. Mannheim compared the meanings given to social being to the givenness of language and it is difficult to imagine the individual 'affiliating' to their first language, exactly because of its givenness to the individual as part of social being.

A more recent review of the issue of imputation in the sociology of knowledge by Alan Scott suggests that the problem is with seeing knowledge/ideology as separate from the social grouping to which it has then to be linked by imputation. He argues that the sociology of knowledge must address the process of group formation since this involves the interaction between group identity and belief. Scott points out that social groups are 'symbolic/ideological formations' and the outcome of 'purposeful and discursive action' (Scott 1988: 51). This is a more useful way of linking knowledge to social group than Mannheim's own rather mechanical separation of ideas from utterances and utterances from empirically constituted social groups. Scott's point that groups are formed through discursive action and the sharing of knowledge, as well as other social practices, supports the link between knowledge and social processes that will be established in this book.

The threat that the sociology of knowledge posed to philosophy did not apply equally to all types of philosophy. As well as the acceptance by Child of a valid philosophical position for the sociology of knowledge,

Jacques Maquet suggested that it was only a threat to those philosophers who saw humans as provided with a spiritual nature that entailed the possibility of transcending economic and social determination through a theoretical 'faculty of the true' (Maquet 1973: 100). More recently Susan Hekman has interpreted Mannheim's role as a forerunner of 'anti-foundational' social science in that he substantially rejects epistemological grounding for sociology. What Mannheim provides is a 'groundless philosophy of social science' (Hekman 1986: 79) that provides a link with modern hermeneutic, critical and structuralist approaches.

Maquet, like Child, brought the philosophical debate about the sociology of knowledge down to differences in philosophical positions, differences due to different ontologies of social being and of knowledge. These commentators implied that the differences are irreconcilable within philosophy; they are beyond analysis or logic precisely because they are prior to the application of philosophical methods. Though irreconcilable, these differences are none the less very much at the centre of philosophy's concern with the possibilities of 'knowing'.

THE RESPONSE FROM FUNCTIONALIST SOCIOLOGY

It is with the publication of *Ideology and Utopia* in an English translation in 1936 that the sociology of knowledge begins its uncomfortable incorporation into the discipline of 'sociology'. This discipline was more particular in the English-speaking world than in European academic circles where the distinction between sociology, philosophy and history was blurred. In Britain, while there was little institutional separation of sociology, there was a sociological tradition deriving from the work of Herbert Spencer. But it was in the USA that sociology was emerging as a separate discipline both academically and institutionally. The struggle of American sociology to establish itself as a distinct 'scientific' discipline dominates the early reactions to Mannheim's work. In 1936 Alexander von Schelting reviewed the German edition of *Ideologie und Utopie* in an American journal, marking both its impact on the English-speaking sociological community and the, then forthcoming, English translation. His comments were uncompromising:

> Yet Mannheim's fundamental views on the problems of ideology and the sociology of knowledge cannot be accepted, because of their basic lack of logical and epistemological consistency and their incompatibility with empirical facts.
>
> (von Schelting 1936: 664)

Von Schelting's principal problem was with the difficulty of maintaining the possibility of a social science in the face of the sociology of knowledge because Mannheim had destroyed 'its objective, impartial validity' (von Schelting 1936: 666). While disputing the basis of Mannheim's critique of the limits of epistemology, von Schelting did tolerate the idea that there is some social basis of knowledge. However, he insisted that this could be distinguished from the cognitive validity of knowledge. Von Schelting's most powerful criticism was that the sociology of knowledge undermined its own basis – it was apparently making a claim for its own truth that it argued was not available for knowledge in general. Mannheim's reflexivity, his willingness to tolerate the limits of any claim to truth in his own work was unrecognizable to the epistemological scientism of American sociology. This scientism took as axiomatic that systematic and reasoned study, its methods reflected upon and sanctified by epistemology, could generate 'truth'.

The interpretation of Mannheim's project that von Schelting initiated set the scene for its incorporation into mainstream functionalist sociology. The sociology of knowledge was deemed to have a role in grasping the social basis of knowledge but this task was to be clearly distinguished from any comment on the validity of knowledge. The latter was properly the business of epistemology and to be excluded from the scientific practice of sociology.

There was a fundamental difference between Mannheim's understanding of the status of knowledge and that of American functionalism but because of the respect for the ideas generated in the European tradition of sociology and the importance of the topic of 'knowledge', the sociology of knowledge was incorporated into American sociology by what Stehr and Meja refer to as a process of 'normalization' (Stehr and Meja 1984: 6). This process involved the shedding of 'the epistemological baggage with which it was freighted at its inception' (Coser writing in 1971, quoted by House 1977: 222n). In effect this meant accepting that the sociology of knowledge must not concern itself with the truth of knowledge being studied but analyse the 'norms of thinking' for the participants under study:

> we can say generally that whatever is regarded as a truth functions as a norm of thinking, [and] imposes upon the conscious agent who recognizes it a distinctive selection and organization of some data of his experience.
>
> (Znaniecki 1970: 310)

This gave the sociology of knowledge a specific task in studying the sociological features on which systems of knowledge were dependent but the critical edge and the proposition of relationism had disappeared. Znaniecki was able to introduce a 'conscious agent' and 'norms of thinking' with which to investigate the socially inscribed function in relation to knowledge of individuals (as in *The Social Role of the Man of Knowledge* – the title of Znaniecki's 1940 book). Knowledge was returned to the individual knowing subject so that it could be analysed (regardless of its truth or falsity) as a product of the 'norms' within which the individual must operate. At the same time scientific method could protect the individual from the effects of social norms, thereby providing a context where they did not determine the content of thought.

What the sociology of knowledge became concerned with was the social processes that interfered with the production of true knowledge. Merton for example discusses the social role of the intellectual in public bureaucracy – the 'technological' wing of social science where the social function of the individual introduces a bias which becomes apparent to the objective scientist. He differentiates between the production of knowledge within the constraints of a bureaucratic context, with its practical demands for public policy, and the academic context of the 'unattached intellectual' for whom knowledge production is relatively unaffected by institutional constraints (Merton 1957: 218).

The difference for Merton between the European variant of the sociology of knowledge (i.e. the Mannheimian project) which considered the total structure of knowledge and the American variant which studied isolated fragments available to masses of people, was both in the object of study and the way it would be studied (Merton 1957: 441). The Mertonian project was intended to distinguish the social processes that generated scientific knowledge from those that distributed information with bias and distortion. The study of communication was to be a scientific project with research techniques and attention paid to the reliability of empirical data. The lack of these features in Mannheim's project were the basis for Merton suggesting that the American variant was better (Merton 1957: 446–9). It could be compared with chemistry because of its systematic techniques such as content analysis but the European techniques of interpretation had no such systematicity.

This positivist and functionalist adaptation of the Mannheimian legacy did not so much stand Mannheim's programme on its head as turn it inside out. Merton's interpretation of Mannheim's project; as doomed to fail while it continued not to differentiate between scientific and other types of knowledge, was probably very influential. The fact that Mannheim considered as 'knowledge' the presuppositions which constitute the world-view of a social group and consequently affect all knowledge seemed to escape Merton who categorized knowledge as ideas that 'perform different functions' (Merton 1957: 497). Merton was dismayed that Mannheim distinguished between 'cultural science' and 'exact science'; for Merton they should be treated as similar forms of knowledge because they are based on equivalent epistemologies. None the less, he did confirm that there was a place for the sociology of knowledge – provided it lost its 'epistemological impedimentia' (Merton 1957: 508).

Consistent with his view that science was a special form of knowledge potentially free of social determination, Merton initiated the socio-logical study of science. This was to be a form of the sociology of knowledge that had off-loaded the epistemological baggage by operating within epistemologically established categories. Merton proposed a study of the 'reciprocal relations between science and society' (Merton 1957: 531). That is, sociology could study the effects of science on social structure and the effects of the social context on the operations of science. But by definition, science itself was not considered as penetrated by social context; if it was it would no longer be science, at least not 'pure science':

> Science must not suffer itself to become the handmaiden of theology or economy or state. The function of this sentiment is likewise to preserve the autonomy of science . . .. The exaltation of pure science is thus seen to be a defence against the invasion of norms which limit directions of potential advance and threaten the stability and continuance of scientific research as a valued activity.
>
> (Merton 1957: 543)

The sociology of science was to articulate the 'ethos of science' (Merton 1957: 552–61) that guaranteed the exclusion of non-theoretical factors in the practice of science. The task of the sociology of science was to study the social context that permitted science to proceed according to the norms of this ethos. Merton, for example, was clear that totalitarianism was more likely to foster an attack on the ethical independence and institution of science than was liberal democracy. But there was no room in his account of the sociology of science for a review of the meanings that constitute the presuppositions of science even in a liberal democracy. This was an issue for epistemology; sociology presumed that the epistemology of science which gave rise to its norms of practice had eradicated the influence of presuppositions on the form and final content of scientific knowledge. Merton's proposals for the sociology of science are so limited as to be unrecognizable in terms of Mannheim's formulation of the sociology of knowledge. By according a special priority to the practice of science, the relationist and perspectival impact of the sociology of knowledge was made redundant.

Znaniecki's response to the sociology of knowledge dates from 1940 and Merton's is from a similar period – a later functionalist response was that of Parsons in 1959. While Parsons maintains a special epistemological prerogative for science, his interest is in the operation of 'values' in the field of knowledge. With a typically Parsonian neologism, 'value-science integrate', he expresses a connection between values and objective knowledge. Values, he argues, select problems and attach significance to items of knowledge and so constitute a basis of meaning that is tied to the social function of knowledge. Parsons compares his value-science integrate with Mannheim's 'general' (as opposed to particular) conception of ideology. The value-science integrate was socially situated in that the values were seen as specific to a given social structure. But Parsons protects the special nature of science through a distinction of levels of selection. The 'primary selection' achieved by values in the value-science integrate does not distort knowledge content. There is a secondary selection that leads to distortion and produces what Parsons calls 'ideology'. The thing which links but separates these two modes of selection was of course the epistemological primacy of empirical science:

> The criterion of distortion is that statements are made about the society which by social-scientific methods can be shown to be positively in error, whereas selectivity [i.e. primary selectivity] is involved where the statements are, at the proper level, 'true', but do not constitute a balanced account of the available truth. It is clear both secondary selectivity and distortion in an ideology violate the standards of empirical social science, in a sense in which the value-science integrate does not.
>
> (Parsons 1967: 153)

In other words science is seen by Parsons to be free from social determination as long as it is not penetrated by secondary selectivity or 'ideology'. The critique of epistemology involved in Mannheim's sociology of knowledge is again being firmly rebutted. Parsons holds that the sociology of knowledge should be concerned with the value-science integrate and distinguished from the study of ideology which should be a problem for the sociology of culture. This means that the sociology of knowledge is to be predicated on the distinction of true and false knowledge, a stricture that Mannheim sought to avoid. Like

Merton, Parsons highlights the sociology of science as a study of the cultural threats to the maintenance of objectivity and impartiality in scientific practice. Similarly, he proposes the study of ideology in relation to the professions; ideology is seen as the interpenetration of distortion into processes of applied knowledge.

The predominant response to Mannheim's proposals for the sociology of knowledge in the English-speaking world was to incorporate it into the programme of 'scientific', functionalist sociology. There were exceptions however. C. Wright Mills's 1940 review of the 'Methodological Consequences of the Sociology of Knowledge' disagrees with earlier responses (e.g. those of von Schelting, Grunwald, Merton and Parsons). Drawing on a cultural relativism implied in the work of Dewey and Pierce, Mills finds Mannheim's relationism quite 'tenable' (Mills 1940: 322n). Far from attempting to dismiss the epistemological baggage from the sociology of knowledge, Mills argues that the production of knowledge, including philosophy and epistemology, takes place in discursive contexts. These have the social features of a specific group of participants with a shared intellectual history, regardless of any particular methods for generating knowledge (Mills 1940: 324–5). This approach is consonant not only with Mannheim's project but also with the way that knowledge will be construed later in this book.

THE RESPONSE FROM HISTORICAL SOCIOLOGY

C. Wright Mills's interpretation of the role and relevance of the sociology of knowledge was not however one that received much support. Other responses that seemed sympathetic to Mannheim's perspective doubted its role as a foundation for sociological work. For example, Wagner explicates Mannheim's project in terms of his historicism but concludes that for an inquiry into 'the sociological aspects of ideologies and of knowledge . . . it might be advisable to select a theoretical basis less dependent on historicistic presuppositions than that offered in Mannheim's system' (Wagner 1952: 321).

The most important exception to the functionalist incorporation of the sociology of knowledge was the comprehensive review of the field by Werner Stark. Stark however was keen to distinguish knowledge from ideology and in this he differentiated himself from Mannheim's position which he regarded as too dominated by Marxism (Stark 1958: 104). Instead his theory of social determination transformed the Kantian 'a priori', the human capacity to reason, which then filled a role similar to Mannheim's presuppositions available to social being. The 'social a priori' were associated with the value system of the society and the 'seeker after knowledge' was located firmly within society and its value system (Stark 1958: 107).

There is however also a connection with Parsons's concept of 'primary selection'; in both Stark's and Parsons's accounts the social basis of knowledge is determinative of the topics of knowledge rather than the content. Stark not only claims that the value-facts are a priori to rational cognition but also claims that the 'axiological system' (the social a priori) only determines what is to be selected for knowledge. He is very clear that the orientation of the human mind to the natural world is consistent and not subject to social determination (Stark 1958: 166). This leaves him free to claim also that scientific objectivity can lead to the discovery of truth (Stark 1958: 126). This argument puts epistemology beyond the realm of the axiological system – exactly the opposite point from that which Mannheim made with his critique of epistemology.

For Stark there is a systematic and progressive development in the natural sciences organized by the desire both to understand and to dominate nature. The truth produced by science is universal – 'In the sciences the truth is always the truth' (Stark 1958: 167). While he did not propose any form of relativism, Stark did suggest that, unlike the natural sciences, the human sciences have yet to grasp the absolute – that which is 'universally human'. But the sociology of knowledge was to have a bridging role in the progress towards a scientific truth that would lead to a revelation of human essence (Stark 1958: 209).

Though Stark's understanding of the sociology of knowledge was both more detailed and more sympathetic than that of the functionalist commentators, it owes little to Mannheim. Stark admitted the influence of Scheler, the phenomenologist who wrote on the sociology of knowledge. Scheler was anti-positivist and opposed to the 'cult of science' (Hamilton 1974: 75) which would appear to be at odds with Stark's position. Scheler's phenomenology was based on a metaphysical hierarchy of values orienting the human being. Frisby points out that Scheler's phenomenology was at odds with Husserlian phenomenology in its dualism of spirit and drives (Frisby 1983: 31) and that there is little 'sociology', in the sense of an explanation in terms of social formation or social structure, in his sociology of knowledge (Frisby 1983: 33).

It is because of Scheler's assertion of a metaphysical, philosophical anthropology with no basis or interaction with sociological categories that I have chosen to ignore his contribution to the sociology of knowledge. Mannheim's comments on Scheler's position seem to be justified in their irony:

we might say: according to our view, God's eye is upon the historic process (i.e. it is not meaningless), whereas Scheler must imply that he looks upon the world with God's eyes.

(Mannheim 1952: 178)

Though Stark does not seem to share Scheler's ambitious project completely, he is willing to import the essentialist and absolutist components of Scheler's work, derived from their shared Catholicism (Hamilton 1974: 87).

THE RESPONSE OF MODERN SOCIOLOGY

There have been a number of other reformulations and reinterpretations that have done less violence to Mannheim's legacy than did the early sociological and philosophical responses. Neisser (1965) and later Eriksson (1975) engaged in methodological excurses exploring how the sociology of knowledge could become scientific. Gurvitch (1971) produced a classification of different types of knowledge, though not supported by empirical analyses.

Frisby (1983) and Jay (1974) have described the Marxist reception to the publication of *Ideologie und Utopie* in German, which sought to distinguish Mannheim's project from the theory of ideology. More recently however, Abercrombie has suggested that the theory of ideology could fill a lack in the sociology of knowledge by linking ideology/knowledge with the social process rather than merely with classes or social groups:

> The critical Marxist position, then, takes ideology as a concept formulable at the level of the mode of production, considered as a set of underlying structures, rather than at the level of class or social group. At this underlying level, ideology functions as a condition of existence of the economy.
>
> (Abercrombie 1980: 174)

Abercrombie sees this modern, critical theory of ideology as an advance on traditional Marxist accounts that were in terms of base and superstructure. While it needs to be developed in terms of the production of ideologies by class formations, he regards it as a corrective to the view, often attributed to the sociology of knowledge, that a particular ideology belongs to a class.

Abercrombie's work is not alone in its attempt to salvage the sociology of knowledge in recent years. Shmueli for example argues that 'relationism' deserves more credit than it traditionally receives and that a 'dynamic synthesis' can lead to a new type of objectivity in the social sciences (Shmueli 1977). Bouchier undertakes an analysis of 'radical ideologies' in the USA and Britain in the light of Mannheim's comments on utopian ideologies (Bouchier 1977). Kettler (1975) builds on his earlier work (Kettler 1967) that explored Mannheim's sociology of knowledge as a perspective within sociology, by arguing that Mannheim's work was consistently within a tradition of liberal political theory. House suggests that the reliance on rationality leading to objectivity that dominated early responses was out of date:

> Mannheim's message is that it is time to move from a Newtonian to an Einsteinian social universe. There is no Truth, nor any unambiguous criterion for agreeing upon what constitutes correct knowledge about society. Knowledge, rather, is an emergent of an interactive process between a collectivity of subjects and the objects that constitute their environment.
>
> (House 1977: 220)

These works are often engaged in relocating and reinterpreting Mannheim's work on the sociology of knowledge after the assault it received from functionalist sociology and philosophy when it was first introduced into the English-speaking academic community. This task has been both theoretical and investigatory. Work by Kettler (1967; 1975), Frisby (1983), Kettler, Meja and Stehr (1984) and Loader (1985) has explored original German writings, studied and translated unpublished notes and lectures (e.g. Mannheim 1982; 1985) and criticism to build up a fuller and more subtle context in which to understand Mannheim's sociology of knowledge.

THE RESPONSE FROM INTERPRETATIVE SOCIOLOGY

Perhaps the most innovative exploration of Mannheim's work, both in scholarly terms and in the light of contemporary sociological theory is by A.P. Simmonds (1978). I have already disputed Simmonds's account of interpretation based on authorial intention (see Chapter 2), but his account of the sociology of knowledge both as a hermeneutic and a critical theory is most interesting. He argues that the sociology of knowledge is a hermeneutic approach aimed at understanding rather than evaluation and as a critical theory it creates a level of communication and understanding across different perspectives. The synthesis that the sociology of knowledge attempts is not, he stresses, a harmonic synthesis in which contradictions are eradicated and differing perspectives merged. It is a dynamic synthesis that the sociology of knowledge aims for, a context in which critical debate can continually reformulate the problem and its resolution:

> Thus the hermeneutic moment makes critical thought possible; as long as the phenomenon of 'talking past one another' is not overcome, criticism remains imprisoned in a solipsistic self certainty, and the consequence of this condition (whether it take the form of cynical passivity or dogmatic and manipulative activism) cannot but be destructive of a genuinely emancipatory praxis.
>
> (Simmonds 1978: 184)

Simmonds's interpretation of the sociology of knowledge is derived from contemporary work by Gadamer, Appel and Habermas. Susan Hekman (1986) has also built on the links between Mannheim's sociology of knowledge and Gadamer's hermeneutics. She argues that they can constitute a new perspective for the social sciences and goes on to show a continuity with the anti-positivism and rejection of the knowing subject in structuralist and post-structuralist approaches to understanding.

THE SOCIAL CONSTRUCTION OF KNOWLEDGE

A major problem with the Mannheimian proposals for the sociology of knowledge is that they utilize a conception of social being that does not easily fit with an account of individual human beings. So, for example, Stern questioned whether Mannheim's account of consciousness was adequate. If the dependency of thought on social situation is asserted then

> something is indirectly asserted about existence, about the situation. Now, from the outset, consciousness or self-interpretation, etc. must conversely be taken into account as contributory factors in existence in the situation, etc.
>
> (Stern 1930 – quoted in Frisby 1983: 207)

If Mannheim's programme for the sociology of knowledge is not to have the nihilistic effect of reducing consciousness to the material content of history, then some degree of agency must be permitted to the human individual to affect both the production of knowledge and the process of history.

Peter Berger, like Child and Goff, brought the social psychology of Mead to bear on the sociology of knowledge which emphasized the role of socialization in constituting individual identity; 'psychological reality is an ongoing dialectical relationship with social structure' (Berger

1970: 374). Berger's 'socialized' conception of human being was a principal feature of his main contribution to the sociology of knowledge written together with Thomas Luckmann – *The Social Construction of Reality* (1971). Following the phenomenological approach of Schutz, Berger and Luckmann began by establishing a knowing and intending subject in a social context of meaning that was common to all consciousness. There were 'spheres of reality' within which conscious-ness could operate (i.e. distinguish, recognize) and there was one sphere that was common to all:

> Among the multiple realities there is one that presents itself as the reality par excellence. This is the reality of everyday life. Its privileged position entitles it to the designation of paramount reality.
>
> (Berger and Luckmann 1971: 35)

There are other ways in which human beings experience life (religious experiences, or sensual experiences for example) but the mode that is most common to most people is the sphere of everyday life. The flow of everyday life provides a context in which individual human conscious-ness usually operates. The sphere of everyday life is experienced as ordered and consistent which is because it is shared with other people and what is shared is, precisely, knowledge of everyday reality:

> Most importantly I know that there is an ongoing correspondence between my meanings and their meanings in this world, that we share a common sense about its reality . . .. Common-sense knowledge is the knowledge I share with others in the normal, self-evident routines of everyday life.
>
> (Berger and Luckmann 1971: 37)

It was to this common-sense knowledge that Berger and Luckmann directed the sociology of knowledge. They regarded as 'ill-chosen' the focus of the traditional sociology of knowledge on intellectual history and theoretical thought (Berger and Luckmann 1971: 26). While different perspectives might be characteristic of different groups, a realm of knowledge utilized by all is that of everyday life. It is in terms of the common-sense meanings and presuppositions of everyday life that other sub-versions of reality are socially constructed.

In approaching the common-sense knowledge of the everyday sphere, their position claims that language plays a crucial role:

> It can, therefore, be said that language makes 'more real' my subjectivity not only to my conversation partner but also to myself.

This capacity of language to crystallize and stabilize me for my own subjectivity is retained (albeit with modifications) as language is detached from the face-to-face situation.

(Berger and Luckmann 1971: 53)

It is through language that 'typifications' are generated in micro-social situations and become habituated with continuous usage. When typifications are shared reciprocally by typical actors then they become institutions (Berger and Luckmann 1971: 72). This process constitutes an objective social reality for individual consciousness. The meanings and typifications of institutions are unquestioned in the course of everyday life for the people who use them. Berger and Luckmann equate the institution as a social form with 'knowledge', as a body of truths about reality that guide everyday life (Berger and Luckmann 1971: 83).

It is into this context of historically constituted institutions making up 'reality', that the individual is socialized. Institutions provide a context for individuals to take on 'roles' in which their actions can be recognized as meaningful by themselves and others. The network of institutions constitutes a 'stock of knowledge' available to members of the society. Socialization involves giving the individual access to the stock, both learning some of its contents and how to gain access to further contents.

The role of consciousness in the socialization process is not clear; socialization, at least when it is successful, appears to take the form of filling a 'tabula rasa'. There seems to be no place in successful socialization for creative interaction that produces new meanings.

Holzner (1972) put forward a theoretical position for the sociology of knowledge that has many similarities with that of Berger and Luckmann – both texts derive their conception of 'everyday life' from Schutz. Holzner however describes the cognitive processes of the individual, borrowing both from cognitive psychology and from the phenomenology of Merleau-Ponty. He describes the individual interacting with the social world by filling roles that constitute an identity for her:

The most prominent orienting devices remain the symbolically defined frames of reference of social roles, which are integrated by the constant process of the individual's or the group's construction of his own identity in the context of the world as he or they know it.

(Holzner 1972: 45)

For Holzner the process of socialization is important for 'orienting' the individual but so is the perception of consensus and, in times of crisis, the authority of a charismatic leader. He also gives some emphasis to channels of communication and their control; the flow of information that is interpreted by individuals according to their frame of reference.

Holzner goes further than Berger and Luckmann by describing two 'foci of reality construction' beyond that of everyday life – specialized knowledge and ideological knowledge. The former are organized around the activities of work that give individuals and work communities a specialized knowledge not available or necessary in everyday life. Ideologies are constructions of reality that serve to support claims to power or authority (Holzner 1972: 144).

Both Holzner and Berger and Luckmann at the level of theory, describe processes by which knowledge is produced, laying an emphasis on the social form of the production and the functionality both for the maintenance of a stable social structure and the needs of the human being. The problems with both of these theories can be discussed in terms of the attribution of agency. The knowing, interacting subject is taken as a fundamental unit of society that has faculties of cognition and the ability to intend. But the description of society progressively erodes the agency of the individual who is inserted into a socially given context of institutions and roles. The structure of society is presumed to be functional for its members since it is derived from the sharing of their human attributes. This in turn describes the function of the individual in relation to society – any agency attributed to the individual is subordinated to the maintenance of social structure. The individual not only operates in a social context but also is determined, to the extent that she is a social being, by that context. Moreover, social process is described in terms of a philosophical anthropology, of human attributes of individuals, attributes that are prior to any consciousness or action:

> While the social products of human externalization have a character *sui generis* as against both their organismic and their environmental context, it is important to stress that externalization as such is an anthropological necessity. Human being is impossible in a closed sphere of quiescent interiority. Human being must ongoingly externalize itself in activity. This anthropological necessity is grounded in man's biological equipment.
>
> (Berger and Luckmann 1971: 70)

This account, in spite of beginning with the faculties of the knowing subject, leaves no room for an account of the individual as creative – as having any autonomy of agency. Sociologically this leaves a gap in the account of social process, of the effects of politics or the ability of groups to acquire power. The phenomenological account of a philosophical anthropology or an ontology of human being, centres the human individual as a subject that is subject to the functions and processes of society.

The conception of social determination introduced by the social constructionists is a much more total determination than that entertained by Mannheim. This is because social being is located in the individual human being and not merely in the set of presuppositions given in the social context to the individual. The consequence is that Berger and Luckmann and Holzner describe not only human being but also society on the basis of phenomenological introspection; society is constructed in their description in accord with their image of the 'human'.

For all its drawbacks as a theoretical base for the sociology of knowledge, the social constructionist accounts do suggest the importance of common-sense knowledge, of knowledge in ordinary social interaction rather than theoretical or scientific knowledge. They locate the category of 'knowledge' in a social context rather than an epistemological one; it is not the validity of knowledge but how it is used that is of importance to the sociology of knowledge. The constructionist accounts also stress the central role of language and communication in the social process of knowledge. The conception of knowledge as everyday communication through language points to the empirical domain that I will argue the sociology of knowledge should study.

CONCLUSIONS

The disciplines of sociology and philosophy are threatened by Mannheim's proposals since, in his account, they are the formal and scientific disciplines whose topics mean they are the most likely to be affected by non-theoretical factors. It is then not surprising that much of the response to the sociology of knowledge is a defence of these disciplines that incorporates the common-sense proposition that social context can influence the form and content of knowledge. While both the philosophical and sociological responses to Mannheim's work was critical and did not exactly embrace the sociology of knowledge as an exciting new project, it has been recognized as a promising new area for development. The philosophers may have been generally unsympathetic to what they saw as an encroachment on their territory, while the sociologists have done their best to incorporate or adapt Mannheim's project to fit with a paradigm in which they were already working.

The crucial difference between Mannheim and most of those who picked up his work was in an attitude towards epistemology. For those sociologists keen to establish the scientific credentials of sociology, both the attempt to comment on epistemology as knowledge and the attempt to found an empirical subject on relationist methods seemed impossible. The philosophers claimed both the privilege to attend to epistemological questions and the privilege of epistemology to be the sole locus for debate about what was 'true' knowledge. The inheritors of Mannheim's legacy were precisely those academics interested in substantive knowledge and the processes, epistemological and sociological, by which 'true' knowledge could be produced. Yet despite the social processes described by the sociology of science or by critical rationalism, achieving 'objectivity' or 'rational truth' relies on an existential transcendence that Mannheim saw was too constricting for the study of knowledge.

What neither the philosophers nor the sociologists seemed to grasp was that Mannheim was interested in a different aspect of knowledge than they were, one which was far more radical than merely arbitrating between truth and falsity. He was concerned with the presuppositions underlying knowledge, the meanings used to create it. He was far less concerned with the 'facts', with the accuracy or applicability of substantive knowledge – these things were important in so far as they indicated the perspective which lay behind them.

The project of Mannheim's sociology of knowledge can be summed up as the attempt to study the relation between knowledge and social structure. In this context knowledge can be understood as the *presuppositions* shared by members of a social group and as the *meanings* through which their action and experience are mediated – as a whole it may be recognized as the *perspective* of the social group. Knowledge is not adequately described by epistemology because all knowledge is *relational* to the social and historical context in which it is generated and used. The methods with which the relation between knowledge and social groups shall be studied are necessarily *interpretative* because there are no objective, epistemological criteria which can arbitrate trans-historically on the nature of truth. The empirical study of knowledge requires a method for *imputing* knowledge to a particular social group in a given context which remains a contentious area.

The perspectivalism that the sociology of knowledge proposed requires suspending a trust in reason and rationality that is necessary for everyday life and in particular for generating applied knowledge. Mannheim's relationism seemed to his detractors like a hollow promise, an attempt to have it both ways. The difficulty with relationism is the limited nature of any claim it makes to generate knowledge. Unlike, say, Popper's critical rationalism, which aims to produce the best knowledge at any one time, objective from a multitude of perspectives, applicable in many contexts, relationism claims a much more transitory understanding. The relational perspective simply explores the social features of any knowledge process, regardless of any claims it might make to be independent of social determination. Although Mannheim suggested that the pure knowledge of some sciences and mathematics would not be amenable to study in this way, accounts of the social and structural features of even such 'pure' knowledge have since been completed (Bloor 1976; Gandy 1973). The radical consequences of relationism and what it overthrows are neatly described by Loader:

> Relationism was the result of the continuation of, and the solution to, the end of existential transcendence (the utopian will) as well as to existential bondedness (the ideological perception). It provided the synthesis of ideology and utopia, theory and praxis, by moving to a new kind of historical dynamic.
>
> (Loader 1985: 115)

The relational perspective builds on the contradictions between different types of knowledge; agreement about the truth is never universal. But universality would be surprising because not only the context of emergence but also that of the dissemination and use of knowledge varies over time and from social location to social location. That certain types of knowledge can be applied effectively in so many different contexts and can endure is a challenge for the sociology of knowledge. Even where knowledge appears the same though, there is often a difference in the way it is applied and understood.

The contradiction between knowledges emerges in everyday life which is also a context characterized by the repair of such contradictions. As the social constructionists have argued, it is through language that meanings are created, sustained, disputed and modified. This theme will be taken up in Chapter 6 when I introduce the structuralist account of the relation between signification and social process.

While I will argue that structuralism offers a way of understanding knowledge as language that can be related to other social practices without reduction to an individual knowing subject, it is to the Marxist theory of ideology that I will turn to help describe the nature of the relationship. The theory of ideology offers an account of the role of knowledge in society that enables its analyses to operate as critique. In pursuing a critical theory of ideology I will be following commentators like Abercrombie and Simmonds, who also felt the lack in Mannheim's schema of a critical edge for the sociology of knowledge.

4 The origins of the theory of ideology

Of course the social determination of knowledge thesis was not original to Mannheim and the sociology of knowledge project. The recognition that ideas are not the pure result of cognition but are affected by the human context of cognition, can be traced back through philosophy – Larrain goes back to the fifteenth century to Machiavelli (Larrain 1979: 17). But it is perhaps in the attempts of Francis Bacon in the seventeenth century that the origins of a concern with social features of knowledge as introducing distortions are to be found. Bacon's theory of 'idols' described influences on the production of knowledge that produced false or distorted ideas. He wrote of the Idols of the Tribe:

> The Idols of the Tribe have their foundation in human nature itself, and in the tribe or race of men. For it is a false assertion that the sense of man is the measure of things. On the contrary, all perceptions as well of the sense as of the mind are according to the measure of the individual and not according to the measure of the universe. And the human understanding is like a false mirror, which, receiving rays irregularly, distorts and discolours the nature of things by mingling its own nature with it.
>
> (Bacon 1985: 277)

He also wrote of the superstition, the human passions and the religious representations that interfered with the observation and application of reason which should lead to knowledge. These influences are human tendencies distorting the cognition of a person in a similar way to the way perceptions are distorted in a 'false mirror'. But such distortions are, at least partly, social in origin; the mechanism of superstition as Bacon describes it, involves a tendency to accept those propositions that have been laid down and established through social recognition and approval. There is in Bacon's theory of idols an early version of what later developed into the theory of ideology. His theory connects with

Mannheim's 'particular' conception of ideology rather than his 'total' conception in that it is concerned with psychological processes. What is most important though is that Bacon was interested in how social and psychological features of knowledge introduced falsification. This is in contrast to the sociology of knowledge which was designed to be non-evaluative and not to distinguish between false and true knowledge.

The coining of the term 'ideology' is normally attributed to Destutt de Tracy whose concern was with the 'science of ideas' which sought the origins of ideas in human sensations. While it is concerned with the roots of true and false knowledge, this approach to studying ideology is very different from the social determination thesis and has not endured. But there has been a continuation of interest in 'ideology' and it is in Marx's work that the cause ceases to be found predominantly in psychological processes leading to false notions. Instead the social and economic relations influencing knowledge are explored so that the ideological process is itself theorized. It is one of Marx's greatest contributions to philosophy and the social sciences to have pointed out the systematic relationship between knowledge and historical and social processes. As we shall see, however, Marx did not describe the relationship in any detail – his primary concern was with describing material, economic relations between human beings. What is more, Marx was not consistent in his account of ideology and while he sometimes seems to be referring to what Mannheim was later to call 'total ideology', at other times he seems to be referring to a 'particular conception' of ideology with its psychologistic basis. Mannheim, clearly influenced by Marx's comments on ideology, distinguished these two types and also distanced his use of the term from Marx's. This was partly because Mannheim did not accept what he read as an overly materialistic account of history in Marx and partly because Marx distinguished ideology as false knowledge from science as true knowledge.

The history of the theory of ideology within the Marxist tradition can be seen as the letting go of the materialist reduction that involved a differentiation between ideology and science as distinct modes of knowing, while retaining an account of ideology as a structural feature of society. It is this grasp of the link between the contents of knowledge and human social relations that is so important about the theory of ideology. It enables analysis to address the role of knowledge as power and leads to a critique of knowledge not based on its truth but on how it affects and is affected by social relations.

IDEOLOGY AND CONSCIOUSNESS IN MARX'S WRITING

In *The German Ideology* (1974) Marx and Engels counterpoise ideology and science. The former is a descriptive term used to refer to and to denigrate the work of the Young Hegelians who see philosophy as an emancipatory force operating through the criticism of ideas. The latter term describes a truer form of knowledge based not on ideas as such but ideas about real forms of existence, that is 'materialism'. While the philosophers saw ideas and thoughts as that which determined human relations and the course of history, Marx and Engels described a material basis for social and economic relations. This meant that ideas and thought were not free and independent of the history of material relations:

> Morality, religion, metaphysics, all the rest of ideology and their corresponding forms of consciousness, thus no longer retain the semblance of independence.
>
> (Marx and Engels 1974: 47)

The concept of ideology here signifies the collection of ideas that are merely the product of thought and that have no material basis. Whereas the idealists pursued the production of ideas as such, the materialism of Marx and Engels sought to ground thought in a concrete world of practical action. Whereas the idealists saw the production of ideas and the development of consciousness through critique as the method by which history would progress, materialism sees the reverse; history progresses through the transformation of the material relationships that exist between human beings and between society and the natural world. From the experience of material relations an abstraction to ideas can be made which will constitute knowledge of the world. The generation of knowledge from practical activity is the basis of science in contrast to ideology which is based on speculation, ideas generating ideas:

> Where speculation ends – in real life – there real, positive science begins: the representation of the practical activity, of the practical process of development of men.
>
> (Marx and Engels 1974: 48)

Marx and Engels' infrequent use of the term ideology in *The German Ideology* is connected to a much clearer concept, that of 'consciousness'. They describe the historical development of consciousness in relation to material activity and mention two crucial stages marked by the division of mental and manual labour. Prior to the division, consciousness and thought were connected to the process of material behaviour; thought and action were part of the activity of all human beings. At the second stage, consciousness became separated from practical action through the division of mental and manual labour. Marx and Engels suggest that priests were the first ideologists who emerged at this stage. With the separation of mental and manual labour, thought could aspire to a 'pure' form, free from the constraints of practical action. This form of consciousness aspired to a representation of the world in its entirety rather than just the sphere of practical action (Marx and Engels 1974: 52).

Consciousness is ideological in the sense that in human, historical life-processes 'circumstances appear upside down as in a *camera obscura*' and the 'phantoms formed in the human brain are also, necessarily, sublimates of their material life process' (Marx and Engels 1974: 47). The difference between materialist, scientific thought and idealist, ideological thought is that the former recognizes the determination of consciousness and so returns to an empirical or 'real' world of practical activity to generate abstractions. In contrast, idealist thought supposes a converse determination and disregards the importance of reference to practical activity for the generation of abstractions, thereby remaining ideological. Materialist thought recognizes that 'Life is not determined by consciousness but consciousness by life' (Marx and Engels 1974: 47).

Language, like consciousness, is a function of practical activity or labour and constitutes its extension into a social form. Language and consciousness emerge simultaneously in Marx and Engels' history of human kind, the former being the material form of the latter. Both are seen as emerging out of a human 'need' to associate with other humans, which in turn leads to increased production, further increased needs and thence to the social division of labour. Although I have chosen to begin reading Marx's theory of ideology by reference to his concept of consciousness, the material form of consciousness and also of ideology is clearly language:

> Language is as old as consciousness, language *is* practical consciousness that exists also for other men, and for that reason alone it really exists for me personally as well; language like consciousness, only arises from the need, the necessity of intercourse with other men.
>
> (Marx and Engels 1974: 51)

The German Ideology was written during Marx's development of a materialist theory of history and his break with Hegelian idealism. It is not surprising that the work is therefore based on a critique of idealism and that the concepts used are rather more 'idealist' than those Marx uses in his later work. This leads to difficulties in deriving a theory of ideology from *The German Ideology* but it is a principal source since in the later, materialist-oriented theory of capitalist political and economic relations, the concept of 'ideology' is marginal and infrequently used. Furthermore, *The German Ideology* was a collaborative work with Engels who, as we shall see, retained more interest in the concept of ideology and is responsible for some of the features traditionally associated with it.

However, there is a section in Marx's own *Preface to the Critique of Political Economy* that illuminates the relationship between thought and consciousness and the material relations of production. Firstly, there is a restatement of the determinate relationship which here includes a wider specification of consciousness than was used in the critique of idealist thought:

> The mode of production of material life conditions the social, political and intellectual life process in general. It is not the consciousness of men that determines their being but on the contrary; their social being that determines their consciousness.
>
> (Marx and Engels 1968: 182)

Besides the materialist assertion of the determinacy of being over consciousness this piece equates 'social being' with the 'mode of production'. This means that consciousness in its ideological form is not merely arbitrarily determined by material relations but is specifically determined by the set of economic relations existing in a given society. The economic relations are also social relations in that the mode of production signifies a particular division of labour and particular class relations. This connection between consciousness and the mode of production provides the basis for the theory of ideology; it is through understanding the mode of production and its social relations that the social determination of ideology can be understood.

In the *Preface* when Marx writes of the 'social, political and intellectual life in general' it is equated with his concept of consciousness as a social process. Further on he refers to the 'legal, political, religious, aesthetic or philosophic – in short ideological forms' (Marx and Engels 1968: 182). These are all forms of consciousness that are not 'practical' in orientation in the way that a skill or a natural science are. Their quality as 'ideological forms' derives from their orientation to social rather than material relations. The production of these ideological forms would be by people whose labour is mental rather than material, whose product has effects in a world of ideas and social relations rather than the material world of objects. Furthermore the raw materials of such labour would be ideas and not material objects or practical action.

So far the concept of ideology as used by Marx is vague and does not lead to a formula of ideology as being 'false' knowledge or untruth. However, the idealist production of knowledge leads to mistaken knowledge because it is based on an incorrect account of the determinate relation between reality (or social being) and ideas. There is not the same implication about all knowledge. The process of abstraction of reality produces the 'phantoms formed in the human brain' which are also 'necessarily, sublimates of their material life process' but which in turn are most significantly 'empirically verifiable and bound to material premises' (Marx and Engels 1974: 47). While the process of constructing abstractions in consciousness is doomed to fail as a representation of reality there is the possibility of testing the contents of consciousness by referring to an empirical reality. It is only in this way that ideology can be distinguished from science. While the former resists the comparison with an empirical reality the latter is epistemologically founded on such a comparison. So too is materialism which is their reason for positing it as a rightful successor to idealism as the method for understanding history.

If the failure of the 'ideological forms' lies in the operation of an idealist epistemology, the specific instances of ideological forms (religion, aesthetics, the law, politics, philosophy) that Marx mentions, seem doomed only to the extent that they depend on an idealist epistemology. But what is it about these forms of thought that is 'idealist'? Both the law and politics for example are concerned with material relations albeit mediated by social relations. The law deals with social relations surrounding the management of material relations between individual subjects (violence, property ownership, theft, rights and obligations to act) and politics deals with the regulation of the material relations between members of the polity and decisions about collection and distribution of shared material (taxes) on its behalf.

The issue is about the epistemological basis of the categories and relations that these ideologies describe. From where does the law derive its categories of the 'person' and 'property' and politics its categories of 'shared material' and the 'polity'? If the answer is that they are idealistic categories generated through consciousness of ideal relations then the idealistic basis of these specific examples of 'ideological forms' can be understood. But the problem then lies in Marx and Engels' implication that there is an epistemological alternative in materialism or science. Are the categories of science any more real, any more observable than those of law or politics? It is even more difficult to grasp as non-idealist the categories of dialectical materialism; 'capital', 'labour' and 'value'. The categories of both science and materialism are abstractions from reality, they are the products of consciousness and as such must be, to follow Marx and Engels' rubric, 'sublimates of their material life process'. The only distinction that they offer between ideology and science is that the latter is 'empirically verifiable'. If it can be accepted, as empiricists do, that the process of empirical verification involves a separate and distinct process of consciousness than that of generating the ideal categories in the first place, then there is a basis for distinguishing between ideology and another form of knowledge, 'science'.

There is a further problem of distinction inherent in Marx's concept of ideology. It presupposes an ontological difference between 'material relations' and 'social relations'. The histories of science and social science demonstrate that empiricism is not so easily applicable to the latter as to the former. Empiricism is a consistent and even dominant approach in the natural sciences while a much more contentious and variable approach in the social sciences. This of itself does not create an ontological distinction; why should social relations be less 'real' than material relations? The difference between material relations and social relations is that knowledge can transform the nature of social relations but knowledge can transform only the specificity of material relations. This means that the application of empirical verification has a different effect in these different types of relations. Part of the manifestation of social relations is as knowledge, shared by human beings and used to inform their actions. Relations in the material world can exist independently of consciousness and are not necessarily affected by it. Consciousness can however manipulate material relations, for example with technology, because of their very consistency and invariability.

I am arguing that the process of creating abstractions at the level of shared consciousness – knowledge – is a social process. The 'reality' in knowledge is constructed in social relations whatever the knowledge refers to. This means that the activities of material science (conductivity physics or dialectical materialism) are social actions and are manifested by social relations in so far as they produce knowledge. This means that the categories available to these forms of thought are generated in the same way as those available to the law and politics though their practical application may have a different type of effect in the world.

There is then a fundamental problem with Marx's empiricist epistemology. It lies with his distinction between a form of consciousness directed to 'practical', 'material' or 'real' activity and a different form of consciousness that is directed to social relations and is taken as constituting ideology. The problem is an epistemological one; the different forms of consciousness cannot be evaluated for their 'truth' value on the grounds of the topic of consciousness or its location in the mode of production. It is important to stress that this dispute with Marx does not extend to his analysis of the mode of production or to the significance that he gives to knowledge as a relation of production. I am merely rejecting the possibility of transcending the constraints on ideology by adopting a materialist approach.

Marx's own, very limited, account of ideology describes its inability to represent real relations because of its generation as abstract ideas and its origin in particular social relations. In this book I will argue not only that these are indeed constraints on the form of knowledge but also that they are constraints on *all* knowledge which should be seen as ideological in the sense in which Marx uses it. Marx's own use of the term is tied up with his critique of idealism and it is not surprising that when in his later work he turned his attention to a materialist analysis of the capitalist mode of production, the term and concept of ideology occurs infrequently. Moreover when he does refer to ideology it is not to develop the concept or incorporate it into his analysis of capitalism but to refer back to the tyranny of ideas and the emptiness of idealism (e.g. in the *Grundrisse*, Marx 1973: 164).

ENGELS AND FALSE CONSCIOUSNESS

It is not in Marx's own writing that the idea of 'falseness' in ideology occurs and it is perhaps surprising that the notion of falseness is attributed to him (e.g. Hirst 1976: 385; Lichtheim 1967: 18). It is in the work of Engels that the concept of ideology is associated with 'false consciousness'. For example, in a letter he wrote:

> Ideology is a process accomplished by the so-called thinker consciously, it is true, but with a false consciousness. The real motive forces impelling him remain unknown to him; otherwise it simply would not be an ideological process.
>
> (Marx and Engels 1968: 700)

This account of ideology is not inconsistent with the account in *The German Ideology* (which of course Engels co-wrote) but the point that ideology is a product of false consciousness is an extension of the concept that Marx uses. The 'falseness' of the consciousness that produces ideology is not a quality of its location in the mode of production but a quality of the individual's failure to understand the 'real motive forces impelling him'. This is a more individualist and

idealist account of ideology than Marx's use in the *Preface*. It is also much easier to grasp and epistemologically almost crass; clearly the materialist who *does* know the 'real motive forces' can avoid producing ideology. At least in Marx's usage, ideology is a part of the structure of social relations and is not overcome by an individual who adopts a materialist account of history.

Engels also credits ideology with a greater role in the dialectical process of history than it seems to have in Marx's determinedly materialist analysis:

> while the material mode of existence is the primum agens this does not preclude the ideological spheres from reacting upon it in their turn.
>
> (Marx and Engels 1968: 689)

This poses an interesting problem; while Marx appears to deal with ideology as so much irrelevance (e.g. the work of idealist philosophers), Engels suggests here that the material process that is the object of study in Marx's later work, can be affected by ideology. It is these two issues of the relation of ideology to social structure and consciousness and the partial determination *by* ideology that are developed in later theories of ideology in the Marxist tradition. It is not clear whether they are issues in which Marx was ever really involved; if he had been, then it would seem likely that they would have played a more important role in his later work.

PREJUDICE AND FALSENESS IN IDEOLOGY

> The word ideology is a pejorative word; it describes unrealistic, prejudice-begotten thought. But ideas which are determined by social reality are not, because they are so determined, necessarily erroneous. On the contrary; determination by – i.e. agreement with – the social basis of life is manifestly a factor making for realism and truth.
>
> (Stark 1958: 53)

While Marx's own writing does not relate ideology directly to 'false consciousness' there is in his use of the term a meaning of distortion and a failure to represent 'reality' while at the same time being determined by material reality. It is not a psychological concept in that it is a product partly of the process of consciousness and partly of the structure of the mode of production (the division of labour, and the domination of one class by another). This makes Stark's reference to ideology as 'prejudice-begotten thought' clearly not a reference to Marx's own writing. Engels in his letters does offer a concept of ideology that is more amenable to Stark's categorization – there is even a sense of morality about 'false consciousness' and 'prejudice-begotten thought' that locates the responsibility for ideology in the individual.

The issues of 'falseness' and 'prejudice' are important because they relate the concept of ideology back to its origins in the work of Francis Bacon and Destutt de Tracy. Destutt's science of ideas was both a scientific study and an aid to policy making through identifying errors in understanding the ways of the world (Lichtheim 1967: 8). As Barth puts it: 'Only success in avoiding false ideas could assure scientific progress' (Barth 1977: 2). Both Lichtheim and Barth relate Destutt's 'ideologies' to Bacon's pursuit of 'idols' and to the aim of dispelling 'prejudices' with the application of reason that is stated in the work of Holbach and Helvetius. Furthermore, both Lichtheim and Barth provide a critique of Marx's concept of ideology that treats it as similar to that of Destutt. Lichtheim describes Marx's concept of ideology as illuminating the fact that human beings do not have 'true consciousness' (Lichtheim 1967: 22). Barth suggests that in pointing to the delusional nature of ideology he is indulging in an idolatory of science characteristic of his time but equally delusional (Barth 1977: 110).

For both these commentators Marx's concept of ideology fails to be useful because of an overarching problem in his claim to have transcended the problem of ideology by the application of a materialist and scientific method. But this criticism unfounds Marx's concept of science rather than his concept of ideology. Marx's contribution is to see ideology as having its origins in the social relations characteristic of the mode of production and not the result of prejudice in the individual. The process of consciousness involves abstraction and consequently distortion of the reality it purports to represent. The material being of humans (their location in the mode of production) determines their consciousness (the ideologies they absorb) but the process of determination does not extend to the particular content of ideology, rather to the forms it takes (philosophy, religion, law, politics, aesthetics, intellectual production in general).

IDEOLOGY AND THE MODE OF PRODUCTION

A more recent commentator on Marx's concept of ideology, Jorge Larrain, accepts that the concept is vague and that it has to be worked out from what little Marx wrote (Larrain 1979: 36). This Larrain does by attempting to understand the concept so vaguely used in *The German*

Ideology in terms of the more specific materialist theory of the *Grundrisse* and *Capital*. This involves trying to grasp Marx's concept not solely by referring to previous conceptions of ideology but by relating it to his analysis of the mode of production. Larrain's first point is that Marx approaches the concept of ideology on the basis of the contradictory character of social reality 'which is brought about by the restricted productive forces and the division of labour' (Larrain 1979: 45). This leads to a characterization of ideology:

> Ideology is, therefore, a solution in the mind to contradictions which cannot be solved in practice; it is the necessary projection in consciousness of man's practical inabilities.
>
> (Larrain 1979: 46)

This way of understanding ideology emphasizes both the process of its determination by the sphere of material relations and the process of distortion. In smoothing over the contradictions in practical, material relations, ideology legitimizes the class structure and the social structure of the mode of production.

The legitimizing effect of ideology is tied to its production by the dominating class. In so far as a class dominates social relations it dominates the production of ideology. Thus the form of dominant ideas is to express social relations in terms of the interests of the dominant classes as if they were the common interest. Marx and Engels are indeed clear about the role of the ideas of the dominant classes:

> The ideas of the ruling class are in every epoch the ruling ideas. . . . The ruling ideas are nothing more than the ideal expression of the dominant material relationships, the dominant material relationships grasped as ideas.
>
> (Marx and Engels 1974: 64)

Before a non-dominant class can become the dominant class it has to 'give its ideas the form of universality and represent them as the only rational universally valid ones' (Marx and Engels 1974: 66). Asserting the universality of ideas is the way that dominant class interests are maintained – ideology is about power and the continuation of particular class relations. It is through the representation of the ruling class's interests as the interests of the whole society that any threat to class power is contained (Marx and Engels 1974: 64). The way that ideology serves the interests of the ruling class, by obscuring the contradictions in the lived relations of the mode of production, is through the generation of ideas and explanations – knowledge. This knowledge characterizes the contradictions experienced under the capitalist mode of production as 'normal' or as 'glitches' or 'hiccups' in a system that is fundamentally sound.

An important feature of Larrain's analysis of Marx's concept of ideology is that it is not directly determined by the material relations of production. He proposes that the production of consciousness must be seen in terms of two relationships that Marx analyses independently. One is the base/superstructure relationship that considered alone appears a mechanistically determined one. The other relationship is that of practice and consciousness that considered alone is the product of humankind's free will. Together the two relationships take on a more dynamic quality and the determinate relationship is mediated by human practice. Practice is in turn constrained by how material relations appear to human consciousness, including their contradictions. It is important to note that the contradictions are not in the appearance of material relations but in their concrete essence.

Larrain is careful to point out that this analysis is his interpretation of Marx's use of particular concepts and that the relations between concepts is not thoroughly analysed by Marx (Larrain 1979: 55–67). The analysis is useful however because the generation of ideology is not left as a mechanistic determination. The introduction of human practice as a mediation in the production of ideology explains why it is not a simple reflection (albeit distorted or inverted) that can be decoded to reveal the essential relations of the material sphere. There is also the possibility of practice expressing the free will of the individual even though it has no other form of expression than the appearances available to consciousness. As Larrain points out, for Marx a particular form of practice, revolutionary practice, was the only way to overcome ideology:

> Revolutionary practice changes the condition within which reproductive practice must necessarily reproduce misleading appearances. ... Revolutionary practice is a conscious, a theoretically informed practice.
>
> (Larrain 1979: 60)

This creates a role for the critique of ideology, not to transcend ideology as Marx's claims for science and materialism in *The German Ideology* suggest, but to engage with ideology and consequently inform an emancipatory human practice.

The tradition of the theory of ideology has attempted this, though with perhaps little effect on practice. The tradition has however tended to assume that by adopting a particular perspective (Marxism) it can escape the ideological effect much in the same way as science appears at times to escape from ideology. I wish to argue, following Mannheim's relationist sociology of knowledge, that while Marx's account of ideology is a useful introduction to the process of the social determination of knowledge, there is no escape from the form of ideology as the only available context of expression. This does not rule out the possibility of critique which by investigation of the structure and forms of ideology as materialized expression (discourse), can affect the forms of human practice.

Before considering subsequent developments in the theory of ideology it is worth presenting a summary of the contributions to a theory of knowledge that Marx provides (and Larrain's analysis illuminates). Marx's concept of 'ideology' adds five things to a general concept of knowledge. Firstly, ideology is determined by material conditions of existence, which are also determinative of social relations. Secondly, ideology is a social production and those who dominate social production also dominate ideological production. Thirdly, ideology is necessarily a distortion of reality insofar as: it is an abstraction, it is socially determined and its production is dominated. Fourthly, ideology legitimizes social relations and covers over contradictions in the material relations of social being. Fifthly, the production and determination of ideology is mediated through human practice which cannot be reduced solely to the reproduction of material relations.

The link between ideology and material and social relations is an important feature of the theory of ideology. That the link is distorted by human power relations and serves human group interests is also important in establishing a link between knowledge and power. What is dangerous about the theory of ideology is that having described the structural relationship between knowledge and extant social relations, it is presumed that a correct attitude will enable the 'true' account of the world to emerge.

LUKÁCS – CLASS CONSCIOUSNESS AND REIFICATION

The development of the Marxist theory of ideology after Marx and Engels pursues the logic of Marx's epistemology in two directions. In one direction was a scientistic development in the work of Engels, Kautsky and Bernstein (Hamilton 1974: 38). Larrain calls it 'positivist' referring to Lenin, Plekanov and Labriola (Larrain 1979: 68). This line of development underlines the base/superstructure dichotomy and reduces consciousness to a simple reflection of the material base of society. The pursuit of this economic determinism allowed little, if any, active role to ideology in the process of the development of the mode of production. It was founded on the scientific validity of dialectical materialism and relied on the distinction between ideology and science for its own validity.

The other direction of development was a 're-Hegelianization' of Marx's concept of ideology. Georg Lukács exemplifies the beginning of this development. As it had for Hegel, consciousness again becomes a significant element in the process of history for Lukács. His historicist account of the role of consciousness was in turn influential in the development of Goldmann's 'genetic structuralism' and the Frankfurt School's 'critical theory'. In a straightforward sense Lukács's account of ideology is at odds with the conception of ideology that I am attempting to develop. However, his work does draw attention to the contents of consciousness and offers an account of their 'truth' and relation to specific historical subjects – classes. Ideology becomes not a mechanistic side-effect of the material relations but a dynamic process that is part of the practice of human beings.

As a student of Lukács, Mannheim was influenced by his treatment of ideology, history and the problem of relativism. But Lukács's importance here is not so much for his influence on the sociology of knowledge as for his merging of a Marxist conception of the relations between classes with concepts derived from the historicist tradition. Lukács is described by other commentators (Hamilton 1974; McDonagh 1977; Giddens 1979) as bringing to Marx's ideas a German idealist interpretation that drew on Hegel, Dilthey and Simmel. Frisby suggests that Lukács's concepts of alienation and reification derive from Simmel's work and in *History and Class Consciousness* they are put into a Marxist context. Frisby also points out that Lukács's Marxism avoids consideration of exploitation or the theory of surplus value (Frisby 1983: 84–95). Lukács neither studied class consciousness empirically nor considered the structural constraints on its development; stratification within the working class, the social reproduction of the labour force and the political legitimation of capitalist domination (Frisby 1983: 93).

His concern was with the consciousness of groups, specifically classes and particularly the proletariat. This brings the concept of ideology into the centre of his work unlike Marx's writings where it remains peripheral to the account of the material relations of the process of production. He begins a description of class consciousness by showing the limitations of bourgeois thought as an explaining away of the existing order of economic relations and an assertion of the immutability of institutions (Lukács 1971: 48). Lukács describes how bourgeois thought thus transforms history into eternal laws of nature that are static and formal and impervious to the 'real' nature of history that is to do with relations between men.

The concept of 'reification' is, for Lukács, one of the key aspects of the ideological or distorting nature of bourgeois thought. It refers to the tendency to transform social relations into relations between things. In classical economics, for example, the structure of capitalist production is described in terms of money and commodities which have systematic relations as things. For Marx however capital is not a thing but a 'social relation between persons mediated through things' (from *Capital* Vol. 1, quoted in Lukács 1971: 49).

The Lukácian reading of history is through Marx's analysis of the mode of production. It is in terms of the relations between worker and capitalist and tenant and landlord rather than between psychologically given individuals. In contrast, bourgeois thought demonstrates 'false consciousness' because it is thought which fails to recognize 'the essence of the evolution of society' and fails to grasp phenomena 'in relation to a society as a whole' (Lukács 1971: 50). Lukács believes in a 'true consciousness' that can grasp phenomena in a holistic and historical way. The concept of 'false consciousness' plays a similar role in Lukács's writing to that which 'ideology' plays in Marx's.

The form of class consciousness is not however available to historical subjects, such as the members of a class, but has to be derived from an analysis of the totality. Lukács points out that this is why what appears 'subjectively' to be true while:

> At the same time, *objectively* it by-passes the essence of the evolution of society and fails to pin-point it and express it adequately. That is to say, objectively, it appears as a 'false consciousness'.
>
> (Lukács 1971: 50)

The understanding of 'objective' categories is Hegelian and not the same as positivist or materialist references to 'objective'. It enables the analyst to:

> infer the thoughts and feelings which men would have in a particular situation if they were able to assess both it and the interests arising from it in their impact on immediate action and the whole structure of society.
>
> (Lukács 1971: 51).

This possibility of inferring is the basis of Lukács's concept of 'objective possibility'. The analyst is able to understand in a way that subjects cannot, what is 'objectively possible' for a class consciousness at a particular point in history. This analysis provides the basis for being able to recognize 'true' consciousness and distinguish 'false' consciousness.

The historical location of the class takes into account its power, interests and organizational structure which all determine specific forms of class consciousness. 'Ideology' remains a conceptual category for Lukács but is limited to the accounts of material, social relations that distort their true nature. For example in describing the apparent mastery of economic theory in bourgeois thought as the 'crassest form of false consciousness' Lukács says:

> From the point of view of the relation of consciousness to society this contradiction is expressed as the *irreconcilable antagonism between ideology and economic base*.
>
> (Lukács 1971: 64)

Lukács's theory of class consciousness is predicated on a teleology: that the process of history is determined by the development towards truth. There is a similar teleology present in Marx's historical materialism that says there are a series of economic modes of production that societies must pass through until socialism is reached, when the economic contradictions of all previous modes are resolved. Lukács borrows the structure of Marx's economic argument and applies it to the process of knowledge/consciousness/ideology, supporting his own argument with Marx's economic theory. Indeed Lukács's theory of class consciousness is impossible to swallow (or follow) unless one accepts that Marx's analysis of the material base is a scientifically given truth. That is, it must be considered as historically transcendent in the sense of being unaffected by the same, historical, process that Lukács describes for class consciousness. Larrain interprets Lukács as giving a primacy to knowledge: 'It seems as if thought could change the world' (Larrain 1979: 79). Lukács makes it clear that 'knowledge' here is not of the 'abstract kind', rather it is:

> knowledge that has become flesh of one's flesh and blood of one's blood; to use Marx's phrase, it must be 'practical critical activity'.
>
> (Lukács 1979: 262)

He is not suggesting that it is 'thought' that is the main determining force. Both the bourgeois ideology and the proletarian false consciousness are products of particular social relations present in capitalism. It is only through consciousness in action arising out of the contradictions of the real relations, that any transformation of either class consciousness or economic relations will come about.

Lukács tells us remarkably little about the structure and process of 'ideology' or knowledge. Perhaps this is because his problem is not a sociological one; he is engaged in polemic rather than social theory and his work is built around an apocalyptic vision of the future of capitalism rather than a series of questions about social phenomena. His vision leads him to seek a saviour that he finds in the proletariat, albeit heavily cloaked in 'ideology'. His interest is in how the proletariat would (or should) speak if the cloak were thrown off. Lukács's history is spiritual rather than sociological.

What is perhaps most useful in Lukács's account of ideology is the concept of 'reification'. This concept refers to the way ideology covers up contradictions and how it legitimizes by treating human social relations as things. To human beings the existence of exploitative relations of production would be agonizing were they perceived simply as exploitative. If the form of such relations is in fact reordered at the level of consciousness to appear as an exploitation of *things*, then the effect is to reduce the sensation of the violence of exploitation and also to legitimize the relations of dominance. As Frisby points out (Frisby 1983: 94), Lukács is taking Marx's concept of 'commodity', which describes how social and economic relations are frozen in the material products of capitalism, and extending it to show how by treating social relations as things, their social and economic character is obscured. What is a fundamental problem in Lukács's account is how an effective analysis can be achieved. He envisaged an emancipation from reification would come not through abstract reflection alone but through 'praxis':

> Reification, is then, the necessary, immediate reality of every person living in capitalist society. It can be overcome only by *constant and constantly renewed efforts to disrupt the reified structure of existence by concretely relating to the concretely manifested contradictions of the total development, by becoming conscious of the immanent meanings of these contradictions for total development*.
>
> (Lukács 1971: 197).

For Lukács it was the proletariat who were to achieve this praxis. But his programmatic statement also lays the foundation for a critical theory of ideology and suggests a relevance for the critique of ideology that is absent in Marx's own work.

GOLDMANN

Goldmann developed a humanist form of Marxism that continued a direction of development begun by Lukács, emphasizing the role of philosophy and cultural analysis in understanding the 'totality' of history. Goldmann attempted to recover an Hegelian 'Subject' in which history and consciousness are one and his 'genetic structuralism' analyses a process of social evolution realized in the material relations described by Marx. His interest in the emancipation of a class subject, as bringing about an historical synthesis, owes much to Lukács's version of Marxism. Goldmann specifically rejected a Durkheimian approach to sociology, recognizing that the facts are always approached using the researcher's 'categories and implicit and unconscious preconceptions' (Goldmann 1969: 41).

For Goldmann, any claim to 'scientificity' in sociology resides in its reflexive awareness of its own social determination which leads to his interest in the sociology of knowledge. The recognition of the effects of conscious or unconscious value judgements on scientific theories raises the question of relativism as it occurs for the sociology of knowledge: 'Are all ideologies of equal value, at least, as far as the search for truth is concerned?' (Goldmann 1969: 51).

Here Goldmann is opening the question that is closed for Marx and Lukács; is science merely a form of ideology? Goldmann rejects Mannheim's position as having offered the most traditional and unreflexive criterion of truth by making the free-floating intelligentsia its arbiters. Instead he incorporates an evaluative criterion by arguing that a value orientation is more appropriate than others if it:

> *permits the understanding of the other as a social and human phenomenon, reveals its infrastructure and clarifies, by means of an immanent critical principle its inconsistencies and limitations.*
>
> (Goldmann 1969: 52)

The value orientation that meets this standard is, he asserts, one based on Marx's analysis of the class struggle. However, Goldmann suggests objectivity is only available to the individual; by effecting a synthesis of elements of truth from the perspectives of different classes and by preserving elements of understanding already expressed by other thinkers but abandoned under the influence of social, economic or political changes, the individual may be able to 'arrive in the realm of scientific thought' (Goldmann 1969: 58).

Central to Goldmann's interest in the sociology of knowledge is the concept of 'potential consciousness' that he derives from Marx. As a sociologist, what he is interested in is the knowledge of a social group and as a Marxist he is interested in the 'maximum potential consciousness' of a group or class – what it could know and still remain a coherent group. While 'real consciousness' might be what people in a given group actually think, it does not necessarily correspond to what they will do or how they will respond to changes either in their situation or in the information they have. For Goldmann then, 'potential consciousness' is a way of understanding how knowledge is related to social and political change. He is interested both in the future – how political changes might be brought about through information that stretches potential consciousness and causes a group to transform – and in the past. His analysis of French literature (e.g. Goldmann 1964), both the studies of classic writers (such as Racine and Pascal) and of more recent literature, is constantly searching for the world-views of the epoch in which the literature emerged:

> I want to point out that philosophical, literary and artistic works prove to have particular value for sociology because they approximate the maximum potential consciousness of those privileged social groups whose mentality, thought, and behaviour are oriented toward an overall world view.
>
> (Goldmann 1977: 39)

Although Goldmann accepts the significance of the social determination of knowledge thesis for epistemology he does not pursue its implications for the Marxist concept of ideology. His detailed studies of great writings involve trying to uncover the world-view of an epoch and the relation between knowledge and cultural creation, but they are neither in terms of the presuppositions given to social being nor in terms of the relation between ideology and the contradictions in the material conditions of existence.

CONCLUSIONS

The account of ideology that Marx offers does not really amount to a 'theory of ideology'. It is through an interpretation in the light of his account of class power and the contradictions inherent in the capitalist mode of production, such as that undertaken by Larrain, that his comments about consciousness and the idealist philosophers can be construed as a theory. This theory of ideology introduces a distorting dynamic in the process of knowledge that is not due to mistakes or faulty thinking but is systematically related to the social and material relations of society. The analysis of ideology then takes on a critical role by describing the social determination of knowledge in terms of particular social forms that both give rise to the contradictions present in ideology and are legitimized by its content.

The problem raised by the theory of ideology is the analysis of knowledge as true or false, according to its social determination. This was indeed the origin of the concept of ideology and the thesis of social determination. Marx's distinction between science and ideology seems crude in hindsight, but the identification of 'false consciousness' using a

Marxist analysis is more properly associated with Engels and Lukács. Both found their analyses in a non-reflexive mode which presupposes the truth of a Marxist analysis of power. Lukács's concept of reification extends the theory of ideology by showing one of the mechanisms by which it is effective in obscuring class relations. But his belief in the ability of the proletariat to see through their false consciousness through 'praxis', relating knowledge to the material context of action, seems a vain hope – especially with hindsight.

The influence of Hegel's theory of history on both Lukács and Goldmann has denuded the concept of ideology of any analytical power in their work; neither use it to examine the relation between thought and specific conditions of existence. Despite his association with the sociology of knowledge, Goldmann's work represents a point at which the Marxist theory of ideology is furthest from the project of the sociology of knowledge. The social determination of knowledge is supported not as a basis for analysing knowledge or ideology but as a basis for disputing with the positivist tendency in social science in order that an idealist and historicist account of the process of history can be recovered.

Although Goldmann does introduce a measure of reflexivity not present in Marx, Engels and Lukács, it is as a characteristic of the sociology of knowledge which allows for a variety of competing perspectives. Goldmann's reflexivity does not however lead to a 'total conception of ideology'; he, like all the early Marxist theorists of ideology, does not reflect critically on the 'science' of Marxism. It is for later developments in the theory of ideology that we have to wait for an account that does not raise Marx's materialism to a status such that it cannot itself be analysed as ideology.

5 A modern approach to ideological critique

Althusser's brand of Marxist structuralism and Habermas's development of critical theory take the Marxist theory of ideology into new areas. Both work on the tension between science and ideology present in Marx's work and both try to avoid the reduction to class consciousness present in the writing of Engels and Lukács. Structuralist Marxism and critical theory remain committed to Marx's analysis of the material relations of production but both are concerned to address other aspects of human social life about which Hegel had more to say than Marx. These modern versions of Marxism are not attempting to reintroduce 'idealism' in which thought and ideas are given a central role in the determination of history. However, they do involve exploring the role of knowledge and ideas in society and do not accept that all aspects of social relations can be reduced to the economic relations of the mode of production. They address the political processes of capitalism, attempting to understand the part played by knowledge and ideology in the maintenance of the mode of production and its characteristic social relations. In the hands of Althusser and Habermas, the critique of ideology becomes not just a basis for pouring scorn on the thinkers who have rationalized an exploitative economic and class system. Their concern is to understand the mechanisms that keep capitalism going and make it resistant to challenges – so that they might strengthen those challenges.

While there are many areas of common ground between Althusser and Habermas, both are very different writers in style and tradition and they do not refer to each other's work. Both are influenced by Marx and Hegel but their work progresses in different directions. Habermas develops the notion of ideology from critical theory's broad concern with culture to an analysis of its role in sustaining rationality and resisting the economic and political crises characteristic of capitalism. He goes on to develop a theory of communicative action which focuses on the exchange of ideas and meanings in contrast to the exchange of goods. Before looking more closely at Habermas's contributions to the theory of ideology I will first consider Althusser's briefer but still significant analysis.

DETERMINATION AND STRUCTURE

In the dogmatic account of the base/superstructure model entrenched in Marxist political theory, Althusser sees both a philosophical failing and the roots of a failure in political practice. In the Marxist theory of the Second International the economic base is dogmatically described as determining the superstructure (Callinicos 1983: 62). This had the effect of denying any historical role to philosophy; since philosophy is at the level of the superstructure it is therefore determined by the base. The work of philosophy had been completed, it was claimed, by Marxist theory's recognition of the material base as the level of determination. All that remained for theory was to explore the details of determination while avoiding the tendency of bourgeois ideology to obscure determination by the material base.

The materialist 'inversion' of the Hegelian dialectic that Marx took over from Feuerbach involves, according to Althusser, an 'epistemological break'. Prior to the transformation of the dialectic, Marx's work is under the shadow of the Hegelian dialectic and the transformation brings about a new problematic and the possibility of an emerging science. However, Marx himself did not philosophize the inversion or discuss the philosophical form of the transformed dialectic (Althusser 1969: 174).

Althusser points out that historically, contradiction alone (the contradiction between the forces of production and the relations of production, the contradiction between two antagonistic classes) is insufficient to bring about revolution. This is the political failing of a materialist reduction; history shows that it is inadequate to view the determination of events in terms of contradictions in the base. He argues that there must be an accumulation of 'circumstances' and 'currents' that 'fuse' into a 'ruptural unity' that involves not only the level of the relations of production but also the conditions of existence prevailing at the time and the international conjuncture (Althusser 1969: 100).

Althusser's concept of the dialectic involves various levels of social formation that have a 'relative autonomy', that is to say, they are to some degree self-determining. It is the partial intra-determinacy of different levels that prevents reduction to a single force. The categorial distinction between the 'levels', and what constitutes them empirically, is not clear. However, the base, or economic structure, seems to be one level and the political and ideological seem to constitute two other, superstructural, levels (CCCS 1977).

The fact that contradiction at the different levels can bring about a unity of effect is what Althusser means by 'overdetermination':

> the 'contradiction' is inseparable from the total structure of the social body in which it is found, inseparable from its formal conditions of existence, and even from the instances it governs; it is radically affected by them, determining, but also determined in one and the same movement, and determined by the various levels and instances of the social formation it animates; it might be called overdetermined in its principle.
>
> (Althusser 1969: 101)

It is the overdetermined character of the materialist dialectic that distinguishes it from the Hegelian dialectic. The latter is a process within one level, that of consciousness, and involves 'no true external determination' (Althusser 1969: 102). Althusser describes the distinction between the two dialectics as being in the 'centres' of their circles of determination. There is only one centre in the Hegelian version, the emerging totality of history, but the materialist dialectic because of the different levels of social formation, has a 'decentred' quality that leads to its overdetermined process. The centredness of the Hegelian dialectic Althusser presents as having an 'internal spiritual principle' which in its abstract simplicity can only realize itself as ideology (Althusser 1969: 103).

This accounts for the smoothness, the lack of 'rupture', end or radical beginning to history in the idealist dialectic. For Althusser the crucial distinction between Marx's dialectic and Hegel's lies in the relation Marx describes between his concepts. These concepts (the mode, forces and relations of production) are not the product of a mere inversion of Hegel's concepts of civil society and the individualized satisfaction of needs by '*Homo oeconomicus*'. The different concepts are a product of theorizing a different form of determination that is by the mode of production in the 'last instance' but includes a relative autonomy of the superstructural levels. Althusser puts the claim that overdetermination is universal, and not merely applicable to aberrant historical situations, with ironic grandeur:

> the economic dialectic is never active in the pure state; in History, these instances, the superstructures, etc. – are never seen to step respectfully aside when their work is done or, when the Time comes,

as his pure phenomena, to scatter before His Majesty the Economy as he strides along the royal road of the Dialectic. From the first moment to the last the lonely hour of the 'last instance' never comes.

(Althusser 1969: 113)

The conception of overdetermination is a notable development in the theory of ideology. It makes meaningful an analysis of the level (or levels) of ideology and relates it in a non-reductive way to the economic base – the mode of production. Ideology, or the superstructural levels, in Althusser's rendering of the dialectic remains a constitutive part of a process that is characterized by unequal power and domination. Although his analysis is principally philosophical and occasionally historical, the concepts and theoretical relations between them that he develops are relevant to understanding specific instances of ideology.

IDEOLOGY, KNOWLEDGE AND SCIENCE

The problem remains though that Althusser has begun to theorize ideology in a way that is dependent on some other form of knowing being possible. He wants to grasp the nature of the practice of ideology scientifically and characterizes 'ideology' as whole, unified by its problematic and dependent on the social situation in which it occurs. Moreover, ideology is driven from outside, by the underlying political and economic context (Althusser 1969: 62–3). He articulates a distinction between scientific theoretical practice and ideological modes of thought:

Theoretical practice falls within the general definition of practice. It works on a raw material (representations, concepts, facts) which it is given by other practices, whether 'empirical', 'technical' or 'ideological'. In its most general form theoretical practice does not only include scientific theoretical practice, but also pre-scientific theoretical practice, that is, 'ideological' theoretical practice (the forms of 'knowledge' that make up the pre-history of science, and their 'philosophies').

(Althusser 1969: 167)

There is then a sequential and hierarchical distinction between science and ideology; science follows ideology, the discontinuity being marked by an 'epistemological break'. Althusser describes the ideological form of Marx's early work as humanist in that it addressed the problem of *human nature* or the essence of being human. Marx's epistemological break involved a rejection of this 'empiricism of the subject' and the emergence of a new problematic:

a theory of the different *levels* of human *practice* (economic practice, political practice, ideological practice, scientific practice) in their characteristic articulations, based on the specific articulations of the unity of human society.

(Althusser 1969: 229)

Although this amounts to a transformation of theory and its object it is not clear in what sense it is an *epistemological* break. The transformation of the problematic does not necessarily lead to a transformation of the form of validity of knowledge. If it did it would involve a transformation of the human practices that produce knowledge, that is the transformation of ideological practice into scientific practice. But this transformation is merely asserted by Althusser's claim of the epistemological break – he fails to describe the transformed practice, that of science, except in terms of what it is not (i.e. ideological practice).

In *Reading Capital* (Althusser and Balibar 1970), Althusser explores the development of Marx's scientific exposition of historical materialism, stressing the point that the raw materials of knowledge production are not things, not essences of the material world, but concepts and abstractions that are ideological or scientific. Furthermore, he locates knowledge production at the level of thought, as it were, untainted by the influence of ideology which operates in a practical world (bound by social practices and traditions). Not only does this sound like a reverse of Marx's critique of idealism but also there is no description of the process of knowledge or its relation to the 'real' world. Althusser rules out epistemology as a solution to the problem of ideology, arguing that there are no guarantees. The only criteria of 'science' we are left with are its 'openness' and the fact that it takes place 'entirely in thought'.

KNOWLEDGE AND THEORETICAL PRACTICE

Althusser develops a position that, as Callinicos (1976) describes it, is dependent on the autonomy of theory even though the scientificity of theory is difficult to guarantee if epistemology is rejected. Impressed by the form of the material sciences, Althusser follows Engels in comparing the development of Marx's 'science' with the development of the discovery of oxygen by Lavoisier and the relationship between the planets and the sun by Galileo. The comparability is that all three were involved in a 'break; the mutation by which a new science is established in a new problematic, separated from the old ideological problematic' (Althusser and Balibar 1970: 153). The difficulty with this is that Althusser (and Engels) are convincingly describing a change in problematic, perhaps even a paradigm shift, but it is not clear that what went on before is contrastable as ideology, as non-science. It may be accepted that Althusser is describing science by its theoretical practice, its 'labour of theoretical transformation', but this is not adequate to distinguish it from ideology as a practice. It also fails to explain how the theoretical practice of science can be separated for the purposes of knowledge production from other practices that are the hallmark of ideology in Althusser's account. Geras makes a similar point by emphasizing the idealism inherent in Althusser's separation of theoretical practice (science) from political practice (Geras 1977: 268).

Both in his foreword to the Italian edition of *Reading Capital* and his *Essays in Self Criticism* (Althusser 1976), Althusser points out his own 'theoreticist tendency' in equating philosophy with science as the 'Theory of theoretical practice' (Althusser 1976: 124). This account of science is indeed overly optimistic but at the same time limited. As we shall see in Chapter 8, the sociology of science does not provide evidence to support his belief in the independence of science from social structures and ideological processes. His account of ideology on the other hand is much more rewarding, locating it as he does in the presuppositions necessary for social life and avoiding the philosophical consequences of attempting to privilege one perspective.

IDEOLOGY AND STATE POWER

In the essay on 'Ideology and Ideological State Apparatuses' (Althusser 1971: 123–74) Althusser starts to describe the reproduction of the means of production and to articulate the form of the institutions that achieve this reproduction. These institutions, the Ideological State Apparatuses (ISAs) are listed by Althusser as: the religious, the educational, the family, the legal, the political, the trade union, the communications and the cultural. The ISAs are distinguished from the Repressive State Apparatus (RSA) in that the former are plural and private while the latter is unitary and public. The RSA (the government, administration, the army, the police, the courts, the prisons, etc.) functions, at least ultimately, by repression and violence. In contrast the ISAs function predominantly by ideology and derive a unity through the dominance of ideology by the ruling class:

> To my knowledge, no class can hold State power over a long period without at the same time exercising its hegemony over and in the State Ideological Apparatuses.
>
> (Althusser 1971: 139)

The ruling class may be an alliance of classes and the maintenance of hegemony is not the same thing as a monolithic dominant ideology. This means that the ISAs are one of the sites of class struggle and although there is a continuity amongst the ISAs Althusser suggests that some are more dominating than others in the sense that they play a larger role in the reproduction of the relations of production. Under feudalism there was a dominant ISA, the Church, which worked in concert with the family. With the development of capitalism and the shift of power from the aristocracy to the bourgeoisie, many of the functions of the church were devolved onto other emerging ISAs, the most important being the educational.

Pointing to social institutions that are empirically recognizable is a refreshing change in Althusser's style but it is not just the identification of the institutions that is important. Describing the mechanism by which ideology works is the only way that we can be convinced by Althusser's institutions since he has defined them theoretically by their functions. Hirst (1976) takes exception to Althusser theorizing the ISAs as the means by which the relations of production are reproduced. He disputes the distinction between production and reproduction of the *relations* of production and argues that Althusser is actually describing the reproduction of the *agents* of production; human socialized individuals. Furthermore these economic agents are not necessarily human subjects; capital can be an anonymous economic agent, in the form of the managed enterprise.

Hirst's criticisms point to the inherent functionalism of Althusser's conception of the ISAs. The state has a function, the reproduction of relations (or agents) of production, that the ISAs fulfil. The functions of the state and the ISAs are unified by the ruling class and its ideology. This scheme in which power operates uniformly in direction and function, echoes economistic versions of the mechanics of ideology. As social institutions the ISAs are 'driven' by a force beyond them – the contradictions at the base.

The theory of the ISAs would indeed be very crude if Althusser left it at that but he completes the essay with a discussion of ideology, the mode in which the ISAs function. Here Althusser attempts to analyse the general form of ideology as opposed to theorizing particular ideologies 'which in whatever their form (religious, ethical, legal, political), always express class positions' (Althusser 1971: 150). Ideology in general has no history in the sense that its structure and form is immutable throughout history. Althusser compares this characteristic to Freud's proposition that the unconscious is eternal. He offers two remarkable theses that describe this trans-historical form:

Ideology represents the imaginary relationship of individuals to their real conditions of existence.

(Althusser 1971: 153)

Ideology has a material existence.

(Althusser 1971: 155)

The second thesis is perhaps easier to grasp. 'Ideas' or 'representations' do not have a spiritual existence, their existence is material and the materiality of ideology is marked by its existence in 'apparatuses' and 'practices'. The first thesis is more difficult in that it does not express ideology as mere illusion nor as a reflection of real conditions. The imaginary aspect of ideology is to do with the *relationship* between individuals and real conditions. It is interesting to note that an objective reality is presupposed by this thesis – there is a real existence of an individual that is material and is separated from the ideological consciousness of the individual by an 'imaginary' relationship. For Althusser, the 'real conditions' are, in the last instance, relations of production and class relations. The 'imaginary relation' is a material one, that is, it is the actions or practices of the individual that flow 'freely' from her ideas. Althusser has constructed a subject that is endowed with consciousness which 'believes' freely in ideas or 'forms' ideas freely. But the actions that must be consequent on those ideas, Althusser asserts are:

> inserted into *practices*. And I shall point out that these practices are governed by the *rituals* in which these practices are inscribed, with the *material existence of an ideological apparatus*.

(Althusser 1971: 158)

These apparatuses need not be major institutions; Althusser offers as examples of ritual practices a funeral, a school day, a political party meeting. One of the consequences he claims for this theory is the disappearance of ideas 'to the precise extent that it has emerged that their existence is inscribed in the actions of practices governed by rituals defined in the last instance by an ideological apparatus' (Althusser 1971: 159).

Althusser's thesis is a version of the social determination of knowledge that relies on the socialization of human subjects into ritual practices. There is implied the possibility of a break in this functionalist account of the determination of ideas, beliefs and actions. But if ideas can escape the chain of determinacy, what is their form? The production of discourse, especially scientific discourse, would seem to comply with Althusser's concept of 'ritual practice'. The very science that he is, presumably, engaged in can itself be recognized as existing as a practice within three of the ISAs he refers to; the educational, the political and the communicative ISAs.

But Althusser's principal hypothesis is that 'ideology interpellates individuals as subjects' (Althusser 1971: 161) by which he means that the subject and ideology are mutually constituting categories. It refers to the fact that subjects do not engage in ideology but are 'always already subjects'. Even the unborn child is 'expected' and constituted as a subject by its having a name and a sexual destiny thrust upon it at birth by the family and community that expects it.

Althusser's description of ideology in general in the ISA's paper seems to cover all possibilities of discursive action and some cognitive action (believing; having, creating and accepting ideas). The process of interpellation of subjects involves a 'recognition' that constantly transforms individuals into subjects. Ideology, whether in the form of religious cant or a friendly greeting creates a location for the individual which she/he fills by recognizing it as their place (as a servant of God, as the person hailed). It is in that recognition (Althusser calls it a 'mirror structure') that the subject is constituted. Moreover, the recognition process is a double mirror structure in that a Subject is also recognized and thereby constituted. The Subject is the category that marks the place that the individual must fill to be constituted as a subject. So, the Subject is constituted as a centre of authority to which the subject must be obedient: 'God', 'the boss', 'their [i.e. the subjects'] conscience', 'de Gaulle', 'the priest', 'the engineer', 'thou shalt love thy neighbour as thyself' (Althusser 1971: 169).

The imaginary relation between individuals and their real conditions is founded in the illusion that the 'recognition' is free; what is obscured is the subjection to the Subject that is necessary and unavoidable. Even in denying the relation, by refusing to 'recognize' (God, a friend, the law) the individual is recognizing the place they are refusing to fill and thus is still constituted as a subject. What ensures this is that the ideological apparatus responds (damnation, approbation, incarceration). The individual cannot disengage with the apparatus.

Althusser has all along promised an escape through scientific practice, an escape that may be brief and ineffective in itself but which leads to a transformation of other practices – especially political practice. But the conditions of science as a practice which may escape the functional determination of ideology, are not explained. Althusser asserts that all ideology is 'centred' while science is 'decentred' and has no subjects and no Subject but it remains unclear how science might escape from ideology. He merely proposes that:

while speaking in ideology, and from within ideology we have to outline a discourse which tries to break with ideology, in order to dare to be the beginning of a scientific (i.e. subject-less) discourse on ideology.

(Althusser 1971: 162)

The conception of ideology that Althusser offers involves a social determination thesis that avoids mechanistic determination through the possibility of science. Like Habermas's 'ideal speech situation', the fact that scientific practice can never be realized is not the point. It describes a possibility, endemic to the social form of ideology, that determination is not total and mechanistic.

This is to read Althusser's distinction between science and ideology as being finally not one between equivalent categories. 'Science' describes the ideal form that motivates struggle within ideology. In this sense science is not a sociological category (i.e. one that can be used to describe specific social forms) nor is it an epistemological category (i.e. one that can be used to account for the form or validity of knowledge). Instead, 'science' can be understood as a response to the conditions of existence (material and ideological) that resists the givenness of those conditions. It is clear that while Althusser compares the 'science' of Marxism with the 'science' of the material sciences, he is not describing the same features as would traditional sociologists or philosophers. He characterizes science by its epistemological break with ideology, a moment in the production of knowledge not indicated by a new theory of knowledge or a new sociological form. The moment of the break is not transcendent but it is a breaking free of the determinations of ideology – a moment in which the presuppositions that determine ideology are transformed by a critical response to them.

THE CRITIQUE OF SCIENCE AND CULTURE

The work of the Frankfurt School as a whole can be seen as a critique of ideology. In developing 'critical theory' the writers of this group confronted the social role of knowledge and ideology using a framework for analysis and an approach very different from that of the sociology of knowledge. Their critique of ideology is derived from the social, historical and philosophical insights of Marx and is concerned with the process of contemporary ideology, although they do not present a theory of ideology as such.

There are two particular knowledge systems that attract the attention of critical theory: science and mass culture. For Adorno and

Horkheimer science becomes ideological because of the change in the relationship between humans and nature that accompanies it. As humans liberate themselves from the constraints of nature (scarce resources) through technology, there comes about a domination of nature. The domination of nature generates a dominating mentality so people dominate each other and accept domination in the name of technological reason and scientific rationality. While scientific rationality can produce 'enlightenment' about nature it also alienates human beings through the social relations consequent upon the domination of nature. These social relations are specifically class relations that replicate the domination of nature in the domination of one class by another.

Marcuse takes up the theme of domination through the ideological form of technological reason and shows how it is legitimized by the widespread consumption enabled by increased production. Domination by political repression, the open domination of one class by another, is no longer necessary. Manipulation of 'needs' by both creating them and satisfying them is the process by which social control is effected. Marcuse points out that:

> the technological controls appear to be the very embodiment of Reason for the benefit of all social groups and interests – to such an extent that all contradiction seems irrational and all counteraction impossible.
>
> (Marcuse 1972: 22)

The effect is that the individual identifies herself with an existence which is imposed upon her. Ideology becomes 'reality' as it is absorbed by the individual. The ideology which both constitutes existence for the individual and imposes social relations upon her is mediated through the culture:

> The means of mass transportation and communication, the commodities of lodging, food and clothing, the irresistible output of the entertainment and information industry carry with them prescribed attitudes and habits, certain intellectual and emotional reactions which bind the consumers more or less pleasantly to the producers and through the latter to the whole.
>
> (Marcuse 1972: 24)

This critique of the consequences of science and consumption culture as ideology comes from a method that is 'dialectical'; there is a two-sided discourse that through the effect of criticism on consciousness changes over time. The principal object of the critique is an ideological structure that is 'one dimensional' (Marcuse 1972: 79) in that it has no reflexive or critical aspects but is uniform in its mode of rationality.

CRITICAL THEORY

Horkheimer in his essay on 'Traditional and Critical Theory' outlines the features of a critical theory and its methods. In rejecting traditional theory as a 'mathematical knowledge of nature which claims to be the eternal logos' he suggests that the self-knowledge of present-day man is 'a critical theory of society as it is, a theory dominated at every turn by a concern for reasonable conditions of life' (Horkheimer 1972: 199). Critical theory questions not just isolated elements of the society which it takes as its object; it is the whole historical structure which is being criticized. Thus it questions the values of the existing order of 'better', 'useful', 'appropriate', 'productive' and 'valuable' and is 'wholly distrustful of the rules of conduct with which society as presently constituted provides each of its members' (Horkheimer 1972: 207). The thought of the critical attitude is marked by a tension in the identity of the critical thinker with his society. Such thinkers:

> interpret the economic categories of work, value, and productivity exactly as they are interpreted in the existing order ... [but] ... the critical acceptance of the categories which rule social life contains simultaneously their condemnation.
>
> (Horkheimer 1972: 208)

The 'dialectic' method thinks through the contradiction between categories given to the thinker that also subordinate her. The critical theory that derives from dialectical thought uses the given categories to criticize both the categories and the social structure which generates them. However, the power of critical thought lies not in any aspiration towards 'absolute truth' (for which Horkheimer criticizes bourgeois methods) but in its merging of the experience and action of the thinker and the categories available to consciousness. Bourgeois thought indulges in an abstraction of the process of thinking from the total process of being, thereby reifying thought and setting it above being. In this way traditional theory 'explains' in the absence of experience (i.e. in abstraction) and so merely confirms the ideological categories given to its consciousness. Scientific rationality for the Frankfurt School involves the domination of experience by purporting to describe and explain it whereas critical theory engages in the dialectic between lived experience and the categories given to describe it. The validity of critical theory lies not in the adoption of a method, vindicated by epistemology, but in the enlightenment that is successful in generating a political practice that moves towards emancipation, the liberation of human beings from domination.

In a collectively written paper, the members of the Frankfurt School confront the concept of ideology, both criticizing its historical development as a concept and the role of ideology in contemporary society. The Enlightenment doctrines had included the belief:

> that it was sufficient to bring order into consciousness, for order to be brought into society. However, it is not only this belief which is bourgeois but the nature of ideology itself. As a consciousness which is objectively necessary and yet at the same time false, as the intertwining of truth and falsehood, which is just as distinct from the whole truth as it is from the pure lie, ideology belongs, if not to a modern economy, then, in any case, to a developed urban market economy. For ideology is justification.
>
> (Horkheimer 1972: 189)

For the Frankfurt School, 'ideology' is a concept to be used in the political interpretation of social forces and is predicated on a Marxist theory of the political history and structure of society. But there is inevitably a claim to truth involved and the critical content of theory alone is not sufficient to justify its acceptance:

> what is required, and what is lacking in the *Zeitschrift* essays, is a philosophical elucidation of thought on materialist presuppositions, which while overcoming Hegel's idealism, does not fall below the level of insight he achieved.
>
> Habermas attempts to accomplish this through a linguistic reformulation of the philosophical foundations of historical materialism.
>
> (McCarthy's introduction to Habermas 1976: xii)

The early critical theorists (Horkheimer, Adorno, Marcuse) gave an insufficient philosophical basis on which to found the status of critical theory in their essays on aspects of critical theory (the *Zeitschrift* essays). To put it simply, in criticizing ideology, critical theory has to establish itself as not prone to the same failings as ideology.

It was left to Jürgen Habermas to establish a more comprehensive account of the basis of critical theory. The Hegelian tendency in Marcuse's work suggested that contradictions in the conditions of existence could be conquered by raising contradictions at the level of consciousness. The failure of this approach as a political strategy led to a review of its idealist formulation. What was needed was a theory of the material conditions, including social and political relations, that inhibit the emancipation of human beings through their own actions.

HABERMAS

The early work of Jürgen Habermas develops the Marxist theory of ideology in a particular way. Firstly, the role of 'consciousness' as an historical force is reformulated without recourse to Hegelian idealism or historicism. Secondly, the epistemological problems that such a reformulation generates are confronted without creating a division between 'science' and 'ideology' or 'true' and 'false' consciousness. Habermas's theory involves a reflexive moment that was present but unsatisfactorily worked out in the earlier versions of critical theory. Thirdly, the way these issues are dealt with is by developing a theory of communicative action. Fourthly, Habermas develops a theory of the processes of advanced capitalist society that is both 'critical' and yet optimistic.

This range of issues dealt with by Habermas extends way beyond the tradition of the critique of ideology or the sociology of knowledge. But there is an interdependence between the various themes in his work that makes it difficult to deal with them in isolation. The theory of communicative action is perhaps the crucial and radical component in Habermas's work but it is not a discrete theory; it develops in response to a number of problems both theoretical and empirical raised in a variety of contexts. This makes it difficult to offer a succinct exegetical account of Habermas's work but I shall pursue three problems to try to present his contribution to the theory of ideology: the problem of epistemology, the problem of ideology and the problem of communication. I shall also briefly refer to the reformed roles that ideology/knowledge have to play in Habermas's account of advanced capitalism.

THE SUBJECT AND SIGNIFICATION

Habermas interprets Hegel's early work on the philosophy of mind (the Jena lectures) to offer three dialectical relations that constitute a systematic basis for the formative process of spirit:

> symbolic representation, the labour process, and interaction on the basis of reciprocity; each mediates subject and object in its own way.
> (Habermas 1974: 142)

The significance of these three relations is that through them subjects are constituted and although the relations have a relation to each other, none is reducible to any other. Symbolic representation refers to the category of language and is one of the ways that a knowing subject, the 'I', is constituted.

Language orders the world of perception and at the same time constitutes a knowing subject that perceives and yet is distinguished from that world. Labour produces a parallel relation in that 'it breaks the dictates of immediate desires and, as it were, arrests the process of drive satisfaction' (Habermas 1974: 154). The dialectic of labour produces a different effect, on a differently constituted subject, than that of language in that it involves subjection to the world of nature. Whereas the dialectic of language (in its proto-form, a 'name giving consciousness') generates a relation from within the subject, labour is a subjection to the causality of nature. But labour has consequences for consciousness in that rules for instrumental action are developed which enable the subject to have a measure of control over nature through the use of tools.

The third dialectic involves the subject recognizing itself through interaction with other subjects. The subject is able to constitute itself as an 'I', an abstract, self-knowing subject, in an interaction that recognizes an 'other' that is a similarly formed subject. This dialectic means that the constitution of a universal category of subjectivity that includes all other subjects at the same time, is also part of the process by which an individual is constituted, as an 'I' that distinguishes itself as non-identical with all other subjects.

The dialectic of the relation of reciprocal interaction is potentially the area of distorted communication but there are tendencies in all the subject constituting relations which contribute to the distortion in relations of reciprocal interaction. In symbolic representation the tendency 'indicates an object or a state of affairs as something else' (Habermas 1974: 153) and in the labour process it involves a 'subjection to the causality of nature' (Habermas 1974: 154).

By adopting this early phenomenology of Hegel, Habermas generates a theory of the knowing subject that is sociological with its reference to the social activities of labour and communication, and yet retains a tension between the individual subject and its location within social formation. He carefully avoids a Kantian reduction to a knowing subject founded on self-reflection or a Hegelian reduction to a universal subject constituted as the absolute spirit of history. Either of these two formulations would require a transcendental knowing subject and would constitute knowledge as a special phenomenon abstracted from the material level of human action. Habermas's knowing subject is materially grounded in the actions of human subjects but there is no reduction to concrete material relations as in Marx. He suggests that Marx's interpretation of Hegel (even without the benefit of access to the Jena lectures) produced an account of the formation of the human species that reduces communicative action to instrumental action – labour (Habermas 1974: 169).

Perhaps the most important consequence of Habermas's 'rediscovered' dialectics of the subject is that he has distinguished his version of critical theory from any possibility of material determination – even in the last instance. This does not amount to a rejection of Marx but points to an absence in his work and leaves Habermas free to retain a basically Marxist account of the forces of production and at the same time develop a theory of social relations of communicative production.

THE PROBLEM OF IDEOLOGY

With his account of the three categories, Habermas has also substantially altered the way in which 'ideology' can be considered. The determination by the material base having been displaced, the form of ideology (distortion) can no longer be explained merely by reference to contradictions in the material base although Habermas incorporates Marx's critique of the commodity form of labour as ideology (Habermas 1972: 59). In developing the critique of political economy as a critique of ideology, Marx retained some aspects of the dialectic of Hegelian critique, but did not offer a philosophical foundation for it within his own materialist system. This leads to a tendency to reduce the form of critique to the form of natural science which, Habermas argues, would not have happened if Marx had maintained a distinction between instrumental and communicative action. The failure of Marx to be clear about the epistemological basis of his critique led to a possibility of misinterpretation:

> And later Marx never explicitly rejected the naturalistic version of the doctrine of ideology which Engels supplied . . . . As long as historical materialism no longer saw itself as involved in the objective crisis complex, as soon as it understood its critique exclusively as positive science and the dialectic objectively as the law of the world, then the ideological character of consciousness had to take on a metaphysical quality . . . . Within this superficial understanding, the correct ideology was distinguished from the false solely according to the criteria of a realistic theory of knowledge.
>
> (Habermas 1974: 238)

The reference to the 'crisis complex' is to a further failing in Marx's analysis. By accounting for the development of the mode of production in terms of economic relations only, Marx failed to take account of the development of political forces which also have an effect on the development of the mode of production. These political forces develop, of course, in the dimension of communicative action, the absent category in Marx's phenomenology. Habermas describes how the concentration and centralization of capital leads weaker parties in the market to assert their claims in a political form. The same features of the mode of production also lead to the state intervening in the process of commodity exchange and social labour. Habermas incorporates Marx's critique of political economy but makes 'ideology' an effective force in the development of the mode of production.

SCIENCE AND TECHNOLOGY

In going beyond Marx's analysis of liberal capitalism, Habermas points out that the bourgeois ideology of 'just exchange' (Habermas 1971: 101) breaks down and with its collapse, political power requires a new source of legitimation. The development from liberal to advanced capitalism has two characteristics. Firstly, the state takes on the role of intervening in the relations of production to control the dysfunctional aspects of capitalism; the contradictions of capital that Marx described. Secondly, the state intervenes in the forces of production by organizing science to generate technology (research and development programmes). This process Habermas calls the 'scientization of technology':

> Thus science and technology become a leading productive force, rendering inoperative the conditions for Marx's labour theory of value.
>
> (Habermas 1971: 104)

In advanced capitalism these two aspects, state intervention and the scientization of technology, create the appearance of social evolution being determined by science and technology. Politics becomes an issue of solving the technical problems of advancing capitalism rather than the realization of practical goals. At the same time the imperative of economic growth to minimize the contradictions of capital, creates an apparent dependence on the logic of scientific and technological progress.

Technology serves as a 'background ideology' that takes on legitimizing power and Habermas writes of the fetishization of science as a 'new' ideology. The 'technocratic consciousness' that takes the place of the old bourgeois ideology is not based on collective repression.

Instead there are rewards for privatized needs that occlude any practical questions about the organization of social life.

Marcuse saw a possibility for developing a new, critical, science not dependent on instrumental reason or the ideological form of modern science and technology. His analysis of the development of instrumental reason, however, was as a consequence of the development of the forces of production. Habermas rejects this analysis because the level of communicative action can have an impact on the process of modernization that Marcuse ignored. In Habermas's account, 'work' and 'interaction' are relatively separate processes with the latter not reduced to the former. The development of rationalization brings about a change in the relationship of these two processes. This more complex account of the process of levels of social formation interacting is reminiscent of Althusser's theory of overdetermination.

IDEOLOGY AND LEGITIMATION

In traditional societies the legitimacy of political power is maintained through 'mythical, religious or metaphysical interpretations of reality' (Habermas 1971: 95) including the divine right of those who rule to continue to rule. They are also interpretations that do not tolerate challenges – either in the form of offences against the king or blasphemy. Habermas describes this as domination 'from above' because the cultural tradition that legitimizes power is generated and passed down through those who exercise it.

Things change when a different mode of knowledge based on purposive-rational action reaches a certain stage of development. Purposive-rational or instrumental action is governed by technical rules based on empirical knowledge that implies conditional predictions about observable events, physical or social. This mode of rationality, whether it is applied to scientific or technological problems or to problems of economic production is governed by 'strategies based on *analytic* knowledge' (Habermas 1971: 92). Strategic and instrumental rationality achieves economic growth and at a certain point, for Habermas the point of modernization, the new mode of knowledge challenges the traditional form of legitimation of power.

Capitalism, Habermas argues, replaces the traditional mode of domination from above with a new mode of domination from below – bourgeois ideology. It is based not on the mythico-religious system resistant to challenge but on the exchange relations of the commodity market including the labour market. Bourgeois ideology takes over the legitimizing functions of traditional society and thereby keeps power relations inaccessible to analysis and public consciousness. This leads Habermas to a very particular formulation of ideology:

> It is in this way that ideologies in the restricted sense first came into being. They replace traditional legitimations of power by appearing in the mantle of modern science and by deriving their justification from the critique of ideology. Ideologies are coeval with the critique of ideology. In this sense there can be no pre-bourgeois 'ideologies'.
>
> (Habermas 1971: 99)

Habermas's analysis is more optimistic than Marcuse's. The emergence of science and technology as legitimizing forces not only signals the transformation of the traditional form of ideology to a modern, rational, form but also signals the emergence of the critique of ideology.

KNOWLEDGE AND INTERESTS

One line of epistemological inquiry leads Habermas to explore the developed forms of knowledge in a way that locates them in terms of his phenomenological grounding of knowing subjects. This investigation produces what Habermas terms 'knowledge-constitutive interests' (Habermas 1972: 191). Habermas reveals three such interests. The technical, which corresponds to the activity of the nomological sciences, the practical, which corresponds to the hermeneutic sciences, and the emancipatory, which corresponds to the critical sciences.

In developing a critique of scientism (which Habermas regards *Knowledge and Human Interests* to be) he is not rejecting the epistemological validity of the nomological sciences or the hermeneutic sciences but is trying to orient them in relation to the critical sciences. It is the scientism of Marx and Freud that has to be rejected and a status found for their critical theories through their interest in emancipation from domination (economic domination and domination of the individual through neuroses). The importance of his distancing from earlier critical theory becomes clear; 'science' as a form of epistemology cannot be dismissed as ideology but a tendency to 'scientism' can be treated as obscuring knowledge-constitutive interests and as potentially ideological. Habermas's grounds his own claim to generate knowledge in two ways. Firstly, he is clearly operating within the area of 'emancipatory interest' and maintaining a position within critical theory. This means that the claim to validity of his work is postponed until its success is demonstrated through its effects in an emancipatory practice. The process of critical theory in the area of sociology involves a particular attitude:

Critical of ideology, it asks what lies behind the consensus, presented as fact, that supports the dominant tradition of the time, and does so with a view to the relations of power surreptitiously incorporated in the symbolic structures of the systems of speech and action.

(Habermas 1974: 12)

Secondly, Habermas points to a methodological possibility that could have far-reaching epistemological effects. The structure of ideology, that which has to be got behind, is created by blocks in communication that limit the options between 'verbal and nonverbal forms of expression', and between 'communication and discourse' (Habermas 1974: 12). The way to analyse ideology is through a theory of communicative action.

COMMUNICATIVE ACTION

Habermas's early work on the theory of communicative action involves establishing the role of a 'universal pragmatics', linked to an analysis of the 'ideal speech situation' and 'systematically distorted communication' (Habermas 1970a; 1970b; 1979). The aim of a universal pragmatics is to reconstruct the rules by which adult speakers are able to:

embed sentences in relations to reality in such a way that they can take on the general pragmatic functions of representation, expression and establishing interpersonal relations.

(Habermas 1979: 32)

The universal pragmatics is an attempt to describe the process by which people interact and establish their identity through communicative action. But, according to Habermas, implicit within the form of communication are claims to validity at a number of levels: 'truth' (representing facts; referring to the extended world of nature), 'rightness' (establishing legitimate interpersonal relations; referring to our world of society), 'truthfulness' (expression of the speaker's subjectivity) and 'comprehensibility' (the domain of language). For Habermas, speech acts or utterances aimed at achieving understanding contain these universal claims to validity (Habermas 1979). His interest is not (or at least not merely) to analyse empirical instances of language. The universality of these pragmatic features of communication indicates the possibility of the ideal speech situation or 'discourse', when communication is undistorted. The universality of the pragmatic features of communication means that all communicatively competent speech contains the possibility of the ideal speech situation:

No matter how the intersubjectivity of mutual understanding may be deformed, the design of an ideal speech situation is necessarily implied in the structure of potential speech, since all speech, even of intentional deception, is oriented towards the idea of truth.

(Habermas 1970b: 372)

Habermas is grounding truth in the particular form of human communication. The universality of the orientation to truth makes it as much a part of the genetic qualities of human being as the ability to communicate through language. What is radical in Habermas's proposal is that while the possibility of speaking the truth is enstructured in every utterance, all the other modes of grounding truth become sources of distortion; historical world-view, ideology, scientism, material determinism, reduction to class consciousness.

The validity claims involved in the form of communicative action are given a 'quasi-transcendental' status because they are present in communication even if obscured by distortion:

In place of a priori demonstration, we have transcendental investigation of the conditions for argumentatively redeeming validity claims that are at least implicitly related to discursive vindication.

(Habermas 1979: 23)

Habermas interprets the universality of the pragmatic features of communication to be oriented towards the possibility of 'truth'. I will argue that such a truth is relational; that is, relative to the social and historical location of the intersubjective action, discursive and practical, in which participants find themselves.

There is a tendency in Habermas's theoretical framework to reduce communicative competence to 'norms' which threatens to preclude a critical account of the social production and reproduction of those norms which the critique of ideology traditionally proposes. Giddens comments that Habermas's emphasis upon the normative components of interaction is 'surprisingly close' to Parson's functionalism:

Both accord primacy to the norm in examining social interaction, rather than to power . . . . I should want to make the case for arguing that power is as integral a component of all social interaction as norms are.

(Giddens 1982: 159)

In the two volumes of *The Theory of Communicative Action* (1984; 1987a), Habermas reviews the nature of rationality and modernity through a series of dialogues with and reflections on the work of major social theorists – Marx, Weber, Durkheim, Mead, Lukács, Horkheimer, Adorno and Parsons. As in his earlier work the aim is to analyse the levels of social process that constitute social formations. The concept of rationality, which he promotes as a feature of modernizing societies, is tied to the process of communicative action rather than to the subjective and individualistic premises of much modern philosophy and social theory. As well as providing a means for analysing social process, the rationality of communicative action provides the basis for the understanding of an interpreter of that action:

> The interpreter observes under what conditions symbolic expressions are accepted as valid and when validity claims connected with them are criticized and rejected; he notices when the action plans of participants are coordinated through consensus formation and when the connections among the actions of different agents fall apart due to lack of consensus.

> (Habermas 1984: 115)

The interpreter neither has a special location for undertaking analysis, nor a special method but the reflexive attention to the relation between communicative action and its content. Just like any other agent engaged in communicative action oriented towards understanding, the interpreter makes claims that have to be supported with reasoned argument.

The context of communicative action is the 'lifeworld' that includes culture, society and personality:

> The lifeworld is the intuitively present, in this sense familiar and transparent, and at the same time vast and incalculable web of presuppositions that have to be satisfied if an actual utterance is to be at all meaningful, that is valid *or* invalid.

> (Habermas 1987a: 131)

It is through the processes of cultural reproduction, social integration and socialization that the lifeworld is constantly reproduced. The lifeworld both provides the basis of meaning on which communicative action can draw and it is also a product of the exchange of meaning that constitutes communicative action. The roots of Habermas's concept of lifeworld clearly lie with the phenomenology of Schutz and Berger and Luckmann (see Chapter 3) but his concept is closely related to a theory of social systems that includes the institutional structure of society. Habermas is careful to ensure that neither lifeworld nor system are subsumed by the other category but he explores links between them, including the systematic restriction of communication. It is the set of formal conditions of possible understanding, the rules of discourse, that restrict communication and help to sustain ideological interpretations of the world (Habermas 1987a: 189). In general though, with the theory of communicative action, Habermas is withdrawing from critical theory including the critique of ideology which he suggests has 'become dull' within an inadequate metatheoretical framework (Habermas 1987a: 202). He also argues that the increasing fragmentation and differentiation of the rationalized lifeworld of modernity both takes the place of ideology and at the same time makes it difficult to sustain:

> In place of 'false consciousness' we today have a 'fragmented consciousness' that blocks enlightenment by the mechanism of reification.
>
> (Habermas 1987a: 355)

The proposition that truth underlies the form of communication is not compatible with the sociology of knowledge. Relationism situates both the form and content of knowledge in relation to its social context and while it avoids a reduction to the social basis of knowledge leaves no space for even a quasi-transcendental truth. Communication is a social practice and even if systematic distortion is removed, existential determination is not. Knowledge, as the product of the social practice of communication, is always a product of social being and to some degree determined by the presuppositions given to social being that constitute the possibility of communication.

For both Habermas and Althusser the problem of analysing ideology is bound up with the status of valid knowledge. This leads Althusser into the unrewarding account of 'science' but at the same time his account of the social process of ideology through the concepts of over-determination and the ideological state apparatuses takes the theory of ideology forward substantially. Critical theory offers a more optimistic account of valid knowledge through the postponed validity to be derived from emancipatory practice. Habermas's early analyses of ideology in relation to rationality and legitimation seemed to build on Marx's theory of ideology within a framework of critique. But he seems to have withdrawn from his earlier commitment to critical theory and become increasing involved in the philosophical basis of communicative action.

Habermas's later work has opened up the way for communication to be studied as a social practice and has identified it as a dimension of social being largely absent in Marx's account. His early critique asked 'what lies behind the consensus?', what 'supports the dominant tradition of the time' and proposes an analysis based on 'the relations of power surreptitiously incorporated' in the social practices including communication (Habermas 1974: 12 – quoted above). Such a perspective does not require a universal pragmatics for it to proceed with an analysis of the form of discourse as ideology.

6   From signification to discourse

These 'structuralists' may lack a common programme but they do not lack a common ancestry. It is principally in the genealogy of their ideas that one should look for evidence of their kinship.

(Sturrock 1979: 5)

This is how Sturrock introduces a collection of five essays on Lévi-Strauss, Roland Barthes, Michel Foucault, Jacques Lacan, and Jacques Derrida. I too will treat this group of writers as 'structuralists' and look at some aspects of their work to show how it has created an object for analysis that is relevant to the empirical tasks of the sociology of knowledge. This object, discourse, is at once an empirical phenomenon recognizable without a particular theory, and at the same time a theoretical object that is amenable to analysis.

As an object, discourse is available on two levels. Firstly, to a participant (in a discourse, in a kinship system) for whom the object has a reality that can be described and understood. Secondly, to an analyst (of discourse, of a kinship system) for whom the object has structural features that enable it to be understood in relation to other, similar structural forms. The analyst describes features that the participant need not necessarily be aware of. Awareness of these features may even impair the participant's practice but they are features that enable the analyst to understand, in a more general way, what participation involves.

To explore further what the object of study of the structuralists is, I will first follow its development from a common ancestry in the particular approach to language that originates in the work of Saussure and the members of the Prague Circle.

SAUSSURE AND THE SIGN

Linguistics is the study of the mechanisms of language but Saussure breaks with a traditional concern with grammatical rules. His approach is to study the structure of the elements of language:

> Language is a system of interdependent terms in which the value of each term results solely from the simultaneous presence of the others.
>
> (Saussure 1974: 114)

A traditional linguistics which studies the formal properties of a language (its lexicon, phonology, graphology) assumes that meaning is conveyed through correct application of the rules by users. But for language users, the rules become an issue only when communication breaks down, and even then, language can remain effective communication long after rules have been bent or broken.

By studying the structure of the elements of language Saussure dispenses with the tie between meaning and the exercise of formal rules. Instead he links meaning and linguistic structure through a concept of the sign in which the signified (the meaning) is only arbitrarily related to the signifier (the phonological or graphological form of the sign):

$$\frac{\text{signified (concept)}}{\text{signifier (sound-image)}}$$

The arbitrary link between form and meaning is the radical centre of Saussurian linguistics:

> The idea of 'sister' is not linked by an inner relationship to the succession of sounds s-o-r which serves as its signifier in French; that it could be represented equally well by just any other sequence is proved by the differences among languages and by the very existence of different languages.
>
> (Saussure 1974: 63)

The effect is to focus on the systematic relationship between signifiers that is characteristic of language in general. This focus is at a deeper level than that of grammatical rules that concern specific languages. Although the link between signifier and signified is arbitrary, the relationships amongst signifiers and amongst signifieds are relationships of value:

> even outside language all values are governed by the same paradoxical principle. They are always composed:

1) of a dissimilar thing that can be exchanged for the thing of which the value is to be determined; and

2) of similar things that can be compared with the thing of which the value is to be determined.

(Saussure 1974: 115)

The conception of language that Saussure developed is that of a social phenomenon, realized not in the individual act of speaking, but 'only by virtue of a sort of contract signed by the members of a community' (Saussure 1974: 14). Although Saussure claims the arbitrary and differential qualities of language as 'a priori' they need not appear so for the user. Indeed, the identification of meaning with the material form of language (words, sentences, speech) is a precondition of ordinary language use; to use language is to trust it as a tool that expresses meaning. It is of course possible to use language in a premeditated and reflective way consciously to construct meaning. This use of language is poetic and characterized by the intention being applied not only to content but also to its specific form.

An historical (diachronic) account of the form of language is rejected by Saussure because it implies a less than arbitrary relationship between signifier and signified. He does however describe language as a form in a constant process of evolution that is not tied to corresponding changes in its meaning or vice versa. But he denies any law of evolution; the regularity in synchronic linguistics is not a result of evolutionary continuity.

The structuralists adopted Saussure's conception of an analytical object, language, as structured in itself and not reducible to any external structures. In their hands, structural anthropology and semiology took on the study of the structural form of meaningful systems. But they did not stop at the analysis of the system of meanings, they used this analysis as a basis for recovering 'hidden' meanings – for *interpreting* what they were studying. The structuralists looked at meaningful systems within their social context and analysed meaning as structured in a way analogous to language.

The common ancestry of the structuralists lies in the theoretical form they construe for the objects they analyse. As we shall see, the object for Lévi-Strauss's anthropology and Barthes's semiology is a social form that can be analysed as a language (kinship systems, myth). But for the later Barthes, for Foucault and for Derrida the object is constituted empirically in language but is treated as a system of signifieds – discourse.

The transformation of the object of study from the system of signification to the process of discourse involves a critique of the sign and of structure. It involves the transformation of an object that is meaningful but structured at the level of the signification to an object that is still meaningful but is also structured at the level of the signified.

STRUCTURAL ANTHROPOLOGY

Lévi-Strauss saw structuralism as playing the same role for the social sciences as nuclear physics had for the physical sciences. What he means by structuralism is clearly rooted in structural linguistics and he carefully quotes Troubetzkoy to indicate the programme he will apply to anthropology:

> First, structural linguistics shifts from the study of *conscious* linguistic phenomena to the study of their *unconscious* infrastructure; second it does not treat *terms* as independent entities, taking instead as its basis of analysis the *relations* between terms; third, it introduces the concept of *system* ...; finally, structural linguistics aims at discovering *general* laws, either by induction 'or ... by logical deduction, which would give them absolute character.'
> (Lévi-Strauss 1968: 33; L-S quotes from Troubetzkoy's 'La Phonologie Actuelle', Paris 1933).

This programme does not seem so radical in terms of social philosophies to warrant Lévi-Strauss's optimism for its effects. It is, however, the way he makes a connection between anthropology and linguistics that makes his programme unusual:

> Like phonemes, kinship terms are elements of meaning; like phonemes, they acquire meaning only if they are integrated into systems.
> (Lévi-Strauss 1968: 34)

What is strange about this is that phonemes are no more than elements of meaning but kinship terms also represent real relationships lived by people. The type of formal analysis of meaning that Lévi-Strauss was proposing was very different from the common sense of 'meaning' available to participants in the social events being analysed. Lévi-Strauss is not interested in what it means to be party to a maternal-uncle type of kinship relationship. 'Meaning' has a much more general significance and the search is for a universal meaning, one that crosses the boundaries of distinguishable human cultures or kinship groups.

What excites Lévi-Strauss about the possibilities of structuralist analysis is its potential for a formalized analysis of meaning. The formality of structural phonology lies in the relatively small number of oppositions between distinctive features (grave/acute, voiced/voiceless) that are sufficient to form the acoustic infrastructure of any known language (Wilden 1972: 7). It proceeds not by attempting to describe the essence of units but by arranging the sound units according to a system of 'binary oppositions'. Lévi-Strauss sought to demonstrate that similar oppositions operate in kinship and mythic systems enabling him to compare apparently unlike kinship systems and myths from different cultures and show the structural continuity of mythemes, and kin relationships, across what are, at first sight, very different cultures.

STRUCTURES OF 'MEANING'

The structuralist is an active agent in the process of analysis, exercising not merely mechanical skills of applying a method, but also interpretive skills in constituting the object to be analysed; the terms, units, relations and structures. This is not an aspect of 'structuralism' made clear by Lévi-Strauss although it is a consequence of one of the features of the method; the 'shift from the study of conscious phenomena' to the study of their 'unconscious infrastructure' (Lévi-Strauss 1968: 33 – quoted above). What structuralism studies about cultural phenomena is something not available (or at least not manifestly available) to the consciousness of people participating in the phenomenon under study. It needs the presence of the structuralist to interpret from the concrete, the abstract connections, continuities or 'unconscious structures':

> If, as we believe to be the case, the unconscious activity of the mind consists in imposing forms upon content, and if these forms are fundamentally the same for all minds – ancient and modern, primitive and civilized (as the study of the symbolic function, expressed in language, so strikingly indicates) – it is necessary and sufficient to grasp the unconscious structure underlying each institution and each custom, in order to obtain a principle of interpretation valid for other institutions and other customs, provided of course that the analysis is carried far enough.
>
> (Lévi-Strauss 1968: 21)

I do not wish to reject Lévi-Strauss's 'structuralist method' but call into question the epistemological basis that can be claimed for it. His importation of a structuralist method from linguistics creates a problem of what is to count as 'cultural anthropology'. What is it a study of and to what end? The structuralism that Lévi-Strauss applies in cultural anthropology seems to be asking the question 'what does it mean?' – a very different problematic from that of structural linguistics. But whose meaning, that of the structuralist or of the participants? Or is it a universal meaning that is potentially available to all but in practice is available only to the structuralist? Wilden sees structuralism as a metaphor of the discourse of science which provides the structure which defines meaning:

> As a new metaphor of the discourse of science in our culture, structuralism confuses meaning – which concerns survival, with signification – the instrument of meaning. . . . Meaning – the goal – becomes bounded not by the structure of the context in which it occurs, but by the structure of 'science'. As a result, the methodology implicitly becomes an ontology.
>
> (Wilden 1972: 11)

In the analysis of kinship systems Lévi-Strauss treats the kinship units (such as the terms of the avunculate) themselves as signs. But here the relationship between signifier/signified is not arbitrary. The point of the analysis is to discover an underlying meaning that makes sensible the apparently arbitrary relationship between kinship elements (or mythic elements) and reality. This is a very different sort of analysis from structural linguistics that involves not simply exploring the mechanisms of the system but also 'decoding' its meaning.

Dan Sperber takes Lévi-Strauss to task for claiming that kinship systems should be regarded as a language with the circulation of women taking the place of the circulation of words:

> The structure of a spoken language determines not who says what to whom, but what can be said at all in a given tongue, irrespective of who the interlocutors are. A spoken language is a code which determines what messages are available for (among other possible uses) circulation in the social network(s) to which the speakers belong. By contradistinction, a marriage system is a network, whose structure determines which channels between social groups are open to the 'circulation of women'.
>
> (Sperber 1979: 23–4)

There is then a double confusion in the connection between linguistics and anthropology that Lévi-Strauss attempts:

1 linguistics may study language but it is not a study of meaning in language, rather of language that can be meaningful
2 kinship systems are not analogous to language in the sense that they are not meaningful systems through which messages or communications are exchanged.

MEANING AND CONTEXT

The study of myths, totemism or magic involves cultural phenomena that are signs and symbols for the participants but are not in themselves lived in quite the same way as kin relations. However, what constitutes 'meaning' for structural anthropology is the discovery of that content of the unconscious human mind operating collectively that determines concrete manifestations of culture. The discovery of general laws of structure is only the first step in an interpretive process. Lévi-Strauss makes the final step in his analysis of the Oedipus myth like this:

> we may now see what it means. The myth has to do with the inability, for a culture which holds the belief that mankind is autochthonous . . ., to find a satisfactory transition between this theory and the knowledge that human beings are actually born from the union of man and woman.
>
> (Lévi-Strauss 1968: 216)

For whom is this a level of meaning? It seems unlikely to be a powerful statement of meaning for the participants in a cultural context that tells and hears the myth – the myth has its meaning in its content. To the anthropologist however the myth provides a problem of meaning, because in the context from which the myth is considered (i.e. anthropology/western 'civilization') the meaning is not obvious. The context of anthropology is that of a discourse that attempts to generalize and encompass other discourses, such as those of myth-telling. There is then an attempt to generalize and move towards a universal 'myth' that can stand for all the utterances of a similar type in their various discursive contexts. The context of the discourse of anthropology provides constraints on the form of a statement that will be recognized as meaningful. So, it is not sufficient merely to reduce all Oedipus myths to one, there has to be a retelling in a different form. This form has two distinctive features for cultural anthropology (and perhaps all other sciences):

1 the articulation of a problem or problems
2 the expression of abstract and general relations.

These two features reduce the myth to the level of 'theory' as far as is possible – that is cultural anthropology removes the myth from the context of its telling and translates (decodes) it into an abstract theoretical language. As we have seen with the Oedipus myth, the final move in revealing its meaning informs the anthropologist about features of the culture that are beyond the content of the myth. The need in the case of the Oedipus myth to resolve the contradiction between two pieces of knowledge that are in conflict can be comfortably taken as the signified that lies behind the significations that make up the various versions of the myth. Myth-telling can be treated as one discourse and anthropology as another one. Anthropological analysis need not be seen as the attempt to discover the truth about primitive societies, but instead as the attempt to 'translate' (or transform) the utterances from one discursive context to another.

DISCOURSE AS THE STRUCTURE OF MEANING

Kinship terms are part of a language and operate as signs with signifiers and signifieds – usage of kinship terms indicates membership of a language group. But Lévi-Strauss also claims the structure of actual kinship ties as a system of meaning:

> What is generally called a 'kinship system' comprises two quite different orders of reality. . . . Thus along with what we propose to call the system of terminology (which, strictly speaking, constitutes the vocabulary system), there is another system, both psychological and social in nature, which we shall call the system of attitudes.
>
> (Lévi-Strauss 1968: 37)

There are two types of discourse referred to here as constituting the kinship system. The first is the more formal and apparent and may be considered as a system of nomenclature for kinship relations and rules for its usage. The second level of discourse is constituted less formally in social and psychological practices that facilitate living within the formal system, including ways of breaking the formal rules. To give an example, incest may exist simply as a prohibition at the level of the formal system but at the practical level, breaches of the prohibition are explained, joked about or criticized. In this way the two types of discourse provide a context of meaning for the participants such that kinship relations as practical action can be considered as meaningful. The act of marriage or recognizing an uncle is both a symbolic act within the formal discourse and a practical act given meaning by the less formal level of discourse.

It is relatively easy to see myths as constituting a discourse that provides knowledge for members of a culture of the world around them. But Lévi-Strauss is arguing that kinship systems serve a similar discursive role and that they are similarly constructed out of units of meaning. The prohibition of incest can be found in the utterances within many kinship systems. Lévi-Strauss explains its discursive role in this way:

The prohibition of incest is ... the fundamental step because of which, by which, but above all in which, the transition from nature to culture is accomplished.

(Lévi-Strauss 1970: 24)

It is through the exchange of women in the alliance of marriage that culture and society are founded. For Lévi-Strauss the incest prohibition is both a communication between human beings of the fact that they are no longer bound only by the rule of nature, and the first content of the rule of culture:

the incest prohibition expresses the transition from the natural fact of consanguinity to the cultural fact of alliance.

(Lévi-Strauss 1970: 30)

Lévi-Strauss considers language itself to be one field of communication and the system of exchange and alliance to be 'the other field of communication' (Lévi-Strauss 1970: 496). By comparing different meanings from different contexts he is able to find continuities between meanings and contexts. In this way he is able to satisfy the desire in his own context, anthropology, to 'understand' what is being exchanged as meaningful in strange, alien, 'primitive' contexts.

I have tried to suggest that what Lévi-Strauss is doing is a form of discourse analysis that both attempts to articulate the rules governing the formation of the type of discourse and interpret the 'meanings' of utterances within the particular discourse. These meanings are analytically generated, constructed from outside the discursive contexts under analysis, that is they are not meanings as used by participants. While the methods of structural linguistics seem to have some role to play in studying the structure of meaningful systems, they have nothing directly to offer the unravelling of meaning. The latter is an interpretive task relying on a transformation of meaning from one context to another. In effect Lévi-Strauss is making structuralism do more work than it is equipped for without considerable development. But the unravelling of meaning is in practice the rationale for utilizing the structural method; the reduction to universal meanings makes satisfying and convincing the formal description of the structures of myths and kinship systems.

SEMIOLOGY AND MYTH

The work of Roland Barthes can be read in a similar way although both the style of his approach and the methods he uses are different. For my purposes here it is convenient to regard Barthes's work as having two phases; the first in which he is concerned with semiology, the second in which he is concerned with discourse. In the semiological phase his work is inspired by the success of structural linguistics and he seizes upon the possibility of being able to offer an ordered analysis of meaning. He turns his attention from the production of literary works to the production of 'cultural artefacts'. In the second phase the promise of semiology as a method of decoding significant structures is put aside in favour of an account of a discourse wherein meaning is elucidated by moving in and out of the contexts of utterances. His attention returns to literature (if it had ever really left it) and to the role of the self in relation to discursive contexts. In the first phase Barthes's approach has similarities to that of Lévi-Strauss: the concern to present methods, to be systematic, to draw 'structuralism' from structural linguistics. But in his second phase the issues of systematicity and method become blurred and the connection with structural linguistics becomes vague. His role as an interpreter of discursive structures becomes tacitly accepted and the earlier formalism recedes.

Barthes began the move towards formalism with his collection of essays entitled *Mythologies* (Barthes 1973) written between 1954 and 1956. His aim was to reveal the '"naturalness" with which newspaper, art and common sense constantly dress up a reality which, even though it is the one we live in, is undoubtedly determined by history' (Barthes 1973: 11). The first step in this revelation was the recognition that 'myth is language'. Just as words represent concrete things in the world and the relationship between words in an utterance refers to a relationship between concrete things, so cultural artefacts refer back to the history of culture. The myths that Barthes refers to are contemporary and different from the myths that interest the anthropologist. For example they are not necessarily linguistic utterances with beginnings and ends. Actions and objects are treated as signs that in certain situations form meaningful structures – myths. Their meaning can be unravelled by paying attention to the structure of signifying elements and interpreting from a cultural context constituted by history.

STRIPTEASE

In Barthes's analysis of 'striptease' for example, the cultural context invoked is that of France. It is not merely striptease clubs in general that provide the context for interpretation, it is specifically 'Parisian striptease'. The style of analysis is to answer an unuttered question: 'What is striptease, in what sense is it meaningful, what are the meanings it involves?' The answer is not merely a description of the event but a description of the relationship of signifying elements presented with their decoded meaning, thus:

> Striptease ... is based on a contradiction: Woman is desexualised at the very moment when she is stripped naked.
>
> (Barthes 1973: 84)

The style has tremendous rhetorical power in that the analysis reveals the obverse of the obvious and yet it is treated as still obvious. So, striptease is analysed as a statement that moves towards one thing (sex and evil) only to contradict this and move immediately away.

> French striptease seems to stem from ... a mystifying device which consists in inoculating the public with a touch of evil, the better to plunge it afterwards into a permanently immune Moral Good.
>
> (Barthes 1973: 84)

As the body is laid bare of garments so it is covered with barriers to nudity such as 'exoticism' in the form of furs, fans, feathers, etc. Although the clothes and adornments shed through the striptease are signifiers of luxury, legend or romance, their erotic significance is actually separated from the woman:

> The end of the striptease is then no longer to drag into the light a hidden depth, but to signify, through the shedding of an incongruous and artificial clothing, nakedness as a natural vesture of woman, which amounts in the end to regaining a perfectly chaste state of the flesh.
>
> (Barthes 1973: 84–5)

The rhythmic dancing, the ritual gestures, the professionalism of the stripper all function to de-eroticize the process which for Barthes is a 'meticulous exorcism of sex' (Barthes 1973: 86).

CONTRADICTORY MEANINGS

Barthes's accounts of striptease, and all the other cultural phenomena on which he writes in *Mythologies*, imply that these phenomena are meaningful and that there is a 'true' meaning to which his analysis aspires. Often this seems to involve a contradiction of an accepted meaning (the striptease as non-erotic, the jet-man as having gone beyond speed, wrestling as more to do with *Commedia dell'Arte* than sport, etc.). By 'accepted meaning' I am referring to one accepted by participants in the phenomena – it is clearly constituted for Barthes as an interpretation against which he is speaking. For example Barthes's account of French amateur wrestling asserts that it is not a contest but a spectacle and so the outcome (who wins) is not a significant point in the event. In this example Barthes enlists the assistance of the public and the audience as vindicators of his interpretation:

> The public is completely uninterested in knowing whether the contest is rigged or not, and rightly so.
>
> (Barthes 1973: 15)

> The spectator is not interested in the rise and fall of fortunes; he expects the transient image of certain passions.
>
> (Barthes 1973: 16)

These are not the accounts given by spectators and it is difficult to imagine them offering such accounts. But the power and the point of Barthes's account of wrestling, as a spectacle that re-enacts the battle of good over evil with grandiloquence and excess of gesture and act, is that this interpretation is contrary to an accepted one of wrestling as a sport in which competitors demonstrate skill and strength in their progress towards a victory. The interpretation of wrestling that I treat here as 'accepted' is presented in Barthes's own utterance as an absent speech with which he is dissenting – without its existence there would be no need for his interpretation because the meaning of 'wrestling' would not be an issue. Barthes's use of spectator and public as interpreting agents is a rhetorical device, redolent of the style frequently used in political speeches ('It is quite clear to any reasonable/sensible person that . . .'). The effect of the rhetorical device on the reader is to 'give the benefit of the doubt' to the speaker. Thus Barthes's account of wrestling does not seem so strange and unlikely as if it were merely his own and there were no alternative account against which his was implicitly juxtaposed.

This issue is of importance for two reasons: firstly, whose meaning is the analysis meant to elucidate? (a problem that arose with Lévi-Strauss); secondly, what is the analyst doing? These questions were fairly easily answered with respect to Lévi-Strauss. He clearly was engaged in the analysis of kinship and myth as an anthropologist. This means that he asked his questions from an existing problematic; each question had a history of answers on which he was able to draw and contextualize his own. The answers that his analysis might produce were not intended for the enlightenment of participants but for the enlightenment of anthropologists. This for Lévi-Strauss is tied up with the business of 'science', which aims to discover truths that are universal and that can be seen to be a product of their method.

Now with Barthes the answers are not so obvious. He offers no one problematic of questions or methods in which to ground his analysis.

Clearly some aspects of his approach borrow from literary criticism and his use of the term 'myth' suggests there is some borrowing from Lévi-Straussian anthropology. There is also a connection with the psychoanalytical tradition of interpreting cultural phenomena and personal experiences and a trace of intellectual Marxism that is critical of an existing order and its received interpretation.

THE THEORY OF SEMIOLOGY

Barthes attempts to ground his work in theory in two texts; the article 'Myth Today' written after the analyses in *Mythologies* and published in English with them, and the later *Elements of Semiology* (Barthes 1969). In the first of these Barthes creates his own problematic centred around his own idea of myth:

> what must be firmly established at the start is that myth is a system of communication, that it is a message.
>
> (Barthes 1973: 109)

Treating speech as the paradigm of communication he says that 'myth is a type of speech' but one not confined to the utterance of words:

> Myth can be defined neither by its object nor by its material, for any material can arbitrarily be endowed with meaning: an arrow which is brought in order to signify a challenge is also a kind of speech.
>
> (Barthes 1973: 110)

Just as words are endowed with meaning by the history of social usage so 'myths' gain their meaning; there are no natural or eternal meanings. The process of myths as communication can be studied in a scientific way:

> myth in fact belongs to the province of a general science, coextensive with linguistics, which is semiology.
>
> (Barthes 1973: 111)

Barthes refers to the science of signs, postulated by Saussure as semiology, as a science of forms 'since it studies significations apart from their content' (Barthes 1973: 111). He also refers to research since Saussure that has not necessarily attempted to construct a semiology but has 'referred to the problem of meaning: psycho-analysis, structuralism, eidetic psychology, some new types of literary criticism' (Barthes 1973: 111). Having gestured to a history for his theory Barthes proceeds to describe the structure of myth by borrowing from the Saussurean distinction between signifier and signified as analytical components of the sign.

The system of myth is according to Barthes 'a second-order semiological system' (Barthes 1973: 114). What constitutes a sign in the first order, that of language, is merely a signifier in the second order, that of myth. Barthes represents the relationship between myth and language as shown in Figure 1.

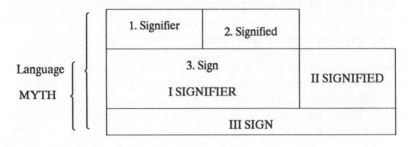

Figure 1 The relationship between the signification systems of language and myth
Source: (Barthes 1973: 115)

This introduction of a second order of system drastically alters what is being claimed for semiology. The issue is one of meaning; Saussure's linguistics and his postulation of semiology is not concerned with meaning itself but with the rules by which meaning is conveyed within the sign. Linguistic analysis may distinguish cases where meaning is not effectively conveyed but it remains unconcerned with what is meant by an utterance; structural linguistics is not an interpretive study.

Barthes's two order semiology suggests that there is a discontinuity between 2. signified (language) and II. SIGNIFIED (myth) and it is the elucidation of the latter that his analysis aims at. The first order of meaning is available to participants but the second order of signification is a 'hidden' level of meaning in that it is not readily available to participants (who might believe striptease to be erotic) and needs to be generated by an analyst who knows that it is there and so looks for it.

The move that Barthes makes to a second order signification has important methodological implications. The second order has to be constructed interpretively while the first order of signification can be constructed on the criterion of meaningful/non-meaningful. If meaning can be derived by participants in the communication then there must be a significatory system operating and it can be analysed at the level of the first order regardless of what the meaning is. But the second order depends on the content of meaning for its existence to be recognized. The second order signification system opens up the possibility of an endless layer of significatory systems each aspiring to a larger context from which meaningfulness is derived. Each level has to be constructed interpretively so that the distinctions between levels cannot be systematically articulated. Finally, after the first order system, the unit on which analysis is based ceases to be a material unit present to the senses (as words, seen or heard) but becomes an ideal, abstract unit created within the mind of the interpretive analyst.

These problems were not strange to the Prague School, who were working on the semiotics of art about twenty years before Barthes. Mukarovsky states that:

> The artifact, thus, functions merely as an external signifier ... for which in the collective consciousness there is a corresponding signification (often labelled 'aesthetic object') given by what is common to subjective states of mind aroused in individuals of any particular community by the artifact.
>
> (Mukarovsky 1977: 4)

The 'collective consciousness' here becomes a repository for the rules of signification and the signifieds of signs and is connected to Saussure's idea of 'langue'. There are of course endless problems for the analyst who wishes to use the concept of the collective consciousness but it does at least involve an attempt to locate the basis of meaning in a social context. It has the effect too of keeping to the forefront the meanings recognized by participants. Prague School semiotics deals with signs as first order systems and takes as its aim the analysis of signs and their relations as they are available to participants. In so far as meaning is a problem for semiotics it is not a question of discovering 'hidden meanings' but one of the structure of signifiers that communicate a meaning accepted by participants. This neither has to be demonstrated nor theorized because meaning for semiotics is not the issue, it is the structure of signifiers that is under scrutiny. The form in which meaning is dealt with is that of conventional meanings. Eco says that 'Semiotics is mainly concerned with signs as social forces' (Eco 1977: 65) which indicates that it is the mechanics of signs that his (and Pierce's) semiotics describes. Eco has little to say about meaning but is aware of some of the problems of pursuing it:

> Every attempt to establish what the referent of a sign is forces us to define the referent in terms of an abstract entity which moreover is only a cultural convention.
>
> (Eco 1977: 66)

Following Pierce, Eco recognizes the problem of 'unlimited semiosis', that is that every 'meaning' proposed for a representation is itself a representation that has a meaning, etc., in infinite regression. Unlike Lévi-Strauss or Barthes, semioticians like Eco avoid attempting to interrupt the chain of meaning to discover the universal or hidden meaning.

In the *Elements of Semiology*, Barthes develops his theory of a second order system of semiosis using Hjelmslev's (1953) distinction between connotation and denotation. He also introduces the idea of a second version of this two-level system of signification in which:

> the first system becomes, not the plane of expression, as in connotation but the plane of content, or signified, of the second system.
>
> (Barthes 1969: 90)

This is the system of signification that he refers to as 'metalanguage' and for Barthes, semiology is a metalinguistic description of ordinary language. Metalinguistics investigates and reveals a hidden (connotative) level of meaning whose coherence is independent of the first (denotative) level. Barthes's distinction between language and metalanguage depends on a clear distinction between denotative and connotative levels of meaning and yet it is difficult to sustain these as independent categories. Their relation is far closer than the arbitrary link between signifier and signified so that in some contexts (irony or double entendre for example) connotative meanings are part and parcel of the denoted meaning.

It is arguable that the theoretical trappings of semiology have nothing to do with the interpretations of striptease and wrestling. Despite creating a theory with a series of levels of semiosis it fails to support the substantive analyses in *Mythologies* where Barthes's examples show that it is not merely the formal structure of signification that he is interested in. He wishes to *interpret* substantive cases and find out what they mean in relation to their social context.

However, from a sociological perspective there are a number of gaps in Barthes's analyses, both at the substantive and theoretical levels. Firstly, there is no discussion of the link between 'meaning' and its social context and, secondly, there is no discussion of the theoretical status of power, ideology or history. The effect Barthes's substantive analyses have on their readers seems to be at the level of a reinterpretation of phenomena offering a new, plausible meaning. The plausibility stems from the implicit allusion to ideology; there are historical forces at work in human culture that bring about the obfuscation of meanings that are then hidden. The reader responds to another example of the truth emerging as the 'cloud of ideology' is dispelled. The very fact that Barthes does not present his work in terms of a theory of ideology means that the interpretive basis on which he is operating can be withheld from the reader. But what remains important about Barthes's substantive work is that he points to cultural phenomena in the everyday realm that are (or were) regarded as insignificant – they are, he reveals, laden with meaning and social and political significance. This is in itself a more political task than that proposed by semiological analysis.

SIGNS AND DISCOURSE

Up to this point the structuralism of Lévi-Strauss and Barthes has been characterized by a formal interest in the structure of signification which has its clear roots in structural linguistics. I have argued that in spite of the formalism of diagrams, binary opposites, levels and meta-levels, structuralism has really been about a mode of interpretation of aspects of culture.

The concept of structure allows cultural phenomena to be described in a (relatively) context independent way so that general instances can be analysed. The result is to address the issue of the social role of the signifying system; what is the function of the avunculate kinship relation, the Oedipus myth, the Parisian striptease? This functionalist, teleological aim is inappropriate for the systematic analysis borrowed from structural linguistics. But in questioning the way that meanings are structured in social contexts, Lévi-Strauss and Barthes have created a new object for sociological analysis – discourse.

The early structuralists analyse relations between larger elements of meaning than is entertained in structural linguistics. These elements are constructed from elements in a first order system (usually language) with its own structural properties. But in the second order system they take on a different set of structural features. In kinship relations such as the avunculate the first order elements are the family relationship terms of father, uncle, mother, son, nephew. But at the second order the element of maternal uncle/nephew operates within a different structure. With wrestling, the 'opponents' are not simply themselves but taking on the parts of 'good' and 'evil' in a ritual that has a context much larger than the particular match.

In borrowing from structural linguistics the early structuralists took on the task of analysing signs and systems of signification. But in moving to a second order analysis they looked at the relations between groups of signs in discursive systems. I will expand on what I mean by discourse in Chapter 10 but here it is sufficient to say that 'discourse' refers to the structured features of cultural processes when groups of signs become signifying elements in themselves. I have pointed out that the early structuralists treated the discursive elements in their analysis as 'natural', as empirically given. But the interpretations have actually constructed the elements, albeit with some empirical evidence, and a different interpretation may yield different elements and a different type of structure. In Barthes's later work this plurality of structures and elements becomes a strength of the analysis.

INTERPRETING TEXT

The text is a 'galaxy of signifiers, not a structure of signifieds' (Barthes 1975: 5) to be approached by the operation of interpretation:

> To interpret a text is not to give it a (more or less justified, more or less free) meaning, but on the contrary to appreciate what plural constitutes it.
>
> (Barthes 1975: 5)

The search for plurality both evaluates the text and yet leaves it intact so that it can yield more possibilities. *S/Z* deals with a specific text, Balzac's *Sarrasine*. It is however the interaction of 'texts' that is the subject of Barthes's book. Firstly, the text is plural in itself with different sub-texts, and secondly, the reader brings to the text a plurality of texts. Barthes approaches the 'tutor text' (Balzac's story, *Sarrasine*) and breaks it into fragments which he calls 'lexias'. He, literally, interrupts the tutor text to explore the codes working within it. When he refers to the 'discourse' Barthes seems to be evoking the flowing character of the text, suggesting its dynamic, alive nature rather than its stolid, object nature as a text (e.g. Barthes 1975: 44, 51, 58, 178, etc.). When the text has a reader it ceases to be a mere object and takes on anthropomorphic form; it has a voice or voices (the 'codes'), it creates its own history (the history of the already-read content), it 'plays', 'creates', 'lies', etc. The 'discourse', then, is the active intertextuality of the texts that occur between reader and tutor text.

Barthes develops an idea of discourse that is evocative of the text as something being read, or being written to be read. While the text may be mere words on a page the discourse takes on a deeper and more determinative role. The author has followed a form, that of the narrative, which is a form not of words but of discourse. It has a history that limits what the characters and the author can do with words.

Although Barthes retains the semiological jargon of 'codes' from his earlier work, they serve a different function in the analysis in *S/Z*. In the earlier work the analysis of semiological codes led to the discovery of hidden meaning in the cultural creations of literature, advertising, theatre, sport, etc. In *S/Z* the codes are more like ways of speaking that together make up the discourse. They do not necessarily reveal hidden meanings but do reveal the structured nature of the discourse and its constraints on author and characters – and reader.

Barthes finds five codes operating in the story of Sarrasine: the hermeneutic, semiotic, symbolic, proairetic and cultural codes. Where a lexia is indicated by Barthes to be functioning within one of these codes it is making a reference beyond its own immediate confines. That is, the word or words of the lexia are doing more than giving up their meaning as words. For example, the title of the story, 'Sarrasine', is, according to Barthes, operating in both the hermeneutic and semiotic codes. The title raises a question of what Sarrasine might be: a noun, a name, a thing, a man, a woman? The question is to be answered later in the story; the title creates an enigma that is to be solved. The hermeneutic code raises questions, delays their answers and leads to solutions and as such structures in some measure the succeeding narrative. 'Sarrasine' as a title also works in the semiotic code because in French the structure of the word is feminine – the semiotic reference is to femininity. The title is, as the story reveals, the name of the principal character who is a man.

> Femininity (connoted) is a signifier which will occur in several places in the text; it is a shifting element which can combine with other similar elements to create characters, ambiances, shapes and symbols.
>
> (Barthes 1975: 17)

Barthes's five codes work both within the text and without it; they refer forward and backward within the text joining parts that are discontiguous. They also refer outside the text to the cultural and symbolic codes that the reader (Balzac's, if not Barthes's) might be expected to know.

There was in *Elements of Semiology* and even in *Mythologies* the promise of a 'scientific' method of analysing meaning by developing the methods of linguistics and semiology. In *S/Z* there is no such promise and in its place is an attempt to show that texts are structured beyond their structure as language. As Barthes wrote in 1974, four years after the original publication of *S/Z*:

> I no longer believe – nor do I desire – that Semiology should be a simple science, a positive science, and this for a primordial reason: it is the responsibility of semiology . . . to question its own discourse . . . finally, science knows no site of security, and in this it must acknowledge itself as *writing*.
>
> (Barthes 1988: 8)

By proposing discourse as the object of analysis, Barthes shows that language, when it is used in certain ways (in this instance a story), has levels of structure that operate beyond the level of structural linguistics or even semiology.

THE LIMITS OF STRUCTURALISM

I have taken a particular reading of the work of both Lévi-Strauss and Barthes that emphasizes the influence of structuralist linguistics but points to the progression of these writers' 'structuralism' away from linguistic analysis. This is a result of their field of interest not being in language as such but in cultural forms (myths, literature, etc.).

The relationship between meaning and structure is different for language and discourse. It is the structure of language that creates meaning – analysis can work back from a recognizably meaningful form to discover its structure. The structure of discourse is created by the relationship of meanings in utterances. The relations that constitute the structure exist in the exchange of meanings; their creation, dispersal and variance. The analysis of discourse cannot then be agnostic about meaning in quite the same way as can linguistics.

Early structuralism was attractive because of its potential for analysis of cultural forms without reliance on a pregiven set of cultural values. The functionalist tradition of anthropology had interpreted the culture of 'primitive' societies in accord with a model taken from the anthropologist's own, 'civilized', society. The presumption was that there were certain universals of social organization, functions that could be recognized in a variety of cultural forms; myths, kinship orders, etc. The tradition of literary criticism had developed with a comparable aesthetic presumption. The good books were accepted as good (because they endured, because they were readable and re-readable). The problem was to explain why. The structuralist work of Lévi-Strauss and Barthes interrupted these traditions, raising questions about their presumptions and, most importantly, demonstrating a different way of doing anthropology or cultural criticism.

The eventual acceptance of Lévi-Strauss and Barthes by their respective disciplines indicates the value orientations that made their interpretation possible. Lévi-Strauss accepted the traditional role of anthropology to 'explain' the differences of alien cultures in ways that make them recognisable as the same 'underneath'. Barthes managed to leave the great works of literature intact. Having killed off the author and dragged all manner of cultural forms into the debate he finally reaffirms the text and its readability.

What then were the limits of early structuralism? Firstly, there is a tyranny of the signifier; the over-emphasis of the relation of signifier to the signified. Signs are to be seen everywhere and they all need to be decoded. To read Barthes's *Mythologies* is to make going on the London Underground an agonizing assault of messages begging to be decoded; advertisements and dress styles proclaim loudly while faces remain blank and meaningless. What is oppressive about the emphasis on the sign as a signifier is that human action and the operation of power are overlooked.

The second limit is the essentialism of the notion of 'structure' (Boudon 1971: 136). There is an implication that there is one original structure; the one that endows the set of specific signifiers with their meaning. What constitute the elements of a structure, its units, never seems to be a problem for the structuralists because they are taken as an empirical property of the medium of signification (the text). The fact that the structure revealed enables analysis to proceed is taken as sufficient evidence of the right elements having been extracted. Structure becomes a given for analysis and is treated as an essential feature of the object being analysed.

There is a third limit to early structuralism and that is its failure to deal with the historicity of structures. There is little or no sense of diachrony or process in the work of Barthes or Lévi-Strauss. Both were escaping from an historicist notion of evolutionary development, traditional to their disciplines. For Lévi-Strauss the search for universal structures meant that the issue of functional development could be put aside. With Barthes the situation is more complex. The politically oriented, even Marxist basis, of his critical and ironic interpretation is obscured and scientized by the structuralist conceptualisation of method. It is as if he is most careful to avoid reference to ideology because that would imply a determinacy that his analysis would have to confront.

These three limits to structuralism are not the marks of failure. It is ironically at the points at which Lévi-Strauss and Barthes transgress 'structuralism' that their work is most successful; when they produce inspired accounts of the hidden meanings of cultural forms that have been taken for granted.

7 Discourse, knowledge and critique

In this chapter I will explore the work of two writers who continued with the structuralist project of directing attention not to the world described by language but to the world constructed within language itself. Structuralism undermines the taken-for-granted fit between signifiers and signifieds necessary for using language in everyday life. For Lévi-Strauss and the early Barthes structural linguistics seemed to promise a technical solution to the problems of interpretation; once the structural relations could be revealed then the code of meaning could be unravelled. But for Foucault and Derrida, any interest in structuralism was not with the promise of a technical solution. They both began analysis of the object clarified by the structuralists, discourse, using whatever techniques disturbed a taken-for-granted reading of its meaning. Their aim was not interpretation in the sense of laying bare the truth behind the utterances in language. Their analyses attempted to reveal the contingent nature of discourse, contingent not on a real, stable, natural world represented in discourse but on an historical and social world, fluid and changing. Contingent also on the process and human practice of discourse; the need to make sense, to show cause and demonstrate rationality.

I will first look at some features of Foucault's writing that seem especially relevant to the programme of the sociology of knowledge and then mention some of the techniques employed by Derrida to highlight the perspectival quality of accounts.

FOUCAULT AND HISTORY

Foucault does not write as a sociologist of knowledge and yet his topic is the social process of knowledge. He writes about how knowledge is construed through discourse, the exchange of speech and writing between members of society, and has effects on the lives of people. In later reflective work he recognizes that what concerned him from the beginning was the conjunction between knowledge and power (Foucault 1980: 109).

The position from which Foucault's work develops is similar to the origin of the sociology of knowledge: the breakup of a unitary religious world view that centred on god's perspective of human beings and their society. His work explores the emerging human sciences that develop a humanist perspective. Foucault is not concerned with discovering the 'true' perspective or the underlying logic which links a perspective with reality but takes it as axiomatic that perspectives are historically contingent and that they emerge as competing views rather than revelations about the true nature of the world.

In *The Archaeology of Knowledge* Foucault criticizes the traditional problematic of history and proposes a new one. Traditionally, history was designed to mark out the continuity of perspective and reveal its systematic development from recognizable origins. Foucault, however, rejects the historicist theories of history that seek some essential dynamic of development. The new theory of history develops around a new set of questions to do with discontinuity; 'threshold, rupture, break, mutation, transformation' (Foucault 1972: 5). The domination of the study of history by chronology is replaced by a variety of time series reducible to no particular origin. For the new history of ideas there is no single, linear schema but series that are juxtaposed to one another, that overlap and intersect. Gone are the themes of origins and consciousness, of spirit and, most importantly, the aspiration to any form of absolute truth. Foucault's anti-historicism follows Nietzsche's rejection of the search for origins:

> because it is an attempt to capture the exact essence of things, their purest possibilities ... because this search assumes the existence of immobile forms that precede the external world of accident and succession.
>
> (Foucault 1977: 142)

The search for origins relies on a metaphysics, an 'image of primordial truth', and the traditional historian's task is to disclose this essence. Nietzsche discovered that the history of reason arose from chance and that the concept of liberty is an invention of the ruling classes. The genealogical method turns from the presumption of essence and continuity, contingent upon origins, and discovers a social setting in which categories emerge. Emergence, a 'non-place' for Nietzsche who points to its lack of closure, is the 'endlessly repeated play of dominations' (Foucault 1977: 150). Domination through history is marked by rules and rituals, rights and obligations. The rules, of law for example, do not put an end to the violence of domination but sow the seeds for reciprocal domination. The genealogy of emergence is then the history of the seizure of the right to dominate. Genealogy not only breaks with a traditional approach to history but also is the tool with which Foucault makes the discourse he studies contingent on the social context in which it occurs.

THE DECENTRED SUBJECT

The analysis in *The Order of Things* is of the emergence of life, labour and language as the objects of knowledge within the nineteenth century. It was the period when the human subject became the centre of attention. In the classical episteme, discourses of 'nature', 'grammar' and 'wealth' had been organized around a world of natural objects that could be grasped by classifying and describing rules of association. The human subject had but a marginal role to play in this world of things deemed to have an order immanent to them and exterior to human history. With the emergence of the study of life, labour and language, however, there was a discovery of a human knowing subject at their centre. These new practices were, apparently, in the control of human beings; no longer did human beings live out the order of god or nature, they were located at the centre, creating their own order. The study of human beings took on a new quality because the object in the human sciences was self-determining, the subject of its own destiny. And yet, as Lemert and Gillan point out, there was an irony in the fact that once human beings became of scientific interest because of their influence on history, the only way to study that history was to 'objectify' human agency:

> Man became the object of thought by being made the subject of history. Knowledge of the human required, contradictorily, the transcendence of the human. Man can only think himself by, simultaneously, recognizing himself in going beyond himself.
>
> (Lemert and Gillan 1982: 18)

As human beings, with the agency they displayed in the activities of life, labour and language, could not be studied scientifically, an idealized subject 'Man' was centred as the focus for the human science. 'Man' was invested with essence on behalf of all human beings and yet as a construct of the discourse of the human sciences it was a limited and finite form compared with the possibilities of concrete human beings.

The process that Foucault describes in history is described in individual development by Lacan. In a famous paper, 'The mirror stage as formative of the function of the I as revealed in psychoanalytic experience' (in Lacan 1977: 1–7) Lacan suggests that the recognition of itself in a mirror by a child is exemplary of the formation of the human subject, the 'I', that is the object of psychoanalysis.

The behaviour that inspires Lacan's analysis is that of the human infant who, between the ages of 6 and 18 months, is able to recognize as such its own image in a mirror. This behaviour discloses, for Lacan, 'an ontological structure of the human world' (Lacan 1977: 2). The recognition of itself by the child is the beginning of the constitution of the being as a subject: a human being as opposed to any other sort of being. The 'mirror stage' is a pre-requisite for constituting the subject in relation to other beings:

> This jubilant assumption of his specular image by the child . . . would seem to exhibit in an exemplary situation the symbolic matrix in which the I is precipitated in a primordial form, before it is objectified in the dialectic of identification with the other, and before language restores to it, in the universal, its function as a subject.
>
> (Lacan 1977: 2)

It is through the mirror stage that the infant grasps herself as a totality. Prior to recognizing and identifying with the image, the body is viewed as fragments. The mirror stage comes to an end when there is a recognition of other 'I's that are equivalent as subjects. It is entering into relations with these others that mark the transformation to social being and the decentring of the subject.

Lacan's highly compressed account of the human subject is based on the 'mirror stage' which happens some time after birth. In other words the characteristics of human beings that constitute them as subjects are not present in the organism, though a tendency or an ability to 'recognize' or 'identify' might be deemed to be inherent. That the subject is constituted after birth by two stages (the mirror stage to constitute the 'I', the dialectic with the 'other' to constitute the social being) means that the subject is constituted through the relations it has with its environment.

The point at which the subject ('Man' for Foucault, the 'I' for Lacan) recognizes its power over its destiny and therefore its own identity, is the same point at which that subjectivity has to be decentred to understand the world in which it operates – through objectification in the emerging human sciences for Foucault, through the objectification through the dialectic with the other for Lacan. It is not clear to what extent Foucault's work is influenced by Lacan's account of the mirror stage. He does however give psychoanalysis a 'privileged position in our knowledge' (Foucault 1970: 373). In its analysis of the unconscious through the conscious, the practice of psychoanalysis moves towards 'man's finitude'. In contrast to the human sciences which operate with the representable, psychoanalysis 'leaps over representation' and reveals the possibility of signification, of conflict and function (Foucault 1970: 374).

The infinite bounds of possible forms and the limited knowledge possible during the Classical Age was exchanged for the finite bounds of 'Man' and the positive but still limited knowledge of 'Man'. God, the infinite and unknowable was replaced by Man the finite and knowable, a form that in its possibility imposed its own limits. The limitation on knowledge was not a determination from outside human existence, but was fundamental to the possibility of positive knowledge. In a way it is the price of positive knowledge, a corollary that seems inescapable:

> Hence the interminable to and fro of a double system of reference: if man's knowledge is finite, it is because he is trapped, without possibility of liberation, within the positive contents of language, labour and life; and inversely, if life, labour and language may be posited in their positivity, it is because knowledge has finite forms.
>
> (Foucault 1970: 316)

It is perhaps important to note that 'Man' in the discourses of which Foucault writes included women – in so far as they were the same as men in their humanness. But the discourse was of course dominated by men and it was literally Man that was centred rather than human kind. We could perhaps criticize Foucault for treating the human subject as equivalent to Man and were his analyses sensitive to gender they would rapidly reveal the differences between men's and women's location in the discourses he studies. However, his point is that the human sciences had not explored these figures and had centred as subject an idealized construct of Man. By addressing the finitude of Man, Foucault not only destabilizes the nineteenth-century discourse but also opens the way for a gendered critique of the human sciences.

KNOWLEDGE AND TRUTH, TRANSGRESSION AND CRITIQUE

The organization of knowledge around the simultaneous decentring of concrete individuals and the centring of 'Man' in its finitude makes possible the emergence of a division 'that distinguishes illusion from truth, the ideological fantasy from the scientific theory' (Foucault 1970:

320). Such a division between truth and illusion may not be new in the knowledge of the nineteenth century but it takes on a particular form in that period:

> there must also exist a truth that is the order of discourse – a truth that makes it possible to employ, when dealing with the nature or history of knowledge, a language that will be true.
>
> (Foucault 1970: 320)

The feature of the nineteenth-century discourses is that they do not merely need to be true, they need to have their truth articulated in their very structure. In other words the statements of truth need a foundation in an epistemology and a method. There are two forms where statements and discourse demonstrate the truth of each other. One is positivist and based on empirical truth, the truth of the object lying beyond the discursive account of it. The other involves a transcendental system for establishing truth that is characterized by a teleological structure. These forms occur together, rather than as alternatives – Foucault refers to both Comte and Marx as providing examples of this sort of duo-form discourse (Foucault 1970: 320).

The tension between these two modes of truth leads Foucault to search for another form that would separate the empirical and the transcendental while being directed at the contents of both these forms of discourse. A possibility lies in the return to 'actual experience' (that is, a phenomenology) but he rejects this as merely providing the roots of positivism and eschatology. Instead he proposes a critical position based on the question 'Does man really exist?' (Foucault 1970: 322) that suspends the centring of the human knowing subject and instead addresses the structure of the discourse.

The archaeological method involves studying the regularities of discursive practices. The archaeology of knowledge does not privilege 'truth' or particular epistemologies; it is not only concerned with the structure of 'sciences'. Foucault uses the term 'positivity' to express the regularity of statements in a discursive formation prior to the establishment of epistemology or science. The regularity of the positivity is that of the will to truth; statements may not be 'true' in the sense that they are systematic products of a specific epistemology but they are dealt with by practitioners as if they are true (Foucault 1972: 190–1).

Archaeology deals with discourse as having a system of rules that generate the positivity. Genealogy on the other hand is concerned with the operation of power, of the dynamics that orient regularities:

By comparison, then and in contrast to the various projects which aim to inscribe knowledges in the hierarchical order of power associated with science, a genealogy should be seen as a kind of attempt to emancipate historical knowledges from that subjection, to render them, that is, capable of opposition and of struggle against the coercion of a theoretical, unitary, formal and scientific discourse.

(Foucault 1980: 85)

There are the beginnings here of what Foucault is later to develop as the concept of power/knowledge. With the centring of 'Man' and the emergence of the human sciences there is the imperative of choice – political choice. The tension between the modes of truth is resolved only in the recognition that thought has direct consequences on action – that is, that the process of knowledge is at the same time a process of power. This means that knowledge cannot operate reflectively on or above history, unaffected by the social, political and historical process of which it speaks.

Lemert and Gillan interpret Foucault's transgressive strategy as having a political role:

Foucault holds that knowledge is gained only by the criticism of knowledge. Thinking, therefore, is a continual transgression of established norms of truth. Thinking is a political act because these norms are socially constructed and maintained.

(Lemert and Gillan 1982: 137)

This is a clearer statement of Foucault's orientation than any that he makes himself. The notion of transgression of limits is both a topic and a resource for Foucault. His own thought attempts to transgress the traditional limits of conceptualizing social forms. As topics, the transgressions are in discourses that marginalize bodies; the limit between reason and unreason, the well and the unwell, the free and the constrained body, and limits of categories through which humans express themselves – life, labour and language. The human subject is approached not as consciousness but as a body and the limits are not absolute or ontic limits but those created by discourse. The transgressions that Foucault studies are not apparently intended ones but contingent on historical situation. Nonetheless, the discourse has its effect on bodies (the 'treatment' of insanity, the opening up of corpses, the discipline of workers and recalcitrants, the constraints on sexual bodies).

Foucault's analysis uses transgression as a resource to cut across these discourses, demonstrating their situatedness – specifically in relation to other discourses but with allusion to other social forces such as the social organization of bodies required by developing capitalism. Lemert and Gillan suggest transgression is the same as critique, but Foucault avoids critique as such because it has to be founded in the terms of finitude; this is why his account of history seems so negative. So many things are thrown away (continuity, consciousness, truth, origins) and all that is left is vagueness and negative categories (discontinuity, decentred subjects, the unthought, the mass of discourse). The positive form of Foucault's theory is to recover, in small measure, some of the things thrown away – series, contiguity, association, regularity, descent. Without these recoveries there would be no resonance to Foucault's speech; it could say nothing. Transgression is a shifting of boundaries not a kicking over of traces:

> Transgression is an action which involves the limit, that narrow zone where it displays the flash of its passage, but perhaps also its entire trajectory even its origin; it is likely that transgression has its entire space in the line that it crosses. The play of limits and transgression seems to be regulated by a simple obstinacy: transgression incessantly crosses and recrosses a line which closes up behind it in a wave of extremely short duration, and thus it is made to return once more right to the horizon of the uncrossable.
>
> (Foucault 1977: 33–4)

The strategy of transgression aims to disturb not only the contents of discourse but also the structural basis that gives the contents their meaning. The transgression that Foucault embarks on is nothing like as positive as anything done in the name of critique. The aim, however, is not to modify and reconstruct the contents of discourse as knowledge but to make his reader aware of their contingency on historical, social and discursive features.

THE WILL TO KNOWLEDGE

In his inaugural lecture at the Collège de France in 1970, Foucault spoke of 'three great systems of exclusion governing discourse – prohibited words, the division of madness and the will to truth' (Foucault 1971: 11). The will to knowledge (or truth; Foucault exchanges terms apparently without significance) refers to the structure of discourses that excludes that which is false and that which cannot be dealt with in terms of its truth or falsity. In effect discourse is structured positively in terms of how the truth is to be formulated. Thus in the Classical period ('the turn of the sixteenth and seventeenth centuries'):

a will to knowledge emerged which, anticipating its present content, sketched out a schema of possible, observable, measurable and classifiable objects; a will to knowledge which imposed upon the knowing subject – in some ways taking precedence over all experience – a certain position, a certain viewpoint, and a certain function (look rather than read, verify rather than comment), a will to knowledge which prescribed (and more generally speaking, all instruments determined) the technological level at which knowledge could be employed in order to be verifiable and useful (navigation, mining, pharmacopoeia).

(Foucault 1971: 11)

The will to knowledge is the structure of discourse which requires a certain way of thinking, a rationality that is the basis for limiting what is an acceptable contribution to the discourse. Foucault studies these limits and attempts to transgress a contemporary will to knowledge and its system of regularity. Firstly, there is an institutional basis in pedagogy, the book-system, publishing, libraries, learned societies and laboratories. Secondly, the way knowledge is used in society determines how its truth is assessed. Thirdly, there is an internal logic or structure of discourse that articulates its contents as the truth.

Exclusion can follow prohibitions of certain objects or words or of a whole category of presentation – such as that of the madman who is deemed to oppose reason. Links with established discourses may privilege certain utterances. So for example, discourse on economic practices is rationalized with theories of wealth and production, and prescriptive discourse, such as that of the Penal Code, is validated with reference to sociological, psychological, medical and psychiatric knowledge. The will to truth operates also on the internal rules of discourse. Commentary can have the effect both of establishing the authority of original texts and of replacing that authority. The 'author principle' effects a limit in discourse by establishing the name of the author as an index of truthfulness or significance. The 'discipline' of texts organizes and limits discourse on topics; propositions are included in disciplines only when they can demonstrate their identity within the disciplines. For example from the end of the seventeenth century a proposition to be 'botanical' had to be concerned with the visible structure of plants – it could no longer retain reference to its symbolic value or virtues as had been the case in the sixteenth century.

These internal limitations regulate the operation of discourse and are based on tradition; the discourse of the present has, in order to find its space of utterance, to reconcile its statements with those of the past:

Disciplines constitute a system of control in the production of discourse fixing its limits through the action of an identity taking the form of a permanent reactivation of the rules.

(Foucault 1971: 17)

There are rules and practices of qualification that limit the rights of individuals to participate in certain discourses. Ritual determines the roles and possibilities for speakers in religious, juridical, therapeutic and even political discourse. The institutionalization of the act of writing (the separateness of the writer, the intransitive style, the asymmetry between 'creation' and the use of linguistic systems) creates a fellowship of discourse that controls participation.

These forms of exclusion and limitation ground the formation of discourse in social practice; if only in its limits, discourse is socially determined. Both the participant's role and the content of her utterances are limited by the existing social forms of discourse. The content of discourse is also determined more directly through the way utterers orient their contributions:

by proposing an ideal truth as a law of discourse, and an immanent rationality as the principle of their behaviour. They accompany, too, an ethic of knowledge, promising truth only to the desire for truth itself and the power to think it.

(Foucault 1971: 21)

DISCOURSE

For Foucault discourse is, in effect, knowledge, but knowledge with its claims to truth and meaning bracketed (see Dreyfus and Rabinow 1982: 49). His disinterest in truth and meaning turns the attention away from ideas which, as contents of knowledge, need to be grasped at the level of their meaning and (potential) truth. To concentrate on discourse is to take as the object of study a material form and study it as it is without presuming a reality, such as a concrete world, is represented by the statements in the discourse.

That which Foucault treats as discourse is an apparently amorphous mass of statements in which the archaeologist discovers a regularity of 'dispersion' rather than a hidden system of knowledge underlying it. The horizon available to orient and unify analysis is not then one of truth or meaning, of historical continuity or scientificity – merely a pure description of discursive events (Foucault 1972: 27).

Foucault takes as a starting point the unities of statements already given in discourse, such as the disciplines of medicine or political economy. These are immediately subject to question however; the archaeologist takes no connections or continuities at face value except the location of statements as they are found. The metaphor of the method with that other type of archaeology is that the researcher should not presume links between artefacts on the basis of what is already known of them – all that is really available is knowledge of where they were found. Connections between layers may be more significant than connections in place. On the other hand, the inadequacy of an account of the smooth passage of time through apparently successive layers, may be realized only by recognizing the similarities between the structure of artefacts found in the same plane.

The unit or 'atom of analysis' for Foucault is the 'statement' which is not simply a proposition, a sentence or a speech act, but a series of signs that possess meaning within the discourse.

It is then the regularities of the discourse that define the statement but regularity is realised in human practice. While Foucault is not concerned with recovering the authorial intent behind the statement or even the actual author, he says it is important to determine the position that 'can and must be occupied by any individual if he is to be the subject of it' (Foucault 1972: 96). Statements have a material form as objects but their identity is derived from their status within a social practice or institution. The statement operates in an 'enunciative field' of statements in which there is an exchange that 'allows them to follow one another, order one another, coexist with one another, and play roles with one another' (Foucault 1972: 100).

POWER AND KNOWLEDGE

Foucault grounds the formation and regularity of discourse in social practices, both exterior to it (the institution) and interior to it (discursive practices) and so generates a social determination account of the process of knowledge. It is the role of power, both within society and within discourse, that is used to describe the regularity of discursive formations. The introduction of power into the analysis of discourse differentiates between Foucault's formal method of archaeology and his transgressive method of genealogy. For genealogy, meaningfulness is not arbitrary – it has effects that are the result of power operating in social practices. Whereas the archaeological method attempts to achieve some distance from its object with the bracketing of truth and meaning, the genealogical method becomes enmeshed in a politics of discourse:

I believe we must resolve ourselves to accept three decisions which our current thinking rather tends to resist . . .: to question our will to truth; to restore to discourse its character as an event; to abolish the sovereignty of the signifier.

(Foucault 1971: 21)

To see discourse as an 'event' is to recognize it as social practice not as the revelation of essence. The event retains its specificity and discontinuity and does not become merged into the search for an underlying theme of continuity. The will to truth has raised the signifier to the heights of the embodiment of truth and rationality in the word; the discovery of 'a logos everywhere elevating singularities into concepts, finally enabling immediate consciousness to deploy all the rationality of the world' (Foucault 1971: 21).

Since knowledge is power, Foucault's own work seems doomed to reinforce the will to truth and the alliance of power and knowledge – its transgressions have been incorporated and insights gleaned by many texts, including the present one. Foucault showed signs of recognizing the power in the knowledge he produced (e.g. his work with French prisoners' groups) and used his intellectual productivity to undermine claims to truth and power rather than attempting to identify with the interests of the proletariat. So, to intervene discursively is a form of political practice:

if pointing out these sources – denouncing and speaking out – is to be a part of the struggle, it is not because they were previously unknown. Rather, it is because to speak on this subject, to force the institutionalized networks of information to listen, to produce names, to point the finger of accusation, to find targets, is the first step in the reversal of power and the initiation of new struggles against existing forms of power.

(Foucault 1977: 214)

POWER AND BODIES – BIO-POWER

Once power is recognized by Foucault as a crucial component in the analysis of discourse, it might be expected that he would pay more attention to social institutions – traditionally regarded as the sites of accumulated power. However, Foucault does not concentrate on power as such, nor on its accumulation but on its effects; how does power manifest itself? What makes it so powerful? His response is that it is the body that feels the effects of power.

In *Madness and Civilization* (1967), although the topic was the discursive articulation of that space of non-discourse, madness, the effect on individuals was in terms of their bodies. Foucault's story begins with the gathering of bodies together into lazar houses – 'Poor vagabonds, criminals and "deranged minds"' (Foucault 1967: 7). The mad are taken from their exterior exclusion on the ships of fools and confined in an exclusion within society, in the hospitals, where the reasoned articulation of unreason can begin. The experiment of confinement acts on the body of the mad; by definition they cannot be reasoned with. The positive account of the mad (as opposed to that of their lack of reason) is of their bodies; bodies are subjected to the reasoned discipline of work even if minds cannot be.

The development of confinement is a separation of bodies; the mad from the poor and both from the criminals. The institution of the asylum and the discourse of psychiatry are refinements of the discursive pursuit of the categories of reason and unreason and the effects of the increasingly powerful discourse on the bodies of the insane. With the birth of the asylum the discourse of treatment can begin. The unreason of the madman's body is effaced by the silencing of unreason while the behaviour of the mad is observed, reflected upon and subject to judgment ('By this play of mirrors, as by silence, madness is ceaselessly called upon to judge itself' – Foucault 1967: 265). The body is then the 'subject' of society, in both senses of the term; subjection need not be dependent on violence or terror or even ideology.

Foucault wants to reject the traditional separation of power and knowledge, the belief that the 'renunciation of power is one of the conditions of knowledge' (Foucault 1977: 27). He is demonstrating that the meticulous, positive, knowledges developed about the deviant and the normal have powerful effects on bodies. He asserts that:

there is no power relation without the correlative constitution of a field of knowledge nor any knowledge that does not presuppose and constitute at the same time power relations.

(Foucault 1977: 27)

In the *History of Sexuality: Volume 1*, Foucault presents a theory of power (Foucault 1979a: 94–5) that counters the classical approach of power as an accumulated property of the powerful – the ruling class and the state. Instead he argues that power relations are distributed throughout society occurring in all types of non-egalitarian relationships be they economic, sexual or to do with knowledge. It is a theory of micro-power that recognizes the origins of social divisions in the relations between people in the process of production, in the family, in small groups and institutions. Power, he argues, is connected to the intentionality of humans but, like the statement which is meaningful in discursive relations, power is only powerful in human relations and cannot be reduced to a quality of the subject – power is always and necessarily accompanied by resistance.

Foucault's theory of power as instantiated in intersubjective relations is provocative but it does not adequately address the possibility of the accumulation of power. The power exerted by institutions, by bureaucracies, the state, classes and other groupings is more than the sum of micro-power relations. The problem seems to lie with the relation between discourse (power/knowledge) and action – how do discursive practices bring about powerful effects on people?

Foucault writes as if action is analytically reducible to discourse. The pain or pleasure of bodies appears as a discursive phenomenon and apparently has no materiality other than that of the discourse. This means, for example, that while the 'repressive' discourse on homo-sexuality does not (always) have the force of law and may give rise to a discourse of 'resistance', there are possible effects of the 'repressive' discourse on the homosexual as an individual other than those of the law. Foucault has reduced 'repression' to the effects of the law and subjection to it by means that are ultimately violent. The repressive effects of discourse can however operate exactly through creating discursive space for perversions. The response of cultural and social formations can, without the formality of law, be repressive of the individual. Merely to discursively mark particular practices as odd or deviant can be sufficient to repress them.

The analysis of bio-power includes an optimism about the political action that results from using the 'claims of bodies, pleasures, and knowledge, in their multiplicity and their possibility of resistance' to 'counter the grips of power' (Foucault 1979a: 157). This is an unconvincing strategy (see Fraser 1989: 55–66) which is a shame because it is not easy to see how Foucault's work can lead to any other forms of activity than critique. Perhaps his critique can lay the found-ation for resistance by individuals and small groups to the domination of lives by the discursive evaluation of ways of being – but this is a very circumscribed and reactive form of politics.

The attraction of early structuralism was that it provided a method by which the human sciences could proceed without forcing an equivalence with the natural sciences and without relying on an interpretive model of understanding. Structuralism appears, at first glance, not to be a hermeneutic method that engages meaning and interprets. Instead it appears to analyse the structure of signifying units that are grasped as something immanent to the objects under study.

However, the structuralism of Lévi-Strauss, early Barthes and Foucault seems prone to reifying both the sign and the structure, giving these analytic devices the quality of essences of real things. Furthermore, the mechanics of revealing structures and signification systems tends to cover up what is in effect a process of interpretation that is dependent on the perspective of the analyst. Foucault, I have tried to show, has developed ways of avoiding some of these problems by introducing the dynamic of power into his later analyses. Even at his most 'structuralist', Foucault is sensitive to the problems with a structuralist method.

DECONSTRUCTURALISM AND THE METAPHYSICS OF PRESENCE

It is Jacques Derrida who confronts the problems of structuralism directly at the level of philosophy as well as in the practical context of the analysis of texts. The major problem he confronts is the metaphysics of presence that dominates human thinking; the tyranny of the signifier and the sanctity of the structure are dangerous excursions into such a metaphysics. The closure of metaphysics is to begin by attending to two features of presence that we have seen concerned Foucault; the centre and the origin. Derrida sees in structuralism the beginnings of an attempt to break from a chain of determinations of the centre and the origin that are always expressed in terms of presence – it is this history of the centre that Derrida is referring to as metaphysics:

> Successively, and in a regulated fashion, the center receives different forms or names. The history of metaphysics, like the history of the West, is the history of these metaphors and metonymies. Its matrix ... is the determination of Being as presence in all senses of this word.
> (Derrida 1978: 279–80)

The domination of structure by the concepts of the centre has inhibited the 'play' of structures; the dynamic quality of relations within and between structures that creates their forms in a manner irreducible to causes. The system without a centre would be a discourse without a transcendental signifier (such as the key values of philosophy, the laws of science, the spirit of history) to fix the chain of signification.

Derrida recognizes that the closure of metaphysics cannot be achieved by merely abandoning concepts and even involves using the very concepts that are under attack – 'we can pronounce not a single destructive proposition which has not already had to slip into the form, the logic, and the implicit postulations of precisely what it seeks to contest' (Derrida 1978: 280–1). Derrida's work is fundamentally a set of strategies that can circumvent this paradox. The only way of achieving the closure of metaphysics is by using metaphysics in such a way that the emphasis on presence is thrown into question.

DECONSTRUCTING PRESENCE

'Deconstruction' is the name Derrida gives, sometimes, to the critique of metaphysics of presence. It is an approach to texts and concepts that attempts to get inside the text, to utilize its ideas and explore the play between them. Deconstruction can be contrasted either with a Heideggerean 'destruction' which criticizes concepts in order to negate them or a traditional 'critique' that attempts, from beyond the text and its concepts, to render them visible and to throw into relief the play of presence. Traditionally critique operates on the logic of concepts, appraising the consistency and coherence of a text, assessing its value as truth. Such an approach for Derrida is to follow the tradition of 'logocentrism' that never puts in question the logic which organizes the text or its critiques. In contrast, deconstruction aims neither at destroying the text nor assessing it (its truth or consistency are not important issues) but to question its logic by exploring (deconstructing) its central components in terms of their claims of presence. The critique of presence is pursued in deconstruction by revealing the dependence of the centre on absences. The absences take the form of that which is operative as a negative concept, that which the centre is not, that which is not of essence. Derrida's method redresses some of the imbalance, recovering presence for the non-presence of concepts.

For example in *Of Grammatology* (1976) it is the non-presence of writing that receives his attention. Traditional discourse gives a privilege to speech over writing in the consideration of language (Derrida 1976: 27). By deconstructing the concepts of speech and writing, Derrida tries to show that the privileging of speech embues it, as the form of language, with the power of being. The sign uttered phonetically appears to be a direct expression of being, a pure and unmediated signification. This is traditionally contrasted with the written sign which is but a mere dead sign of a sign (the spoken one), a signifier that is a signified first. But Derrida argues that this is an illusion; speech is not pure signification, is not the direct utterance of being, it is not the essential form of language.

He claims that treating speech as primordial derives from the apparent co-presence of signifer and signified and overlooks the temporality of the signification process that operates through speech. In contrast, writing actually reveals through its practice the process of signification; there is quite clearly a chain of signifiers with no final point when meaning and utterance are perfectly conjoined. Writing is, for Derrida, the exemplificatory practice of 'logocentrism' in which meaning is organized according to reason, a logos. In writing, the logos can be separated from the individual subject of the author giving it a quality transcendent of the particular text. But at some point that logos has to be linked with a knowing subject which is why, for Derrida, the very form of language as writing, logocentrism, privileges speech as the point where the operation of the mind and reason is closest to the operation of the sign.

It is dangerous to summarize what is a complicated and often tortuous argument because the importance is often what happens during the process of deconstruction rather than any conclusions that may appear to emerge at the end. Deconstruction is a way of reading texts that attends to that which is normally overlooked. Rather than look for the emerging theme, the logic of the argument or the narrative structure of a story, the deconstructive reading takes notice of the spacings between signs, of the trace of what has gone before, of the play of difference that constructs meaning in the present.

The feature of inscripted language that is so indicative of the trace structure is spacing – the space between words, the marking of absence alongside presence (Derrida 1976: 68–9). Derrida's critique of the sign counteracts the tendency to treat the sign or its signifier as an essential entity. He furthermore establishes a ground from which to displace the 'subject' from the centre of the process of signification.

TACKLING THE TEXT

Derrida utilizes a number of conceptual strategies to bring about the effects of deconstruction. These strategies are designed to destabilize the presence in concepts being deconstructed by pointing out their dependence on a trace of that which is not present. The two most famous of these strategies are 'writing under erasure' and the isolation of 'differance'.

In the first, the sign that is used in writing to represent the concept is literally crossed out. It remains visible and legible but its erasure marks the lack of presence, the effect of the sign as a trace. This is a strategy Derrida develops from Heidegger but where does erasure end? The reader, having been forced to struggle with the graphics of erasure, will raise the erasured sign to a new level of presence; its presence as word plus its erasure. Once the reader has assimilated the device of erasure it fails to interrupt the flow of meaning and therefore fails to force the reader to recognize meaning as a consequence of the metaphysics of presence.

The second strategy, that of 'differance', is like erasure only available at the level of written texts. The shift from 'e' to 'a' that distinguishes the term from 'difference' is silent in both French and English. The semantic effect Derrida intends with differance is to recover an alternative meaning present in 'differ' in its Latin root but lost in the word 'difference' in both French and English. This meaning is:

> the action of postponing until later, of taking into account, the taking-account of time and forces an operation that implies an economic reckoning, a detour, a respite, a delay, a reserve, a representation.
>
> (Derrida 1973: 136)

Most of this meaning is present (*sic*) in the English word 'defer'. Differance, then, introduces a temporalizing quality of meaning that is not available in difference (which is merely expressive of 'not being identical, of being other, of being discernible' – Derrida 1973: 136).

By constantly showing that signs are dependent not only on difference but also on differance for their efficacy, Derrida is destroying the illusion of presence that is involved in the process of signification. He is stressing the trace that is contingent on the signifier and pointing to its causes beyond any relationship it may have with the signified. This stress serves to render the sign inessential by always pointing to its unavailable origins. The sign operates in temporal as well as spatial relations; it is meaningful through what it is not in both relations of space (syntagmatic) and relations of time (paradigmatic). But this does not mean that the sign can be unravelled; the play of differance points to an endlessly receding chain of origins. The determination of the signifier cannot be traced, it cannot be brought into the light of presence.

The problems with using such strategies does not escape Derrida; the strategies change from one of his texts to the next, while all attempt the same task. Each is powerful only as long as the reader struggles with its newness. Once the meaning is stabilized for the reader, the reading is no longer delayed and the strategy joins the lexicon of signifiers available to writers of texts.

If deconstruction is in any way different from critique it is in having an axe to grind. The ground from which it operates is that of the critique of logocentrism. While Derrida appears to be utilizing the structure of truth in a critical manner – much as Foucault does with the 'will to knowledge' – what he effaces is the claim to a superior truth that such a task necessitates. Critique or deconstruction are not agnostic about either presence or truth; if they were then they would have no resonance, they would be illegible; erasure would obliterate.

> If deconstruction poses itself as a strategy then it must have some means of the evaluation of its field, of a calculation as to what is to be undone. Certain problems must have a priority, and that order of priority may be loosely called political.
>
> (Cousins 1978: 77)

I began by introducing Derrida as the structuralist who pursues the issues of the sign and of structure. His claims to method are limited but his critique of the structuralist project of understanding the social world as a structure of signifiers is not without value. The temporal dimension of the sign provoked by the concepts of the trace and differance provides an antidote to the tendency within structuralist thought to reify the sign and the structure.

Derrida's critique throws the 'sign' into disarray, showing that with its trace, structure is more than was bargained for. The sign is not reducible to a signified but nor is it reducible to structure, to the structural relations of signifiers. No set of binary oppositions alone renders the sign meaningful; there is always the play of differance that imbalances the opposites. Although Derrida resists a politics of the sign – it would return too quickly to presence for him – he provides a warning of the effects of scientization, a tendency that in some discourses is counterpoised to politicization.

THE CHAIN OF SIGNIFIERS

Lacan also engages in a critique of the sign that is directed at the Saussurean conception of the relationship between signifier and signified which suggested a correspondence between the two elements that exhausted the possibilities of determining meaning. Saussure's account of the structure of language showed how the arbitrary features of the signifier can carry this meaning. Lacan's criticism is that this implies a unity in the sign that is not borne out by the process of understanding the meanings of specific utterances. For example, any signifier connotes as well as denotes and the range of possible connotations varies with the discursive context (Lacan 1977: 154–5). In its usage in poetry, meaning is culled from connotations and new meanings are evoked out of the particular associations of signifiers.

Saussure's account of meaning in the sounds of language was tied to the thoughts of the individual who speaks them (Saussure 1974: 113) but

Lacan proposes that the meaning carried by signs cannot be reduced so neatly. Where Saussure sees the sign as divided neatly between the 'interior' of the person (signified: idea) and their 'exterior' (signifier: sound) Lacan points to a 'chain of signifiers'. That is, that the signified itself operates in turn as a signifier. The 'idea' (whether speaker's or hearer's) is not the other side of the signifier as word-sound, it is also a signifier in its own right, that is a component of another sign. The structure of the sign does not stop with a single relation of signifier/signified, it is always part of a chain of significations. Lacan's point is made forcefully by stressing the intersubjectivity of language:

> What this structure of the signifying chain discloses is the possibility I have, precisely in so far as I have this language in common with other subjects, that is to say, in so far as it exists as a language to use it in order to signify something quite other than what it says.
>
> (Lacan 1977: 155)

Of course Saussure's concept of the sign is not of a mere unity of signifier/signified. He locates the sign in a language that enables the signifier to be effective. Instead of pursuing the relationship between signs as a further process of signification he describes the relation as one of exchange value. For Saussure the structure of the sign exists in the context of a language in which there is a difference between the values of signs that govern their exchange:

> Its value [i.e. the sign's] is therefore not fixed so long as one simply states that it can be 'exchanged' for a given concept, i.e. that it has this or that signification: one must also compare it with similar values, with other words that stand in opposition to it.
>
> (Saussure 1974: 115)

Lacan's concept of a chain of signifiers seems a substantial advance on Saussure's account because it extends the possibility of exploring meaning in a specific utterance, without it having to be reduced to a standard (the current 'value' of exchange). The concept of the chain of signifiers has some similarity to Derrida's 'trace'. Both are concepts that disturb the possibility of the sign as a phenomenon available for simple decoding. Both describe the structure of the sign, as a unit that carries meaning, as existing in a complex and variable relationship to other signs. Its complexity lies in the irreducibility of the meaning of a specific sign to a standardized signification-plus-value. The structure of sign-as-trace or sign-as-in-a-chain demands that meaning is a property of specific usages that can be approached only by reference to the context of that usage.

In this chapter and Chapter 6 I have looked at the work of four major authors under the heading of 'structuralism' to show how the borrowing of methods and terminology from structural linguistics has generated approaches to social phenomena. I have organized my account around the development of the concepts of structure and signification. As the work of the later structuralist writers develops a critique of the sign and attempts to avoid any reduction to structure, the original conception of culture-structured-as-a-language, characteristic of Lévi-Strauss and Barthes, becomes less central. In the work of Foucault, philosophical issues about the role of the human subject transform the status of meaning and with the writing of Derrida and Lacan the role of the sign itself is transformed from the relatively mechanical role it played in Saussure's work. The most important feature of the development of the structuralist approach is the introduction of other concepts necessary for the analysis of meaning, particularly 'power' in Foucault's work and the 'trace' in Derrida's. If power is used as a concept to interpret or understand discourse it becomes increasingly difficult to abstract the 'structure' of the discourse from its social and historical setting. The concepts of the 'trace' and 'differance' relocate the structure of signification in its specific setting in time and space – with their use, it is more difficult to regard discourse as a disembodied structure, containing pure knowledge or pure ideology.

One of the important methodological consequences of concentrating on discourse as the object of analysis is that the category of the 'subject' has been subordinated to the social practice of discourse. The recognition that meaning is not a quality of the intentions of the individual subject opened the way for meaning to be analysed as a property of discourse. In later structuralist work, the decentring of the idealized subject of humanism led to meaning being seen as contingent on the social and historical specificity of discourse. The position avoids the reduction to ideal or transcendent meanings involved in traditional approaches to interpreting meaning and the very contingency of discourse on its social context means that it can be recognized as being the form of knowledge and ideology.

8 Science and language

I have tried, up until now, to mark out the three themes of knowledge, ideology and discourse as separate and independent, to pretend that there was little cross-fertilization of ideas between the themes and to imply that they had been pursued by different disciplines. While this is a very partial account, it is, for example, remarkable how little reference to Marx's theory of political economy Mannheim makes, how the theorists of ideology did not attempt to specify the concrete form of ideology and how little reference to any traditional social or political theory there is in the work of the structuralists.

More recently, other writers in tackling specific issues have merged these three themes, sometimes citing the specific writers I have referred to, sometimes drawing their influences from other traditions. In this chapter I will mention some work addressing the topics of science and language that begins to draw elements from the perspectives on knowledge, ideology and discourse already discussed. The sociology of science has rediscovered some of the issues of relativism and reflexivity raised by Mannheim and has also begun to address the discursive features of the way scientists present accounts of knowledge. Later, I will look at some explorations of the mechanisms by which ideology is articulated in linguistic and discursive forms.

THE NATURAL WORLD OF SCIENCE

We have seen in Chapter 3 how Merton transformed the sociology of knowledge from Mannheim's programme to one that took account of the special role of science. The view of science that underpinned Merton's approach was that it was 'certified knowledge'. The term 'science' also referred to a set of practices which generated certified knowledge and were characterized by technical methods and institutional imperatives.

The technical norm of empirical evidence, adequate, valid and reliable, is a prerequisite for sustained true prediction; the technical norm of logical consistency, a prerequisite for systematic and valid prediction.

(Merton 1957: 552)

It was the technical norms that provided the criteria for certification and the institutional imperatives (universalism, communism, disinterestedness, organized scepticism) that determined the context in which nothing else could get in the way. 'Universalism' expressed Merton's belief that truth should be arbitrated according to impersonal criteria. 'Communism' was the conviction that scientific knowledge constituted a common heritage and was not the possession of the discoverer. 'Disinterestedness' was the claim that scientists practised science without interest in whether it was they or someone else who discovered the true knowledge. 'Organized scepticism' was Merton's presumption that there was a 'detached scrutiny of beliefs in terms of empirical and logical criteria' (Merton 1957: 560).

The institutional imperatives were about separating the potential personal and human interests of scientists from the technical norms of activity – the belief was that science would discover the truth through empirical evidence and logical consistency provided that the baser concerns of humans did not interfere. Underlying this belief about the power of science as a strategy for generating knowledge was a belief in a natural world which was uniform and consistent and potentially available to human understanding.

The traditional sociology of science proposed by Merton was intended to explore this special type of human behaviour and to describe the social practices which led to the production of certified knowledge. This would clarify what was good about good scientific practice so that its example could be followed elsewhere. Merton's view of science may sound a little idealistic, even pompous today, but it none the less represents a common view of the basis for the integrity of scientific knowledge. In our everyday lives the success of science in generating knowledge, often evidenced by useful technical applications (aeroplanes, telecommunications, computers, medicine) is impressive. The power of science as knowledge derives not only from its useful technical applications but also from its accounts of the material of everyday life that is so much more comprehensive than common-sense knowledge. It would then make sense that a special and different behaviour could lead to knowledge about the natural and material world, so present to everyday experience but also so mysterious to everyday knowledge of its workings. As Michael Mulkay points out, even Mannheim and Stark had regarded science as a special case, a form of knowledge not amenable to the social determination thesis:

> Sociology could deal either with the social conditions which helped to reveal (or to hide) the objective world or with the social consequences of objective knowledge. Sociology could say nothing about the form or content of scientific knowledge itself, *because the conclusions of science were thought to be determined by the physical and not the social world*.
>
> (Mulkay 1979: 60)

The distinctive guiding principle for the sociology of science was what Mulkay calls the 'principle of the uniformity of nature' (Mulkay 1979: 27) and under the dominance of this principle, sociology attempted to produce a normative account that explained the efficacy of science in representing the natural world. But the practice of the sociology of science failed to uncover consistent rules of scientists' action which looked anything like technical norms or institutional imperatives. What positivist philosophers and sociologists had claimed was involved in science did not fit with what scientists actually did. The sociology of science began to undermine the normative basis of science at about the same time as philosophers were questioning its epistemological basis (Mulkay 1979: 27–62); sociology seemed only to find exceptional cases and was never able to describe successfully the regularity of normal science.

Whether or not nature is uniform, the sociology of science showed that the methods of scientists did not guarantee access to knowledge about nature. The practice of science proved to be more varied and complex and more tied up with social features than the functionalist model suggested. The modern sociology of science takes the functionalist view of science in society as a springboard; it has developed as a critique of the normative, rational view of science and in doing so has inevitably re-run many of the questions that concerned Mannheim (Mulkay 1979: 37). The two that I intend to explore here are the question of relativism and the methodological problems of constituting an object for study.

REFLEXIVITY AND RELATIVISM IN THE STUDY OF SCIENCE

The principle that the sociology of science should be reflexive was introduced as a feature of David Bloor's 'strong programme' (1976: 4–5). This was an attempt to found a rational basis for the sociology of science given the threat to the principle of the uniformity of nature. The strong programme was to be concerned with the causes that bring about states of belief or states of knowledge and was to be impartial with respect to truth, falsity, rationality, irrationality, success or failure. The programme was to offer symmetrical accounts of the causes of both true and false beliefs. What Bloor took to be the object of knowledge was perspectival and relational in a way similar to that proposed by Mannheim:

> Instead of defining it as true belief, knowledge for the sociologist is what men [*sic*] take to be knowledge. It consists of those beliefs which men confidently hold to and live by. In particular the sociologist will be concerned with beliefs which are taken for granted or institutionalised, or invested with authority by groups of men.
>
> (Bloor 1976: 3)

While the introduction of reflexivity and the relativist conception of knowledge might be reminiscent of the origins of the sociology of knowledge, the search for 'causes' was even more positivist than Merton's programme – but it was this that gave Bloor's programme its strength. Still underlying Bloor's (see also Barnes 1976) position was a naturalism that accepted the technical criteria of empirical evidence and logical consistency Merton had attributed to science. Bloor's account of mathematics finds in it a variable content that can be attributed causally to its social context and a stable, uniform content that can be attributed to the natural underlying reality:

> Underlying the mathematics which we now associate with the calculus there has been a constant intuition that smooth curves, shapes or solids can be seen as being really segmented. This is a model or metaphor which has frequently appealed to men when they have sought to think about such topics. Of course mathematics is not the same as intuitive thought. It is disciplined and controlled.
>
> (Bloor 1976: 114)

Bloor suggests that there is an underlying reality that is re-presented as knowledge at three levels – as segmented curves, as smooth curves and as a mathematical expression in the calculus. There is a chain of determination from the underlying natural phenomenon, to the intuitive cognitive form as segmented curves, to the disciplined knowledge form as smooth curves and the calculus. These higher levels make up the social and variable forms but they remain, at least to some extent, determined by the natural world. The evidence lies in the regularity with which, whatever the social form of the calculus, the underlying cognitive form perceives segments. What is rejected or overlooked by this analysis is that the regularity might be a construct of the way these things are thought of or rendered into language. That the natural world is regular in a particular way continues to be presupposed although the principle of the uniformity of nature is a possible explanation of the varying social forms of knowledge.

Bloor was not alone in introducing a perspective on science that began to account for the failure of science to live up to the high standards of the 'institutional imperatives'. Harry Collins also accepted a form of relativism but drew the line at reflexivity:

> Indeed, reflexivity is explicitly disavowed. My recommendation is that the social scientist 'should go about finding out things about the social world of the scientist in the same spirit as the scientist goes about finding out things about the natural world.' I'll call this special relativism.
>
> (Collins 1982: 140)

Collins's special relativism applies strictly to the natural world of the scientist – the physical world that the scientist studies. The sociologist suspends the 'natural attitude' adopted by the scientist so that sociology can explore the socially contingent nature of scientific knowledge that the scientist presumes to be a true account of the natural world. But the special feature of this form of relativism is that it applies only to the natural scientist's world. In order to do her job, the sociologist of science must treat the *social* world of the scientist as a naturally occurring reality, independent of the sociologist's knowledge of it. For Collins this is how the sociologist of science can produce knowledge about scientific practice, by adopting the same spirit as the scientist. His approach presupposes the value of the scientific 'spirit' but it also treats scientific knowledge differently from sociological knowledge.

Despite the lack of reflexivity of Collins's position, he does allow the possibility of studying the sociology of science sociologically (Collins 1981: 216). But this would not involve a reflexive dimension in the sociology of science, merely the creation of a meta-discipline; the sociology of the sociology of science. Collins's position did not go uncriticized by other sociologists at the time it was set out (see for example the comments by Laudin, Knorr-Cetina and Chubin in *Social Studies of Science* 12(2) 1982). Of course reflexivity has arrived in spite of Collins and there are indeed sociologists of the sociology of science (Woolgar 1988; Ashmore 1989). Their strategy is to comment on each other's work as sociologists of science – they seem willing to entertain a more thorough-going reflexivity than Collins and are less concerned to demarcate between natural attitudes.

THE SOCIAL CONTEXT OF SCIENCE

The early sociologists of science had presumed that the social context was prevented from impinging on the technical practice of observation and discovery of logical consistency by the normatively controlled practices of scientists. What Mulkay, Bloor, Collins and others have done in their empirical work is to show that social context always impinges on the practice of science and also plays a part in determining what counts as (and is certified by the scientific community as) scientific knowledge. But in the hands of Collins and Bloor the sociology of science attempts to sustain a principle of the uniformity of nature and of the distinctive features of science as a form of knowledge. Both introduce a restricted form of relativism that means science continues to be held as a different type of knowledge from sociology and therefore scientific and sociological knowledge are not relative to each other. This has sustained a thriving industry of studying what it is that is special about what scientists do – and say they do.

For Collins this involves the 'artisanship' of scientists and the description of an 'enculturational model' (Collins 1985: 159) that sociologizes Merton's prescriptions. Collins does not find a set of rigid techniques for empirical observation and for identifying logical consistency amongst scientists but he describes craft skills, passed from practitioner to practitioner. He proceeds to set out ten propositions (logically consistent and derived, of course, from empirical observation) that are characteristic of the forms of life of scientific culture. This cultural account of science covers both the maintenance of conceptual order and the management of change through discovery. Special relativism means that it is the 'Scientists and others' who 'tend to believe in the responsiveness of nature to manipulations directed by sets of algorithm-like instructions' (Collins 1985: 129). While the sociologist is agnostic about the natural world's vulnerability to demonstrating order when experimented on, the sociologist is confident of the vulnerability of the social world of science to render order when subject to observation and logical analysis.

Woolgar (1981) points out that the underlying naturalism in Bloor's approach (shared by Barnes and others) is extended to the use of interests to explain the social basis of science by some adherents of the strong programme. It is not only the natural world that is presumed to be natural in the sense of having a particular order accessible through the metaphors of science. The interests of scientists similarly have a 'natural', that is causal and systematic, effect on the practice of science and the production of knowledge. Woolgar's point is that the use of interests to explain social phenomena is unreflexively taken to be adequate to demonstrate the social basis of scientific knowledge. The relative nature of scientific knowledge is consequently established by referring to the social impact of interests that are treated as natural and unproblematic rather than variable and socially contingent.

Collins's relativism has also come under detailed attack from within the sociology of science for not retaining impartiality when analysing the claims for scientific status of parapsychologists (Mulkay, Potter and Yearley 1983: 182–93). The 'special' form of relativism cannot ensure impartiality because the social processes investigated are both deemed to construct the knowledge of participants *and* are used as a resource by the analysts. So, while Collins presumes the relativism of the natural world he ignores that of the social world and as a consequence there is a problem of constituting the object of study. How can the 'natural' world of scientists' activity be separated off from the 'social' world for the purposes of study? What Mulkay and his colleagues point out is that in different types of social context scientists will account for the process of generating knowledge differently.

Different approaches to the sociology of science have constituted their object differently. Some involve actually observing laboratories and gathering ethnographic data (e.g. Latour and Woolgar 1979; Knorr-Cetina 1981) and some (like Bloor) have concentrated on the historical documents that tend to provide a relatively formal account of what happened. Others (like Collins) have studied the contemporary production of scientific knowledge and have relied much more on informal interviews and participant observation to find out what is going on. The two forms of limited relativism that I have considered have presumed and then bracketed a natural world that can and may determine the content of knowledge.

There is a recurring problem of how to constitute the object of study for the sociology of science. Is it the fullness of action, is it the negotiation of scientific discoveries, or is it the formal debates enshrined in historical documents – what constitutes scientific knowledge? Underlying all these approaches a shadow of the apparently dismissed principle of the uniformity of the natural world remains – the natural world is presupposed to be different from the social world in its relation to the process of knowledge.

DISCOURSE ANALYSIS OF SCIENCE

The presupposition of the difference between knowledge of the natural and social worlds is however suspended by a recent move in the sociology of science. Discourse analysis relocates the object of study away from action and belief or scientific practice in general and concentrates on discourse; that is on scientists' accounts. Nothing is retained in the object of study that is above accounts (such as certified knowledge) or beneath accounts (such as a presupposed natural world). Instead the structures of accounts are analysed to discover regularities and features of scientists' discourse.

In a series of papers and a book Michael Mulkay and Nigel Gilbert adopt this strategy with data gathered about a particular set of scientists working in a common field of biochemistry (Gilbert and Mulkay 1981; 1982; 1984; Mulkay and Gilbert 1981; 1982a; 1982b; 1982c). Their data consist of formally published papers in the field, transcribed interviews with the scientists and less formal documents such as notes and letters.

Discourse analysis involves a more radical relativism than the other forms tried out in the sociology of science. It avoids any reduction to presumed natural or social forces to explain any part of scientists' behaviour or knowledge. But there is a cost; it cannot make claims to explain knowledge production as such. Discourse analysis can operate only as an interpretation of the form of scientists' accounts. It cannot claim to achieve direct understanding of scientific practice in general, scientific technique, rules of procedure or scientific knowledge. It seems however that in the sociology of science, discourse analysis is a step on the way to understanding these things:

> We suggest ... that a systematic investigation of the social production of scientific discourse is an essential preliminary step in developing a satisfactory analysis of action and belief in science.
>
> (Mulkay *et al.* 1983: 195)

Much of Mulkay and Gilbert (hereafter M & G)'s analysis is directly concerned with the problem of truth and error. Their central finding is that there is an asymmetry, a structural difference, between scientists' accounts of correct belief and those of error. The scientists' accounts of error use the non-scientific factors that are contingent on scientific practice to explain errors – this M & G call the 'contingent repertoire'. Accounts of error do not normally occur in the formal literature but scientists seem willing to talk about each other's errors in the informal context of an interview with a friendly sociologist. M & G list the repertoire of interpretive resources used by eight of their scientists in accounting for error:

> failure to understand, prejudice, commitment to one's own theories, reluctance to make the effort, complexity of the theory, dislike of the

new theory, extreme naivety, narrow disciplinary perspective, threat to status, rushing in too quickly, insufficient experimental skill, false intuition, subjective bias, personal rivalry, emotional involvement, irrationality and general cussedness.

(Mulkay and Gilbert 1982: 176)

These reasons offered for other people's errors are all indictments of the person as a scientist. Not one is socially contingent (such as not having sufficient resources, not having access to the relevant data or theoretical material). Each establishes a prima-facie reason for the failure of the other scientist to achieve the single path to correct belief. Each reason is presented as potentially or actually an interruption in the cognitive process by which correct belief is presumed to be arrived at.

In contrast, accounts of correct belief draw on an 'empiricist repertoire' in which there is a single version of the cause of beliefs – they are presented as contiguous with the empirical world as revealed through scientific practice. What the scientists do is to cite experimental evidence as supporting correct belief but claim that there is no such adequate experimental support for incorrect or erroneous beliefs (Gilbert and Mulkay 1982: 388).

There are three features that make for asymmetry between accounting for error and correct belief. Firstly, error accounting draws on a contingent repertoire (i.e. non-experimental factors) while correct belief draws on an empiricist repertoire (i.e. experimental factors). Secondly, there is considerable variability with many different non-experimental factors in the contingent repertoire in contrast to the unitary empiricist repertoire. Thirdly, the accounts of error are produced by someone who holds correct belief – that is they are accounts of someone else's errors. This contrasts to accounts of correct belief that are in accord with the speaker's own beliefs (Gilbert and Mulkay 1984: 69).

There was one scientist, interviewed by M & G, who described two different, experimentally based perspectives in an account which 'was symmetrical in the strong sense that both correct and incorrect belief were presented as scientifically legitimate' (Gilbert and Mulkay 1984: 83). But symmetrical accounting seems to be 'unstable' or 'precarious'; it involves the speaker standing back from his (they were all men) own commitment to the correctness of his beliefs. In recognizing that opponents use the same repertoires in the same way to distinguish the same material but to different effect, the scientist recognizes the asymmetry in scientific accounting for error and correct belief in much the same ways as do the sociologists. Such a recognition does not lead to the scientist giving up the correctness of his beliefs or the appropriateness of the scientific, experimental method. What happens is that deviants who offer symmetrical accounts 'revert back quickly to the dominant asymmetric structure' (Gilbert and Mulkay 1984: 84).

M & G present asymmetry as a property of accounts; the asymmetry is between accounts of error and correct belief demonstrated through the choice of repertoire. This is characteristic of their tendency to 'naturalize' discourse by treating the interpretive categories (truth, error, repertoire, contingent) as properties of the text of the speech. They also adopt an empiricist repertoire themselves to represent formal findings (although Mulkay abandons some of the more formal aspects of it later: see Mulkay 1985).

However, in a footnote M & G do recognize that the asymmetry they find could be a property of accounts of *justifications* of correct and incorrect belief and that a symmetry may exist between accounts of *causes* of these beliefs (Mulkay and Gilbert 1982a: 183). The concept of 'justification' orients the account to a speaker and begins to situate the account in the practices of a discursive context, that is of particular speakers taking turns to utter and respond. Justifications are doing a particular kind of discursive work: to justify is to establish the reasonableness of a claim *within the current context of discourse*. Jonathan Potter in his study of the way that social psychologists use the testability of knowledge claims as a criterion for distinguishing their veracity, has argued that asymmetrical accounting is a resource utilized by participants to:

> legitimate their own position and undermine alternative, competing positions.
>
> (Potter *et al.* 1984: 94)

There is clearly a need to distinguish between accounts that do different types of work in the specific discursive context; making knowledge claims, making status claims and justifying either of these types of claim.

By focusing on 'discourse' as the object of study, many of the problems of analysing action and belief are avoided and a more Mannheimian relativism than that proposed by Bloor or Collins becomes part of the method. Everything within the object of analysis can remain relative with the aim being 'to identify the recurrent structural features of participants' discourse' (Mulkay *et al.* 1983: 200). This opens the way for reflexivity both in the process of analysis and in the status of the results of analysis. M & G have concentrated on grasping the structural features of the discourse at the level of empirical material – this is rather like presuming that discourse is an unproblematic level of phenomenon and that interpretation at this level is independent of theory.

The problem with M & G's approach to analysis is that there is no attempt to analyse power in the discursive process. They distinguish between different types of discursive context – e.g. between the formal context of scientific papers and the informal context of letters – but do not consider the contingent features in terms of the unequal distribution of the power to utter. Those who utter accounts have to demonstrate qualifications before they are permitted to enter the discourse including academic qualifications and a writing style that avoids criticizing the competence of others. In less formal contexts, such as talking at a conference or being interviewed by a sociologist, different conventions apply and it is less difficult to qualify for participation.

These features of discursive practice (that Foucault calls the 'orders of discourse'; see Chapter 7) introduce the social dimension to the analysis – discourse is not simply a natural setting but is one in which human beings are agents with different powers and different resources that they can utilize.

TEXTUAL AGENCY

The different discursive practices used by scientists to establish and justify what they believe to be the truth have been explored in more detail by Mulkay (1985). He has developed a concept of 'textual agency' which refers to the ways participants draw on a range of discursive strategies. The use of personal pleasantries, for example, in informal letters between scientists shows how textual agents 'bring off' an apology at the same time as distinguishing fact and opinion (Mulkay 1985: 22–3). In this interpretation of scientists' discourse the presence of asymmetry is not treated as a function of truth or falsity (accounting for error or correct belief) but as a strategy utilized by agents:

> This strategy, adopted by both authors, seems to be related to the dual conception of fact which has appeared in every letter so far. The interpretive conception of 'fact' is used in criticizing one's opponent. The interpretative basis of the latter's views is made visible and emphasized as the author formulates the inconsistencies, uncertainties and mistakes perpetrated by his opponent. It is always possible for the author to find such errors, because the opponent's claims are inevitably assessed in relation to the author's differing conception of the facts and their scientific meaning.
>
> (Mulkay 1985: 43)

Mulkay has devised or borrowed a number of strategies that serve to de-naturalize the discourse of scientists and to realize a reflective mode within his own text. For example, to undermine the declamatory privilege of his role as author he introduces characters who comment on and dispute the authorial text. They provide an interpretive gloss on the author's own text in a comparable way to the interpretive gloss that the author text offers on the scientists' discourse. He also explicitly recognizes that the comments he makes about the interpretive work of the scientists in their discourse may also apply to his own sociological discourse. So, in reflecting on a chapter that has reviewed how scientists deal with replication he admits that just as the scientists construct accounts with reference to the sameness/difference of experiments he has constructed his chapter by 'identifying, compiling and using a series of similarities/differences' (Mulkay 1985: 152). He goes on to show that his own text is also located in a series of texts within the sociology of science on replication, according to criteria of sameness and difference. One of the characteristics of difference that Mulkay identifies for his own text (or most of it) is that it treats sociologists' discourse as socially constructed and in doing so his text is very different from a previous contribution by Harry Collins on replication:

> Whereas Collins proposes that we should only treat the 'natural world' as interpretively accomplished, whilst treating the attributes of the social world (such as the sameness/difference of texts and actions) as 'real', my conclusion is that both social and natural worlds are variably constructed through participants discourse.
>
> (Mulkay 1985: 154)

At least for Mulkay and some others working in the field of the sociology of science (see for example the contributions to Woolgar 1988), the issues of reflexivity and relativism are an active part of their method of sociological analysis. They have shown how the analysis of knowledge as discourse can illuminate the social practices by which knowledge is construed. Moreover, by treating the empirical object of knowledge as discourse they have returned to a programme for the sociology of knowledge very close to Mannheim's analysis of the meanings and presuppositions that constitute knowledge.

The analysis of discourse as the way to approach scientific knowledge has emerged against a backdrop of changing epistemological concerns about how true knowledge is constituted. The discourse analysis approach has also emerged after considerable sociological investigation of the actions and beliefs surrounding science as knowledge. A similar focus on discourse has also been explored in the study of law (Sumner 1979; Burton and Carlen 1979) and more recently the study of racism (van Dijk 1988; Wetherell and Potter 1989) and health economics (Ashmore *et al.* 1989). These fields have in common that they are areas of social action and routinized practices which draw on a set of ideas and beliefs that may be treated as 'knowledge' by the participants. To outsiders (and sociologists) the practices seem bound up with the knowledge and the only way of studying action and belief together is to study how participants construct accounts of what is going on.

LANGUAGE

The development of the sociology of science has moved away from a belief in the normative social practice of a science and towards a view of science as a discursive practice in which individual utterances are framed, within particular contexts, to present the beliefs of the speaker as true knowledge. What emerges is a focus on language as the mode of articulating and certifying 'knowledge'. It is also clear that the social construction of the contexts of utterance empower speakers with the authority to speak on and certify certain areas of knowledge. It is through the manipulation of linguistic repertoires that scientists lend their authority to particular accounts of natural processes and support their claims to truth. The structural form of these discourses locates truth with the speaker but the content of the discourse locates it in the natural world represented to the speaker through their scientific practice of experiment and observation. This process is ideological in the sense that contradictions between material and social processes are obscured at the level of language.

For Mannheim science was a relatively special area of knowledge (Mannheim 1952: 243) although he was clear that science was subject to situationally determined thought, the theory of relationism and the theory of the changing basis of thought (Mannheim 1952: 274). But the modern sociology of science has effectively brought it within his account of total ideology and perspectival knowledge by explicating its discursive structure. At around the same time that Mannheim was writing in German in the 1920s, V.N. Voloshinov was writing in Russian about the role that language plays in the process of ideology. He pointed out that the contents of language have a material form but that they also reflect a reality beyond themselves. It is the role of words as signs, as carriers of meaning, as representing, depicting or standing for something else, that enables them to function as the bearers of ideology. Voloshinov did not analyse the static, material form of language but stressed the emergence of meaning and its effect as ideology in communicative contexts:

In essence, meaning belongs to a word in its position between speakers; that is, meaning is realized only in the process of active, responsive understanding. Meaning does not reside in the word or in the soul of the speaker or in the soul of the listener. Meaning is *the effect of interaction between speaker and listener produced via the material of a particular sound complex.*

(Voloshinov 1973: 102–3)

This view quite specifically denies the independence of the individual 'psyche' as the determinant of meaning. For Voloshinov, the contents of the psyche are signs that are derived from the individual's social context. He argues that the social determines the individual through the medium of signs so that she is able to make sense of her own experience only through their materiality. This is an extreme materialist and social determinist position, but one that begins to describe the mechanism of ideology in language. The process of signification is for Voloshinov ideological in that experience is not merely reflected in the sign but 'refracted':

How is this refraction of existence in the ideological determined? By an intersecting of differently oriented social interests within one and the same sign community, i.e., *by the class struggle.*

(Voloshinov 1973: 23)

The same sign can then represent different interests – Voloshinov says each sign has two faces – and this embedded contradiction is sustained by the dominant ideology exerting a stabilizing influence on the meaning of the sign. The 'inner dialectic quality' of the sign is able to emerge fully only at times of social crisis or revolutionary change.

Michel Pêcheux, writing much more recently on the ideological role of language is greatly influenced by Althusser's analysis of ideology. Like Voloshinov he sees language as intimately tied up with ideology and meaning as variable rather than an enduring property of the sign or word. He sees meaning as at least partly determined by the socially constructed location of those who utter:

words, expressions, propositions, etc., change their meaning according to the positions held by those who use them, which signifies that they find their meaning by reference to those positions, i.e., by reference to the ideological formations ... in which those positions are inscribed.

(Pêcheux 1982: 111)

Pêcheux not only links meaning to the social position of the utterer but also links it to their status and location within the discourse (Pêcheux 1982: 115). Meanings in this view are not then reducible to words or to

interactive contexts – let alone to individual subjects. Meaning and ideological effect are a product of the particular utterance in its discursive
context which includes the location of the utterer within that context.

Pêcheux and his colleagues attempt to link the project of linguistics
with the insights of dialectical materialism. In doing so they mount a
critique of the Saussurian distinction between *langue* (language as a
system) and *parole* (language as it is uttered) on the grounds that *langue*
cannot be treated as a stable system of meanings. Insisting that problems
of the continuity of meaning exist within *langue* and not simply between
instances of *parole*, they develop a conceptual framework around the
concept of 'discourse' that is summarized by Thompson:

> Expressions 'have meaning' in virtue of the discursive formations
> wherein they occur, for meaning (sens) is constituted by the relations
> between the linguistic elements of a given discursive formation.
> These relations of substitution, synonymy, and paraphrase are called
> 'discursive processes'. It follows that the meaning of an expression is
> not stable and fixed, but is produced in a continuous process of
> 'slipping', of 'sliding', of 'metaphor'. It also follows that expressions
> may 'change their meaning' in passing from one discursive form to
> another: that is what the Saussurian concept could not grasp.
>
> (Thompson 1984: 235)

The links drawn between ideology and language by Voloshinov and
between ideology and discourse by Pêcheux are prescient of some of the
links that will be discussed in Chapter 10. They do, however, represent
an unusually political development in the study of language. As we have
seen in the origins of structuralism (Chapter 6), linguistics has
traditionally focused on the way meanings are constructed within
sentences. The discipline has tended to study the formal properties of
the production of meaningful language and not interpreted the meaning
content of language or its relation to social context. But the
development of socio-linguistics has shifted attention away from sub-
sentence units of words and phrases to larger units of meaning and
begun to explore the connections between meaning and social structure.

Basil Bernstein famously, and contentiously, has explored the notion
of 'elaborated' and 'restricted' codes. These codes or fashions of
speaking are empirically demonstrable by reference to syntactic and
lexical features of utterance and they locate the utterer in not simply a
discursive context but also a social structural one. The restricted code is
characterized by the high predictability of the syntactic elements that
will be used – the user of an elaborated code will select from a relatively
extensive range of possibilities, reducing the probability of prediction.

The restricted code is 'universalistic' in the sense that the models from whom the code can be learned are generally available whereas the models for the elaborated code are 'incumbents of specialized social positions'. Bernstein describes the link between social structure and code like this:

> the use of an elaborated code or an orientation to its use will depend not on the psychological properties of a speaker but upon access to specialized social positions, by virtue of which a particular type of speech model is available. Normally, but not inevitably, such social positions will coincide with a stratum seeking or already possessing access to the major decision making areas of society.
>
> (Bernstein 1974: 130)

The way in which Bernstein links 'code' to 'class' may seem crude and mechanistic with some hindsight but the establishment of ways of speaking as both marked by social position and as being more or less effective in different contexts was a significant development. The conception of different codes illuminates how language might be the medium for realizing power differentials in the negotiation of meaning so bringing about ideological effects.

M.A.K. Halliday's work both contributed to and drew on Bernstein's and is more detailed in its account of the linguistic features that express social relationships and social structures. Halliday spelt out the links between different functional levels of meaning in language (ideational, interpersonal and textual), different grammatical forms and the social context of meaning. He describes language as a social semiotic, as a field that both constructs reality for the language user and enables her to exchange meanings about that reality. In addressing the social process of language at a level above the way meaning is constructed in a sentence, Halliday describes the 'text' of an utterance as deriving its meaning through the contextualizing field of discourse. He describes different levels at which meaning is constructed; the lower levels are the lexicogrammatical and phonological features derived from the linguistic system, the higher levels are to do with society-wide discursive modes of interpretation:

> In its most general significance a text is a sociological event, a semiotic encounter through which the meanings that constitute the social system are *exchanged*.
>
> (Halliday 1978: 140)

This account, like that of Berger and Luckmann (see Chapter 3) locates knowledge about the world we live in, what we treat as 'reality', in the realm of language. For Halliday this is one of the things texts are doing; providing what is effectively knowledge about our environment. This is nothing so grand as the certified knowledge of science, it is knowledge of everyday life and the context of experience. But the account that Halliday offers is of the role of language and signification in constituting *all* of the social system, including discourses such as science and poetry:

> Language has evolved as the primary mode of meaning in a social environment. It provides the means of acting on and reflecting on the environment, to be sure – but in a broader context, in which acting and reflecting on the environment are in turn the means of *creating* the environment and transmitting it from one generation to the next.
>
> (Halliday 1978: 141)

Halliday's emphasis on the 'exchange of meanings' as the process at the heart of discourse is one I shall return to in Chapters 10 and 11 to guide empirical analysis. Here, it is important to note that Bernstein and Halliday shift the study of language away from the sub-sentence units of linguistics towards an analysis of text and discourse. They also connect the meaning and the ways of creating meaning with social context – but they do not analyse power as it is realised through language or introduce a conception of ideology to discuss the role of language as obscuring contradictions in lived experience. However, the analysis of discourse and text has led to an analysis of ideology in a number of different ways, some of which I will consider in the remainder of this and the following chapter.

Critical linguistics has explored the links between ideology and language drawing on a style of analysis that derives from traditional linguistics. However, its critical perspective, which also derives from the theory of ideology, analyses language as not merely constructing reality but as particular constructions of language constructing reality in particular ways.

> If linguistic meaning is inseparable from ideology, and both depend on social structure, then linguistic analysis ought to be a powerful tool for the study of ideological processes which mediate relationships of power and control .... The need then is for a linguistics which is critical, which is aware of the assumptions on which it is based and prepared to reflect critically upon the underlying causes of the phenomena it studies, and the nature of the society whose language it is.
>
> (Fowler *et al.* 1979: 186)

The techniques they offer to achieve this critical linguistics constitute a kind of inversion of transformational grammar. Instead of unravelling the deep structure of language to demonstrate an underlying coherence and continuity of language, they show how the utilization of particular surface structures are compelling in generating particular meanings. By tracing from the deep structure to the surface structure, the selective operation of particular transformations produces a particular perspective that situates speaker and hearer, actors, actions, objects and events. This process of generating a perspective by reference to surface forms is political; the relative situations created in the perspective both reflect and generate relations of differential power within social contexts. These processes are largely unconscious and not the product of contrivance or intention to produce particular ideological effects (Fowler et al. 1979: 186).

The critical linguistic approach begins to make explicit the processes of ideology embedded in our unconscious use of language by showing the link between semantic effect and the structure of language. Texts subjected to critical linguistic analysis are recognized as part of communicative interactions so:

> The texts are not appropriated as sources of data, but are treated as independent subjects for critical interpretation. . . . Interpretation is the process of recovering the social meanings expressed in discourse by analysing the linguistic structures in the light of their interactional and wider social contexts.
>
> (Fowler *et al.* 1979: 196)

Critical linguistics is an interpretive approach that utilizes some techniques from linguistics while breaking with the linguistic tradition that emulated a science by describing the closed system of language. I will briefly refer to two examples of this approach and application of technique.

RELEXICALIZATION

Tony Trew has analysed newspaper discourse to show how variations in linguistic structure produce ideological effects. The principal analytical tool he uses is the structure of causality in descriptions of events that distributes agency. For example, he considers two newspaper headlines reporting the same incident:

The Times:
　RIOTING BLACKS SHOT DEAD BY POLICE AS ANC LEADERS MEET
　Eleven Africans were shot dead and 15 wounded when Rhodesian Police opened fire on a rioting crowd of about 2,000.

The *Guardian:*
POLICE SHOOT 11 DEAD IN SALISBURY RIOT
Riot police shot and killed 11 African demonstrators and wounded 15 others.

(Fowler *et al.* 1979: 98)

The linguistic form of *The Times* headline is passive and that of the *Guardian* active. This means that there is an effect in varying the relationship of agents as perpetrators of an action, to the action:

Using the passive form puts the (syntactic) agents of the killings, 'police', in less focal position.

(Fowler *et al.* 1979: 98)

The report in *The Times* uses the passive form so that the syntactic agent is only weakly implicated in the action of shooting dead the Africans. In contrast the objects of the action are contextualized and described by the adjective 'rioting':

Given that the report focuses on the ones shot rather than the shooters (by the use of the passive), attaching 'rioting' to 'blacks' simultaneously makes 'rioting' the focal action, and also makes those shot responsible for the situation which is both the context of the shooting and a partial explanation of it.

(Fowler *et al.* 1979: 99)

Trew goes on to describe how in the following days, both newspapers progressively removed the focus on the agents of the killings and the killings themselves. The incident became progressively more generalized under a reference to the 'rioting' that stood for the other actions (shooting), agents (police, blacks) and effects (dying).

Trew's analysis, which is of course far more detailed than I have represented it, is persuasive in showing that linguistic choices about structuring a description 'theorize' the event being described. He is not arguing that this is the result of bias, which would involve both intention and the possibility of unbiased description, but that description necessarily involves theorizing and evaluating events. He is also making the point that descriptions alter over time within one perspective (i.e. that of one newspaper). He shows how transformations that are linguistic, such as those from active to passive constructions, alter the evaluation of the description. Semantic shifts (e.g. from 'kill' to 'die') obscure the causes and agents involved. Nominalizations of verbs (e.g. from 'die' to 'deaths') obviate any need for agents, including victims, to be defined.

Structural transformations are part and parcel of semantic alterations that Trew, following Halliday, calls 'relexicalization'. He contrasts this approach with Chomskyan transformational grammar that analyses sentences as discrete entities and considers only the possible transformations in relation to that sentence. What Trew analyses is the change in meaning brought about by different structural forms within the same discourse, but referring to the same actions and events (Fowler *et al.* 1979: 113).

MODALITY

Kress and Hodge (also co-authors with Fowler and Trew of *Language and Control* 1979) have attempted a systematic account of language organized around categories that reveal its ideological effects (*Language as Ideology*, Kress and Hodge 1979). They base their model of language on its function in representing the world, that is how it achieves descriptions of people, things, actions and relations. They distinguish between two models of syntagm structure: 'actional' and 'relational'. Actional syntagms refer to actions that involve people or things either through transactionals ('police shoot demonstrators') or non-transactionals ('demonstrators shot dead'). Relational syntagms do not involve an action but establish a relation between two entities, either equative ('John is Lear') or attributive ('John's Lear is stunning').

Within these two models for representing the world, the speaker controls linguistic features that give a force to their representation which Kress and Hodge call 'modality'. There are modal auxiliaries (can, may, must) modal adverbs (probably, possibly, certainly) and modal verbs which refer to speech or mental processes (think, understand, feel). Hesitations (um, er) and fillers (sort of) as well as intonation can also affect modality. What Kress and Hodge are referring to is the authority claim that the speaker indicates by the modality in her utterances. In its simplest and most unambiguous form modality is expressed in the sentence 'She may possibly come' by the modal adverb 'possibly', which limits the speaker's claim to knowledge of future events.

Modal auxiliaries are ambiguous about whether they are claims to knowledge or to power. 'She can talk' means either that 'she is able to talk' (claim to knowledge) or 'she is allowed to talk' (claim of authority in giving permission). There is also the potential for ambiguity about temporality that depends on context. 'She can talk' refers either to future events if it is giving permission meaning or present states if it claims knowledge. Kress and Hodge are claiming that the ambiguity of modality is functional in the exchange of meanings, to the aims of the speaker:

> A speaker uses modalities to protect his utterances from criticism. A large number of modalizers indicates considerable fear on the speaker's part and vulnerability, rather than intellectual uncertainty.
>
> (Kress and Hodge 1979: 127)

By modalizing knowledge claims the ambiguity diminishes the power status of the speaker. The speaker can create the converse effect by exploiting the ambiguity of modalizers (Kress and Hodge 1979: 125). 'A cat may look at a king' both says that it is an empirical possibility in the sense of is-able-to (a knowledge claim) and it implies that the cat may do this (a power claim). The claim to knowledge partly obscures the claim to power in the exhortation while at the same time creating a basis for it.

At one level, the structural and empirical level, critical linguistics demonstrates the variation in linguistic representation and its ability to remain meaningful while deleting agency and generating ambiguity in its surface form. Trew's analysis of discourse developing over time shows that reconstruction of the 'deep structure' of a sentence is inadequate to this task because some deletions achieved by transformation may not be recoverable without reference to surface forms or to previous utterances in the discourse. The trace of previous meanings exchanged remains in current exchanges though not visible in the surface 'meaning'. The presence of surface forms (e.g. non-transactionals, nominalizations) may be a guide to what features of earlier exchanges are relevant to present meanings.

At a second, interactional level, the analysis of modality can give information about the power relations operating in the discourse that both constrain and enable the exchange of meanings, without relying on reconstructing subjective intentions to understand the meanings exchanged. At a third level though, critical linguistics does not seem so successful. This is the attempt to relate linguistic structure to social structure and would be the basis for indicating the ideological effects of linguistic structures.

What critical linguistics can do is to demonstrate how ideological effects are achieved through the construction of particular interpretations of events and social relations and show aspects of how power operates in the exchange. But there is considerable ambiguity about the relationship between individual agency, social structure and the process of discourse. This ambiguity is expressed in the descriptive language of critical linguistics. The speaker/writer as agent is described as 'selecting' or making a 'choice' but selection operates:

under the sanction of social norms. The process is deterministic. It is also, presumably, more or less unconscious.

(Fowler *et al.* 1979: 194)

MAKING CHOICES

Social psychologists have begun to analyse the processes that lie behind the selections that speakers make. John Shotter argues that the form and content of utterances is shaped by what amounts to a moral imperative:

> what we talk of as our experience of our reality is constituted for us very largely by the *already established* ways in which we *must* talk in our attempt to *account* for ourselves – and for it – to the others around us.

(Shotter 1989: 141)

The force of the imperative lies in the need to feel a sense of identity by sharing a reality with others. This perspective concentrates on how the individual speaker orients themselves in relation to the discourse. What it does not address are the sociological effects of the 'already established' ways of describing the world. Although the discourse analysis approach in psychology has been called a 'radically non-cognitive form of social psychology' (Potter and Wetherell 1987: 178), a theoretical analysis of the cognitive processes involved in how speakers make selections using frames and texts is possible.

Van Dijk (1988) describes a cognitive structure that involves perceptions being interpreted and stored in memory. The process of 'discourse production' involves drawing on previously gathered information and models of relevance and connection between situations and information. This approach highlights discourse as both cognitive, because it involves interpretation and representation, and social, because it occurs as social interaction. But another social dimension of discourse lies behind van Dijk's account of power, cognition and discourse. Ideology organizes group-based general attitudes which in turn define the structure of the thought processes:

> In other words, ideologies define what may be called the 'foundation' of the social cognitions of group members.

(van Dijk 1988: 139–40)

Van Dijk treats ideology as unproblematically linked to social groupings (such as class and gender) whose interests are realized both through the content of social cognition and through the exercise of power in the context of discourse. A more complex view of ideology from a social psychological perspective is offered by Michael Billig and his colleagues (Billig *et al.* 1988). Rather than viewing ideology as a unitary representation of group interests, they draw attention to the dilemmas inherent in ideology, pointing out that 'intellectual ideology', or the debate between different claims to knowledge, does not 'donate a series of solved problems to common sense' (Billig *et al.* 1988: 40).

The thesis underlying the analysis of the various contributors to this work (on topics including education, expertise, health, racism and gender) is that the dilemmas characteristic of intellectual labour are also to be found in the dilemmas of everyday practices. The theoretical perspective is specifically related to the tradition of the sociology of knowledge and to the theory of ideology but the approach is critical of the tendency to treat ideology as:

> one relatively coherent and internally consistent social structure or layer contained within a wider social whole.
>
> (Billig *et al.* 1988: 152)

This is an interesting comment that brings out a tension between using the term 'ideology' to refer to a particular set of beliefs shared by a particular group of people (e.g. a racist ideology) and the use of the same term to indicate a social process by which the lived relations of human beings are mediated in societies. Billig's complaint is that ideologies are not nearly so coherent as sociologists would have everyone believe – in fact they are characterized by dilemmas that are manifest in applications of knowledge/ideology in human experience. He criticizes Mannheim for treating ideologies as unified belief systems, systematically applied to the world. But what Mannheim was trying to show was the disputation *between* social groups with different perspectives of the social order. In doing this he obscured conflicts *within* social groups and, as we have seen, the attempt to impute a unified perspective to a whole social group is fraught with problems.

The persuasive point being made by Billig and his colleagues is that systems of ideas or beliefs cannot be translated into practice without contradictions becoming apparent. These contradictions emerge as dilemmas facing people in everyday life, as they apply what they 'know' to what they do. There are always at least two competing and contrasting versions about how the world could be interpreted or how action should be undertaken. For Billig and his colleagues these dilemmas are related to the contradictions inherent in ideological perspectives. The sociology of knowledge and the theory of ideology do not, however, describe a system of unitary beliefs that present a coherent picture of the world. As we have seen in Chapters 2–5, the concept of ideology has been developed to describe the management of contradictions involved in the social process of knowledge. Social psychology seems to be discovering anew that ideology only obscures contradictions in lived experience – but that it does not make them go away.

What is to count as 'true' or is to be effective as knowledge is contingent on the context of action. The sociology of science has shown that there are no consistent and abiding rules governing actions that produce knowledge. Instead, scientists negotiate what is true in their discursive practices – they have 'repertoires' for dealing with knowledge as they see it and knowledge as other scientists see it. The study of language shows that the way the world is represented can have ideological effects, not by intention but simply in the process of rendering the reality of experience into language. That process need not be intentional but does involve choices – choices that are individually made but reflect the cultural perspective of the chooser including the dilemmas about knowledge that make up that culture.

9 Culture and the perspective of women

CULTURE AS IDEOLOGY

If the discourse analytical approach of sociologists of science largely ignores ideology and the critical linguists and social psychologists provide only a limited view of ideology, a much more comprehensive account has influenced the modern sociology of culture. The cultural orientation of the user of knowledge, the utterer of discourse, is important in understanding what will count as knowledge and how it functions ideologically in rendering the world sensible and free of contradictions. Western culture, in particular the intellectual culture, including sociology, has in recent years been seriously challenged by the critique from a feminist perspective.

The modern sociology of culture has undermined presumptions about what is to count as culture and has challenged the hegemony of a middle-class aesthetics. The emerging feminist perspective has also utilized the field of cultural criticism to undermine the rationality of the dominant culture by revealing the way it structurally favours men and a male perspective.

Stuart Hall has argued that culture is not something different from the social so that the sociological effects are consequently of central importance in any analyses of any cultural phenomenon. In deriving a theory of the sociological effects of culture from Marx, Hall says:

> Here, *culture* is the accumulated growth of man's [*sic*] power over nature, materialized in the instruments and practice of labour and in the medium of signs, thought, knowledge and language through which it is passed on from generation to generation as man's 'second nature'.
>
> (Hall 1977: 319)

The sociology of culture is an approach which includes the analysis of knowledge and language but always in a context linked to the material processes of human, social power exploiting nature. Cultural forms can be understood as having an ideological role and bringing about the ideological effects of masking, fragmenting, and uniting the lived relations of members of a society. The media have, in Hall's account, colonized the cultural and ideological sphere. They provide the social knowledge through which we perceive our lives and those of others. The media also do ideological work, ordering and evaluating social knowledge, distinguishing between preferred and excluded explanations.

This account does not present ideology as a static or unitary phenomenon. Hall writes of a 'plurality of dominant discourses' (Hall 1977: 343) rather than of ideological effects brought about in cultural forms by the mechanical imposition of a 'repressive discourse' (Pateman 1980) in which values are imposed to present a particular and unitary version of reality. The Marxist analysis of culture claims that ideological effects occur in establishing the field of meanings and in distributing value between terms:

> Hence, though events will not be systematically encoded in a single way, they will tend, systematically, to draw on a very limited ideological or explanatory repertoire, . . . and that repertoire will have the overall tendency of making things 'mean' within the sphere of the dominant ideology.
>
> (Hall 1977: 344)

Raymond Williams has developed a Marxist perspective on the process of culture by addressing the social practices through which culture is produced and organized (Williams 1981). One of the issues that interests Williams is the degree to which the intelligentsia are locked into reproducing the dominant ideology. He rejects a broad interpretation of Mannheim's suggestion, following Alfred Weber, that there is an intelligentsia made up of people who are relatively uncommitted to any particular perspective. But Williams accepts that under certain conditions the relative separation of the intelligentsia's account from that of the dominant order can be demonstrated. He offers three sets of conditions under which there is likely to be a relative distance between the dominant perspective and that of the intelligentsia; where there is asymmetry between a capitalist market and a bourgeois social order, where particular institutions are not in phase with the general order and where organizations are based on a different or alternative order (Williams 1981: 223).

SUBCULTURE AS IDEOLOGY

A degree of 'relative autonomy' or 'relative distance' from the dominating social order can be achieved not only through the practices of the intelligentsia but also through popular cultural forms. The analysis of mass cultural and subcultural forms links with the view of culture as ideology by interpreting cultural texts in a specific relation to the dominant social order. In looking at subcultures, a group of writers at the Centre for Contemporary Cultural Studies during the 1970s showed how a relative separation from the dominant order was evident in subcultural forms (e.g. papers by Paul Willis on drug culture, Dick Hebdige on mods' style and Paul Corrigan on street corner kids in CCCS 1976). Their analysis of subcultural groups in the context of particular practices and activities and a set of other signifying contexts (clothes and music) shows how the codes of the dominant culture are transformed. The same words and meanings produce a different ideological effect because of the different discursive and cultural context in which they occur:

> The major element in doing nothing is talking. Not the arcane discussion of the TV talk show, but recounting, exchanging stories which need never be true or real but which are as interesting as possible.... It passes the time and it underlies the group nature of the different ways that the boys have of passing the time.
>
> (Corrigan 1976: 103)

The role of the text for locating the individual in a group and for establishing individual identity, occurs within a subcultural discourse – one which is not the same for everyone and one which can be contrasted with relatively more dominant forms. In the subcultural discourse, the original meanings of the dominant culture are subverted by adding connotations. Meanings are appropriated and utilized in an oppositional cultural form (the 'mod' suit, the 'rocker' motorbike, the militaristic 'style' of skinheads) which invert their effect. Instead of being symbols of inclusion within the dominant culture, key artefacts are appropriated as symbols of exclusion by subcultural modifications. These are often extremes or extensions of the style associated with the dominant form (vents and buttons on the mod suit, studded leather and straight-through exhausts for the rocker's bike, excessively short hair and amateur tattoos in the skinhead style).

The ethnography of subcultures addressed them in relation to the asymmetrical distribution of power in capitalist societies. The subculture could be seen as a basis of critique, undermining the values of the dominant culture:

These cultures reveal the unsuspected power of commodities and of a minutely articulated ideology in everyday life. They also show the room and scope left by them and in them for struggle and change within the cells of everyday habit.

(Willis 1978: 171–2)

However, while the perspective of subcultures provided a basis for a degree of resistance and challenge at the level of ideology, the conclusion of the sociology of culture seems to be that they were an inadequate basis for structural change. At crucial points subcultures mimic and embellish not only the symbols of the dominant culture but also those value orientations that lie behind the extant structure (nationalism, sexism, racism, obligation to work, respect for the rule of law). Hebdige sums up the relationship between subculture and dominant culture:

It is neither simply resistance against some external order nor straightforward conformity with the parent culture. It is both a declaration of independence of otherness, of alien intent, a refusal of anonymity, of subordinate status. It is an *in*subordination. And at the same time it is also a confirmation of the fact of powerlessness, a celebration of impotence.

(Hebdige 1988: 35)

Although feminist sociology has explored women in culture and women's culture they have not accepted a role of insubordination but have challenged the dominant order of (male) rationality.

IMAGES OF WOMEN

The role of culture as ideology has been a site of struggle for feminists because it is a mode in which meanings are formed and transformed:

We have asserted the importance of consciousness, ideology, imagery and symbolism for our battles. Definitions of 'femininity and masculinity, as well as the social meaning of family life and the sexual division of labour, are constructed on this ground.

(Barrett 1982: 37)

A feminist critique has challenged the implication from cultural sociology of unitary spheres of discourse, untraversed by other forms of domination and other ideological effects. Angela McRobbie and Jenny Garber (CCCS 1976) commented on the absence of women in the accounts of subcultural forms – where were the women and what were they doing? While subcultural forms could be seen as resisting some of the ideological effects of mainstream culture and establishing a relative separation, other contradictions were obscured: specifically, the contradictory nature of the lived experiences of women and men.

One of the things girls and young women were doing was reading magazines. McRobbie (1982) analyses the way one particular magazine *Jackie* does the ideological work of introducing the girl reader into adolescence. The magazine provides a way of 'framing' the world for its readers, of presenting them with 'an ideological bloc of mammoth proportions, one which *imprisons* them in a claustrophobic world of jealousy and competitiveness' (McRobbie 1982: 265). But McRobbie's analysis does not only see *Jackie* as merely worthless and manipulative. It is also a resource used by girls to express their subcultural location, albeit in a very limited way. Reading it shows their disdain for other forms of reading, of the lack of relevance to them of other cultural forms – in school it can signal boredom and disaffection. The ideological effect is predominantly to provide a frame of 'romantic individualism' in which the adolescent girl is presented with the prime importance of the private sphere:

> Romance problems, fashion, beauty and pop mark out the limits of the girl's concern – other possibilities are ignored or dismissed.
>
> (McRobbie 1982: 281–2)

The private sphere is one in which the girl establishes her identity by the consumption of certain goods deemed appropriate to her age and gender. In the fields of work and romance her frame of a private world means that she should be passive – waiting for the right boy, accepting routine work. The narrowness of the gendered roles offered, the persistent passivity and location within a private sphere of women, provides little opportunity for appropriation and subversion of cultural forms.

More recently feminist cultural commentators have addressed the gendered representation of women in popular cultural forms that attempts to define the gendered nature of sexuality:

> Women bear the burden of speech in this area. Women are incited to take responsibility for sexual relationships, to analyse, facilitate, interpret and ultimately to lubricate social and sexual relationships which have run into trouble. ... While men are incited to more and more complicated and novel forms of *sexual technique*, women are incited to shoulder the weight of *sexual consciousness*.
>
> (Coward 1984: 139)

Rosalind Coward is commenting on agony aunts and problem pages in women's magazines. There are no male equivalents for *Jackie* or for the problem pages in women's magazines (though there are some men's magazines that address fashion, style and 'general interest' issues from a 'male' view). Magazines addressed to women do however focus on what women, including young women, are and what they should be. This is a very visible process of the culture constructing womanliness. The magazines can be seen as presenting a package of womanliness: the way the face and body should look, the clothes and style that are appropriate, the activities and attitudes to be adopted. Even, it seems, the way to deal with something so 'natural' as sexuality.

There are problems with presuming that these cultural products are read in an accepting and uncritical way, that the message is absorbed, unmodified and that the reader or consumer then lives the image they have read. This is a different form of the problem of imputation that has always beset the sociology of knowledge. In general the analysis of mass cultural products has circumvented this issue by pointing to the volume of consumption. McRobbie begins her analysis by quoting the expanding sales figures for *Jackie*, 'Britain's longest selling "teen" magazine for over ten years' (McRobbie 1982: 263). It is implied that so many people would not keep on buying the magazine if it did not say something they were willing to hear. Consumption of something that is nothing but a text is in some senses evidence of its absorption – the message is received although it is not necessarily applied as knowledge that guides action.

DECODING IDEOLOGY

The analysis of cultural products has not generally been concerned with how much effect they have on readers – it is a difficult if not impossible issue to tackle. Instead the focus has been on how they might be read, on how messages are constructed or 'coded'. An area ripe for such analyses has been advertisements where the aim of selling the product is achieved by linking it to symbols of cultural value. For Varda Langholz Leymore (1975), for example, there are 'exhaustive common denominators' involving binary oppositions (things like life/death, hot/cold, in/out, original producer/final producer, culture/nature) out of which the value of goods is constructed. This sort of approach has its origins in the structuralist analyses of Lévi-Strauss and Barthes. The task of decoding advertisements has also been taken up by Judith Williamson (1978) who argues that the process of encoding has an ideological effect. Among other analyses or 'decodings' she shows how the image of Catherine

Deneuve, at least her face, head and shoulders, becomes entwined with the perfume Chanel No 5. The advertisement connects two things, the face and the bottle, but, Williamson argues, they are not 'logically' connected; they would not be connected were it not for the advertisement:

> Thus once again we see that the *form* of advertisements is a part of ideology and involves a false assumption which is at the root of all ideology, namely that because things are as they are (in this case because certain things are *shown* as connected in ads, placed together etc.), this state of affairs is somehow natural, and must 'make sense' simply because it exists.
>
> (Williamson 1978: 29)

More recently Bob Hodge and Gunther Kress have taken further the analysis of cultural forms as both encoding meaning and having ideological effects. For them, images, including images of women, are not simply related to the selling of products by utilizing the co-presence of received meanings. They argue that gender differentiation, along with other codes, involves a 'logonomic system' that controls who is able or forbidden to produce or receive messages and through what codes and under what conditions (Hodge and Kress 1988: 266). The logonomic system is the means by which cultural definitions are achieved through the exchange of meaning – it is the language of signs.

For Hodge and Kress 'signs' can be seen in any social practice that involves exchanging meaning. Among the things they analyse are components of language as signs (pronouns, gendered word endings), posture in representational images, social rituals including marriage, cartoons, newspaper articles, features in women's magazines, 'familial texts' and classroom exchanges. Each of these fields is vulnerable to a social semiotic analysis that begins to unravel levels of meaning, showing how meaning is achieved through transformation of signs from meaning one thing in one context to meaning something else in a different context. The regularity of these transformations is what makes the cultural world knowable – we recognize and understand the repeated use of signs in different contexts. We are also able to stand back and analyse these transformations by questioning the way that apparently arbitrary or unrelated signs are linked.

A recurring theme in their analyses is the role of gender. It becomes an aspect of interpreting, for example, the meanings carried in a picture of Mary Quant in her boardroom or the categorization of women as 'seductresses' and 'winners' in a women's magazine article on body language. One set of meaning exchanges that recur in their analyses is to do with the tour of Australia by Princess Diana and Prince Charles.

In the analysis of pictures of Princess Diana they link the coding of gender (dresses, primary colours, long hair, make-up as signifiers of womanliness) with codes of relative power and status. The ability to provide images with many different changes of clothing for example signifies 'a plenitude of selves. This plurality is a transparent signifier of power, similar to the royal "we"' (Hodge and Kress 1988: 102).

There is a sense that certain systems of signs are basic in the Hodge and Kress style of analysis. Red signifies female – pink for little girls, blue for boys – for example, and from that other signs can be decoded and related. Red also signifies energy and desire, so, pale blue 'labels the boy with power purely by not labelling him with energy or desire' and 'Adult women signify their sexuality especially through the colour red: lipstick, rouge, nail varnish' (Hodge and Kress 1988: 105). Princess Diana can then signify the restraint of her sexuality with the use of light shades of lipstick and rouge, but can also signify female power by wearing red dresses featured in the picture sequence:

> The dresses marked by colours are marked for energy in other ways. The dress which plunges 15 cm downwards is one of the red ones, and it has a slit at the front rising above the knee.
>
> (Hodge and Kress 1988: 105–6)

The analysis of the 'contradictory gender meanings offered' by Princess Diana's clothes can progress towards an interpretation of them as legitimizing 'a specific gender ideology and specific class message: that women can only be women when the traditional rulers rule' (Hodge and Kress 1988: 106).

FEMINISM AND KNOWLEDGE

While the analysis of images of women has become an important feature of cultural decoding, it is not the same thing as a feminist analysis which is oriented by a particular political perspective. Whereas Marxist critique revealed contradictions in the lived relations of production, feminist critique reveals contradictions in the lived personal relations of human beings. To be sure, these contradictions of gender differentiation are carried into the process of economic production but their original site is in the distinction male/female and its impact on the relations surrounding the reproduction of the species.

The difference between bodies is presumed to be prior to any talk, any social construction. But there is a continuing discourse surrounding the 'natural' difference of bodies. This discourse refers to the anatomical differences, to the different functions of male and female bodies in reproduction. In the past these distinctions would have included reference to women's intellectual or cultural abilities, their 'special' role as carers and nurturers – all of which would have been cited as natural or obvious. But in the face of critique from feminism these distinctions have been challenged and their grounding in a 'natural order' has been undermined. By asserting that the difference between male and female bodies is not necessarily socially significant, the grounding of a social order of gendered relations in a natural, pre-social order of difference fails. Sexual relations, pair-bonding and child-rearing do not require sexual difference. Conception may, but it need be only the most distant sort of lived relation (i.e. artificial insemination by donor). Women have demonstrated their intellectual and cultural abilities in the very process of describing exactly how cultural barriers are established that keep them out of roles of power and authority and in roles as carers and nurturers.

The feminist critique of male discourse of gender difference has increasingly given way to the establishment of a *feminist* discourse of gender difference. In it, women's knowledge of their world is presented as different from men's and as a knowledge that has been distorted and suppressed. In a piece originally published as critical journalism, Judith Williamson has commented on the process by which knowledge of sexuality is generated:

> Ours is a society which speaks insistently of what it doesn't speak of, relentlessly finding things that no-one had lost in the first place.

> And the territory of the great march forward into sexual knowledge always seems to be the *female* body. It is *our* bodies that the pioneers search, for clues into 'the understanding of human sexuality' – yet another case of 'they've got it, she wears it'.

> (Williamson 1985: 39)

Here the process of knowledge, dominated by men and their interest, creates an object of sexuality, and of knowledge, in the bodies of women. The form of knowledge is a mechanical and technical one – not a discursive or negotiated knowledge. Williamson identifies herself as a subject in the ideological struggle, as a woman whose body is objectified and scrutinized in the interests of understanding human sexuality. The particular location of women in the process of knowledge gives her an experiential perspective on the effects of power and knowledge as they are linked together. It is because knowledge about sexuality objectifies women and because women experience the relative lack of power of that objectification, that they are in a position to generate a feminist discourse based on awareness of the process.

There is a parallel here with Lukács's account of the possibility of 'true consciousness' being achieved through the proletariat's location in the class structure (see Chapter 4). There is also a danger in the feminist discourse of establishing a new natural perspective, that which women would have were it not for the ideological effects of patriarchal relations. In relation to understanding women's bodies and their sexuality for example it may seem obvious that women would have a naturally privileged knowledge. But this is not the point being made by Williamson and others who are developing a feminist discourse that critiques knowledge processes. The objectification of women, and indeed the reification of sexuality, is part of an ideological process in which knowledge is generated and distributed to have effects that are related to power and interests:

> In modern jargon sexuality 'frees' us; it has become part of a discourse of 'liberation' which makes repression, rather than oppression, the enemy of human happiness. But is 'sexuality' really the arena in which our well-being is determined in the power-structure of modern societies? And if indeed we overestimate its power, what effect does this have? What is the function of an ideology that keeps everyone looking for the meaning of life up their own or someone else's vagina?
>
> (Williamson 1985: 44)

The taken-as-read answer to this rhetorical question is of course that by keeping women tied up with talking about sexuality and searching in a personal or private domain for sexual pleasure, they will be kept out of the male domain of action and social power.

It seems that the feminist discourse has not fallen into the trap of naturalizing the form of gender relations in the same way as Lukács naturalized economic relations. But the strategy of feminist discourse does follow Lukács's goal of 'practical critical activity', building a consciousness based in action that arises out of the lived contradictions of real relations. The critique of the thing-like rendering of sexuality and other forms of human relation in patriarchal knowledge also seems to have roots in Lukács's concept of reification. The common ground between Lukács's account of 'true consciousness' and the feminist critique of patriarchal knowledge is that the experience of a structural situation of less power enables a potential for awareness about those structures of power. The awareness is not an individual capacity derived from individual differences but is rooted in the commonality of the experience by the group of the situation of less-power.

But the common ground between Lukács and the feminist critique of knowledge should not be overplayed. There are important differences; most notably there is not one, true consciousness that is to be revealed by the feminist understanding. The feminist critique of knowledge is, by and large, concerned with shifting the ideological barriers of patriarchy to understanding the gendered relations of human society. For most, this is not an exclusive understanding, available only to women, nor is a single or scientific account of the true nature of gendered relations revealed.

THE WOMAN'S POINT OF VIEW

One way in which the feminist critique can operate is to distinguish between a patriarchal perspective and a women's perspective. Hilary Graham and Ann Oakley, for example, distinguish the way that doctors and mothers look at the process of reproduction. This includes the ideological perspective and system of values of the groups but also the network of individuals who influence their attitudes and values (Graham and Oakley 1982: 309). The membership of the categories is not simply determined by gender (not all doctors are men, not all women are mothers) but by the experience of having been a doctor or a mother. The two frames of reference produce a different type of knowledge upon which to draw. The doctor's knowledge is abstract, specialist, expert and derived from medical science whereas the mother's is individualized, intuitive and derived from the sensations of her body (Graham and Oakley 1982: 312). The empirical evidence demonstrates the operation of two frames of reference but it is not clear to what extent these are gendered. The perspectives may not, for example, be significantly different from those shown in other studies (e.g. Silverman 1987) that explore the way power and knowledge operates in doctor/patient encounters and reflect a similar imbalance and divergence of perspective not determined by gender.

There are two important issues emerging that a feminist critique of knowledge must address; is women's knowledge determined, at least in part, by the fact of being a woman, and is knowledge of specifically women's experiences dealt with in a different way from more generalized experience? The first part seems to be answered by answering the second – it is not the fact of being a woman that is significant in terms of knowledge and perspective but the experience of being a woman in a patriarchal society. One of the consequences of patriarchal social relations is to de-emphasize experiences particular to women, and to downgrade knowledge based on experience.

Graham and Oakley make no claims for a feminist critique and do not argue that the mother's frame is determined by gender although they do occasionally substitute 'women' for 'mothers' in their account implying the broader category as the frame of reference. What their work is doing is to address the significance of women's experiences *and* their knowledge and perspective of those experiences. This approach has been used as a feminist strategy within the social sciences to reclaim and recast areas of knowledge, taking a different and more substantial account of women's experiences (for example in the field of informal care Ungerson 1985; in the field of domestic economics Barrett and McIntosh 1982; in the field of food preparation and consumption, Charles and Kerr 1988).

WOMEN'S KNOWLEDGE

While these approaches do deal with women's experiences in a different way they do not claim that women's knowledge is determined by their gender. But there is an emerging trend to claim that there is a 'feminist methodology' or at least a feminist approach to defining what is adequate knowledge. This begins with a critique of the traditional survey method which 'restricts access to the very everyday social processes which feminist researchers most want to tap' (Graham 1984: 113). The feminist approach is based on the need to find ways of studying the 'seemingly mundane activities' which 'shape women's identity' (Graham 1984: 112). As Hilary Graham points out, it is the semi-structured interview which has been used to bring out women's experiences. It is a method that allows women to account for their own experiences, using their own categories and language. It is also a method which allows the researcher to empathize and express solidarity and understanding. The research process has more room for reciprocity and sharing between researcher and researched and it is not determined by a rigid research instrument or a set of rules governing the interaction. That this might lead to possibly greater exploitation of the women subjects has not gone unnoted (Graham 1984; Oakley 1981) but this is an issue about how and for what ends the knowledge is being gathered.

Feminists working within sociology have then upturned the traditional approach of empirical methods which concentrate on minimizing bias in order to maximize the objectivity and generalizability of the knowledge generated. Rather than accepting a traditional view of society as a natural form to be disturbed as little as possible by the methods of research, feminist researchers have followed a strategy of stimulating and encouraging the social subjects they are studying to give up their knowledge. This has involved rediscovering techniques and methods that have long been part of the male tradition of sociology (phenomenological, symbolic interactionist, ethnographic and ethnomethodological approaches) but this time with a political edge. The distinguishing mark of feminist research is not method but the concern with the interests of women.

It is difficult to avoid noticing that some feminist approaches fulfil a traditional gender distinction utilized in anthropology that women are closer to nature and men to culture. The scientistic and technicized approach of the dominant (male) approach to social science is over-thrown for a more 'natural', tell-it-like-it-is approach. The topics for research (such as childbirth, caring, and preparation of food in the family) not only are within what is traditionally seen as women's domain but also are more 'natural' than other things that social scientists study, in the sense of having equivalent practices in all cultures and societies and even amongst animals. The view that the particular observational experience of women is based in the distinctive biological, reproductive difference between women and men has been called the 'centre of feminist theory' (Keller 1989). It not only lies behind attempts to claim that women have distinctive experiences that should be an object of knowledge but also implies a fundamentally different perspective and mode of knowing.

The nature/culture distinction itself has not gone uncriticized within feminist discourse. Penelope Brown and L. Jordanova argue that such a distinction is essentialist in its perception of the sexes and is part of a 'dominant ideology which is an impediment to our understanding of the ways societies construct the sexes' (Brown and Jordanova 1982: 390). They suggest that a relativist perspective is more appropriate because it places the emphasis on the social construction of gender rather than on a categorial or biological distinction. Indeed, the content of the studies of childbearing, caring and food preparation specifically problematize the naturalness or taken-for-granted role of women and describe the processes by which these specific roles are constructed. Relativism in feminist approaches is usually linked to the need for knowledge as power:

> The creation of knowledge is a central concern to feminism because knowledge creation means power ... their experiences of the world, and those of other subordinate, disadvantaged groups, have no part in the production of authoritative knowledge of the world.
>
> (Sydie 1987: 211)

Feminists have also begun to review the epistemological impact of the distinctions that emerge in feminist critiques. Judith Grant, for example, tackles the problems of some feminist positions in creating knowledge.

The rejection by writers like Mary Daly, Marilyn French and Susan Griffin of rationality as a male approach, risks falling into the essentialist trap of distinguishing between male and female modes of knowledge. They attempt to revalue as 'feminine' thought, that which is reflective, associative and circular, while devaluing what is characterized as male thought: rational, linear, logical. As Grant points out, these writers have in effect accepted and built upon a male/female dualism which has as its grounding the bodily sex differences of men and women:

> Female experiences are, in this view, radically different from those of men because the primary experience of everyone is of their sexual self and the body. In the end, the male experience of power (of which reason is a part since it has the *power* to exclude) is likened to the male body and conceptualized as monolithic, whereas female experience and female thinking, like the female body, is multicentred and open.
>
> (Grant 1987: 104)

Grant is critical of this reduction to the biological sex of 'Woman' as a crude basis for epistemology. It involves a knowledge claim that collapses as soon as differences between women emerge (she gives the example of different women's views of lesbian sadomasochistic pornography). She argues that reason and rational interpretation are necessary for discourse to be possible and to enable open participation in debate because 'It is faith and intuition which cannot be challenged' (Grant 1987: 113).

Susan Hekman makes a similar retreat from essentialist views and finds an alliance between feminism and what she calls 'anti-foundationalism'. This latter perspective includes the rejection of an absolute grounding of knowledge, of the priority of the scientific method and of the dichotomies of subject/object, reason/emotion. Anti-foundationalism instead embraces a fusing of perspectives and recognizes a plurality of knowledges and truths. She argues that the goal of both feminists and anti-foundationalists is the same:

> Those who call for a feminist epistemology are, quite simply, calling for the reinstitution of a truly 'human' viewpoint. This would entail a pluralistic position in which both ways of knowing (reason, logic, intuition, empathy) and moral qualities would be associated with persons, not sexes.
>
> (Hekman 1987: 81)

This is a rather weak claim and loses sight of the role of power and the effects on women's experiences of a patriarchal social order. There are others who support a longer-term view that knowledge for feminists, including feminist scientists, is to be derived not from a special epistemology but from a reconstruction of the social context in which knowledge is produced (e.g. Longing 1989).

THE WORLD OF WOMEN

Without claiming an epistemologically privileged status for women's knowledge, feminist writers have none the less been articulating a clear critique of rationality that is gendered and involves domination and oppression. Nancy Fraser (1989) shows how the discourse of needs interpretation within the welfare state makes distinctions based on presuppositions of the differential status of men and women. She argues that feminist politics needs to engage with the 'juridical–administrative–therapeutic state apparatus' that positions subjects differentially according to gender and ascribed need. Feminists need to struggle:

> to challenge the apparently natural, traditional interpretations still enveloping needs only recently sprung from domestic and official economic enclaves of privacy.
>
> (Fraser 1989: 158)

The aim of the struggle is to empower women to interpret their own needs – the struggle is precisely over knowledge and involves asserting women's right to know about themselves and their needs.

A number of the issues surrounding the status and importance of women's knowledge have been explored by Dorothy Smith. She draws a bold distinction between the world of men and that of women and uses the example of sociology to show how men as sociologists are part of a ruling group:

> The profession of sociology is predicated on a universe which is occupied by men and is itself still largely appropriated by men as their 'territory'. Sociology is part of the practice by which we are all governed and that practice establishes its relevances.
>
> (Smith 1987: 86)

Women in contrast have a different territory or place which is outside or subservient to this male, ruling culture. Their place as a matter of tradition and occupational practice is at home, a world dependent on the other and subordinate to it, a world organized by the 'natural attitude' (Smith 1987: 89). The organization of work distinguishes between the abstract mode of action, traditionally male, and the local and physical mode of domestic activity, traditionally female. Smith is arguing that the structural location of the sociologist creates a particular perspective that is allied to the process of government and excludes a realm of experience traditionally the domain of women. The possibility of a women's sociology challenges this perspective:

> Women's perspective . . . discredits sociology's claim to constitute an objective knowledge independent of the sociologist's situation. Its conceptual procedures, methods, and relevances are seen to organise its subject matter from a determinate position in society.
>
> (Smith 1987: 91)

For Smith, a feminist sociology must be reflexive and preserve the concerns and experiences of the sociologist as knower. This means that it must begin from where the sociologist is located bodily – in the experience of everyday life. The aim is not to reiterate what is already known but to take it as a starting point. Rather than give up the perspective in favour of one generated by those who rule, sociologists will begin to generate knowledge from everyday experience and will demonstrate that society is known and experienced differently from different positions in society.

This approach to knowledge recalls both Mannheim's relationism and also Berger and Luckmann's emphasis on the situational context of knowledge. But again the difference is that Smith's position is attempting to generate knowledge that grasps the ideological nature of what is taken as authoritative, ruling, sociological knowledge. What is different, not only from the traditional sociology of knowledge but from most of the other perspectives on ideology or discourse considered in previous chapters is the reintroduction of a subject. The subject is a knowing subject but has a specific location that determines her perspective.

The object of study is quite clearly a human, knowing, doing subject but is also specifically a woman or a group of women. The aim of research is to understand her experience and her knowledge of her world as it is rendered through accounts in interviews. Importantly, the subjects are not treated as representative of a population about which generalization can be made. Instead, the analysis will work towards the interpretive frame by which participants (women) make sense of their world and act in it. This interpretive frame will locate the subject in a network of social relations (of work, within the family, in relation to state institutions for example) from which the subject's perspective is derived:

> The movement of research is from a woman's account of her everyday experience to exploring *from that perspective* the generalizing and

generalized relations in which each individual's everyday world is embedded.

(Smith 1988: 185)

The problematic for the researcher is in recovering that perspective from accounts by participants. As Smith describes it, the extended social relations from which the participant derives her perspective, and which constitute her location, are only partially rendered by that practical knowledge of relations which makes up the content of participants' accounts. The textual analysis by the sociologist involves applying an interpretive frame that makes the everyday world problematic. In one example that Smith follows through (1988: 181–205) this involves problematizing the nature of women's work as parents of schoolchildren. The intersections between the spheres of social relations of home and school are the focus of attention. There are spatial and temporal boundaries and distinctions between the work practices of schoolteachers, pupils and mothers. The perspective that Smith is researching is that of the mothers and their work is largely to do with mediating between the sphere of home and school, child and schoolteacher.

The method for studying everyday knowledge that Dorothy Smith is proposing is not new; its roots lie in phenomenological and ethnomethodological sociology. The results of research are also unsurprising since the analysis is not so fine grained as to render the taken-forgranted as strange (one ethnomethodological strategy) or focused on the experiences of an unusual or separate social grouping (another strategy for making the sociological object of study 'interesting'). But the key feature is that the taken-for-granted nature of *women's* roles in everyday life is rendered problematic and is contested:

I am talking about, the way in which a traditional division of labor between women and men in the home has been foundational to the development of the North American educational system, the way in which the division has been built into the system as its working 'assumption'.

(Smith 1988: 203)

The distinction between men and women is not biologically determined in any simple sense. Smith accepts that men may participate in the work of parenting schoolchildren. Women clearly participate in other forms of work including within the male 'ruling' world. But empirically and traditionally the unpaid labour in support of the school system falls largely to women. It is linked to domestic work; to its routines, its lack of payment or other formal recognition and its inclusion in the process of child-rearing. Smith points out that it is also learnt as part of what mothering involves, it is 'an ideology, a discourse, that mobilizes our work and care' (Smith 1988: 205). The exact nature of that ideology, how it operates as knowledge guiding subjects' lives and practices will be further refined by other networks of social relations and divisions including those of class and race.

The feminist critique of knowledge undermines many of the presuppositions associated with knowledge: that it is abstract thought, that it is independent of context and independent of a knowing subject. The sociology of knowledge had of course argued that knowledge was not abstract but was specified in the presuppositions underlying the perspective of particular people. The feminist critique goes further though, pointing to the ideological nature of knowledge in obscuring lived relations, specifically gendered relations. In focusing not on abstract thought but on the knowledge of acting subjects, feminist analysis attends to the contents of discourse. This might be the cultural products of a society or the accounts of individual participants.

What feminist critique brings to an analysis of knowledge, ideology and discourse is a form of reflexivity that undermines claims to a special privilege for rationality. This reflexivity is not simply the referring back of discursive categories to the discourse in which they were produced, it is a reflexivity which takes into account the subjects as people and their perspectives, which generated the categories:

> To be rational in our society is to be impartial and objective – it implies a distancing of the observer from the object of his research, or policy. The cannons of reason, objectivity and clarity are built into our educational practices and into our scientific discourse. Yet, despite their commitment to reason, rational men are often strangely non-reflexive about the sources of their discourse. They fail to recognize their own ambiguities or contradictions. Their commitment to reason is a form of exclusion, a denial of certain kinds of experience.
>
> (Brittan 1989: 199)

The feminist critique of ideology has reintroduced the perspectivalism of Mannheim's sociology of knowledge into cultural analysis. A woman's perspective is not determined by her sex but by her experience of a specific socio-historical situation. That it is women who experience that situation is determined by their sex; structural forces lead them into the situation. But the individual social location is not only determined by structural forces and there are possibilities to challenge both the structural position of women and the ideology that supports gendered roles. The feminist critique goes beyond merely critiquing the ideology as such, which is what the cultural analysis of codes stops at, because it allows for the variation within the lives of women who receive those messages.

What is important about knowledge is not only how it is constructed but also how it is utilized by people. Ideological effects are realized not only at the level of rationalizing the existence of social structural systems but also at the level of negotiating everyday human interaction.

10 Knowledge, ideology and discourse

The perspective of women, explored in the last chapter, demonstrates the links between the issues of knowledge, ideology and discourse that earlier chapters began to establish.

Women's knowledge is different from men's not because of the biological difference of sex but because their situation and experience as women gives them a particular perspective on the world. Within the perspective there is an enormous range of influences and distinctions so that the differences within a gender perspective may be as great or greater than that between gender perspectives. Women's knowledge guides the actions of women and includes practical skills, knowledge about role and style of being, knowledge about sexuality and reproduction, knowledge about work and social institutions and so on. None of this knowledge is exclusive to women but the context of learning and using the knowledge is particular to people who accept recognition as women because it situates them as people, giving them personal and group identity. The perspective of women does not derive from individual or personal experience but is passed on to women through socialization, through the culture of the society in which they live.

What is effective as women's knowledge can be seen to be ideological in the sense that it obscures contradictions in the lived relations of people. Relationships between people are ordered according to gender which has effects in the distinction of roles and resources between the gender categories of human beings. Some lived experience shows that this ordering of identities and social relations according to gender is not a biologically determined feature of human existence; for example, the ability of women to live in roles 'normally' ascribed to men, and vice versa, and the socially made rules and decisions that deprive women of access to resources. The difference between these experiences and the prevailing experience of women reveals a contradiction between what is and what could be, about socially constructed states that follow cultural norms and those that do not. Knowledge, both from a women's perspective and a men's perspective, tends to reinforce what is, rather than open the way to what might be and in this sense it is ideological. This tendency is achieved by smoothing over contradictions to produce a unitary account so that the lived experience (of most) people seems rational and in accord with knowledge about categorial distinctions between gender classes.

The mode in which knowledge/ideology operates is discourse. The perspective of women is passed on through language (and language-like) exchanges of meanings. The realization of roles and the mobilization of resources is largely achieved through discourse – so are the social processes by which roles are constrained and resources limited. Women's current and past experience is described and framed in language; it is, for example, 'explained' and related to 'needs' and 'functions' of families, communities and societies. It is also in the medium of discourse that women's knowledge and knowledge about women has been challenged and criticized. New social practices have emerged that are sometimes labelled 'feminist' and these are always surrounded by text of some sort (it may be a clothes style, or a style of interaction) that situates the practice in relation to knowledge of womanliness. It is through challenging the presuppositions and extant meanings about womanliness, and transforming them through a critical exchange of meanings, that women's perspective and knowledge about women is changed.

The knowledge of women has been used here as an example to illustrate the argument of this book that knowledge, ideology and discourse are different aspects of the same phenomenon. The perspective of women is a good example to take because it is a field of knowledge very much in flux. Since the early 1950s what might count as a women's perspective has changed because of a sustained challenge to the 'naturalness' of a given perspective by demonstrating its social origins.

In using the example of women's knowledge the classic problem of imputation in the sociology of knowledge and theory of ideology is revealed. Not all women share the same unitary perspective or a set of beliefs which could be referred to as 'an ideology'. But even more difficult to deal with is that the women's perspective has been constructed, at least partially, from outside by men – how then can it be imputed to women? Whatever women's knowledge might be, it is certainly exchanged by both men and women and it exists in tension with alternative perspectives (different versions of a women's perspective, versions of men's perspective). A major issue in feminist politics is the ownership of knowledge – women repossessing women's knowledge – but as the power claims are linked to knowledge claims, the problem of imputation becomes political. Which women's knowledge belongs to which women? Who has rights to exchange meanings on behalf of which group within a group?

There are a number of theoretical issues illustrated in this sketch of women's knowledge as ideology and discourse that I will consider in the remainder of this chapter.

THE PROBLEM WITH THE SOCIOLOGY OF KNOWLEDGE

The sociology of knowledge proposes that the category of 'knowledge' refers to the perspective of a social group. The perspective is partially socially determined, that is, the meanings and presuppositions that constitute knowledge are given to social being and are not purely the products of cognition in the individuals who are members of the social group holding the perspective. The category of 'social being' refers to the relationship between individuals and the social group that is indicated by the sharing of a language and a perspective. The perspective or network of meanings is acquired by the individual from the social group in a manner analogous to the acquisition of language. The antecedence of social being has then a determinative effect on the presuppositions or meanings that constitute the perspective available for a social group.

These propositions make up the existential determination thesis which may be contrasted with the immanent determination thesis which describes the contents of knowledge purely in terms of past and present cognitive processes. The existential determination thesis is partial in that it allows that cognition, mediated by social practices constitutive of social being, will affect the meanings and presuppositions available to social being. The material conditions of existence provide the context which, together with social practices, will constrain the limits and possibilities of presuppositions and the production of knowledge.

The project of the sociology of knowledge is to study this process, although its product will be limited to 'relational' knowledge. 'Relationism' enables the differences between different knowledges to be grasped by reference to the social situations in which they occur. The understanding of knowledge in relation to social context is to be achieved by interpretation with reference to that context.

While there is in the preceding three paragraphs a fairly coherent programme for the sociology of knowledge, a number of major problems remain. Firstly, the sociology of knowledge proposed by

Mannheim neither referred to nor included a theory of social structure. Mannheim did suggest that the presuppositions given to social being had to be 'functional' to the conditions of existence. But he did not discuss what would count as functional or in what ways the conditions of existence would determine the form or content of knowledge. In his empirical work, Mannheim does theorize what is to count as social structure for the purposes of the analysis in hand (e.g. he discusses social locations for the problem of distinguishing generational groups – Mannheim 1952: 288–90). He also frequently refers to class locations (borrowing from Marx's account of class) and to the importance of location in the economy (borrowing from Weber, e.g. in his discussion of economic ambition – Mannheim 1952: 235n). But he does not propose a theory of social structure and the relationship of social being to social structure that is to be a part of the theoretical programme of the sociology of knowledge.

Secondly, relationism as a theoretical perspective for the sociology of knowledge has been badly received by the critics of Mannheim's work. On the one hand it is treated as in effect a form of relativism that implies the impossibility of generating acceptable empirical knowledge. On the other hand relationism is treated as dependent on asserting the special position of a free floating intelligentsia such that it is able to transcend the process of determination that the sociology of knowledge itself describes. While I have suggested that both these treatments of Mannheim's proposal of relationism miss the point of his own arguments, it is only recently that relationism has become an acceptable theoretical perspective with the shift towards what Hekman (1986) calls 'anti-foundational' theories and what might also be termed postmodern social thought:

> A postmodern artist or writer is in the position of a philosopher: the text he writes, the work he produces are not in principle governed by preestablished rules, and they cannot be judged according to a determining judgement, by applying familiar categories to the text or to the work . . .. The artist and the writer, then, are working without rules in order to formulate the rules of what *will have been done*.
>
> (Lyotard 1984: 81)

With the increasing acceptance of the loss of foundations or rules, the proposition of relationism is no longer so frightening and the sociology of knowledge's critique of epistemology is not so threatening.

Thirdly, reflexivity is both a quality and a limitation. I have suggested that Mannheim's proposals for the sociology of knowledge were reflexive in that he argued that the sociology of knowledge thesis would apply to the sociology of knowledge itself. This position invites the charge of relativism, but there are two reasons for resisting the charge. The first reason is that the sociology of knowledge does not claim to generate transcendent knowledge but claims a measure of validity for relational knowledge based on the breadth of its perspective. The attempt to understand knowledge in terms of its relation to social context is principally a hermeneutic task and not an evaluative one. Thus the *understanding* of knowledge can tolerate the differences of different knowledges and does not need to reduce all knowledges to a particular perspective. The second reason is that Mannheim accepted that the task of the sociology of knowledge was historically bounded and that its products could not expect to endure over time. The perspective of the interpreter would affect the contents of interpretation and would be acceptable only in particular perspectival contexts.

Fourthly, the failure to develop a convincing empirical sociology of knowledge has limited the whole project. The inadequate conception of an empirical category of 'knowledge' together with the lack of an interpretive method in line with the theoretical propositions have led to the failure of the sociology of knowledge, by and large, to develop empirical analyses. Mannheim's account of the analysis of documentary meaning avoids reduction to authorial intentions but is dependent on the vision of the analyst rather than any defined method.

I shall turn to the theory of ideology to find solutions to the first and second of these problems. The developments, particularly in the work of Althusser, Habermas, and critical theory, have articulated a non-reductive relationship between ideology and social structure. Knowledge produced within the theory of ideology does not claim a transcendent or scientific status but is founded in 'critique' and the emancipation from domination. It is to the developments of structuralism that I shall turn to help formulate a methodological foundation, an empirical object, and a method of interpretation appropriate to the sociology of knowledge.

THE THEORY OF IDEOLOGY

In Marx's formulation 'social being determines consciousness', it is the history of social being and in particular its struggle to meet material needs that determines its specific form. Marx's version of 'materialism' suggested that humans could understand the social relations consequent on a particular historical mode of exploiting the material world. There are then apparently two modes of knowing that Marx refers to: *ideology*, which is determined in its form and content by the conditions of existence of social being, and *science* which, by recognizing the primacy of the material, can describe the social relations consequent on the historical stage of exploiting the material world. What is more, science is effective as a critique of ideology, challenging the account ideology offers of extant relations in the world.

Marx's theory of ideology relates it to the structural features of the society in which it operates. Following Larrain's reading of Marx it is the contradictory form of social relations that ideology conceals:

> In effect, ideology is reaffirmed as a consciousness which conceals contradictions in the interest of the dominant class. The inverted character of ideological consciousness corresponds to the real inversion of social relations, and this inversion is closely connected with their being contradictory or antithetical.
>
> (Larrain 1979: 60–1)

The relation of ideology to social structure is not arbitrary or merely functional, as in Mannheim's account, to the conditions of existence. In the Marxist account, ideology obscures contradictions in social relations. For Marx the obscuring serves the interests of the dominating class but in the reformulations by Habermas and Althusser there is no reduction to class interests – it is the exigencies of the mode of production that determine the obscuring of contradictions by ideology. This is important because these writers are explicitly rejecting a notion of class subjects; both class subjects who perpetrate domination in their interests and the possibility of class subjects who may transcend the false consciousness of ideology.

The claim to scientificity as a way of establishing true consciousness is also rejected by critical theory. Truth as such is not a possible aspiration of human consciousness; to suggest that it is, is to re-establish a Hegelian dialectic giving primacy to consciousness and to resurrect an historical truth above social being. Instead, the negating effect of a critical theory is directed to confronting the contradictions inherent in social being by criticizing the uniform account ideology provides of the real as rational.

Althusser does not, as the early critical theorists do, describe a theoretical practice that is also a political practice. But he does relate the form of ideology to the social structure and to the status of individuals in social being. For both Althusser and early Habermas, the human subject as an individual knowing subject is a product of the form of ideology and the contents of ideology are managed by the apparatuses of the modern capitalist state. The form of ideology is no longer treated as false consciousness associated with a false (i.e. idealist) philosophy as it was with Marx and Lukács. Instead it describes the form of knowledge that is available to human beings.

Insofar as the term 'ideology' no longer refers to a form of thought associated with the interests of one class, Habermas drops it. In both Althusser's theory of 'levels' of social formation and the process of 'overdetermination', and in Habermas's distinction between system and lifeworld, there is a sense of relationism in that a reduction to either the level of concrete reality or the level of ideas is resisted. Knowledge is relational to the material context of social being and is partially determined by it. While for Althusser there are clear hints of an acceptance of the anti-foundational consequences of this position, it is a path that the later work of Habermas expressly resists. In his criticism of Foucault and Derrida (Habermas 1987b), he reasserts the modernist attempt to grasp the nature of rationality. None the less, the difference between levels is, if anything, clarified at this stage in his work. Habermas refers to 'culture' as the store of knowledge from which those engaged in communicative action draw their interpretations. If the level of knowledge/ideology is construed as at least overlapping with his concept of 'lifeworld' which includes culture, then the relative autonomy of the practical level of human action is maintained:

> To the degree that the yes/no decisions that sustain the communicative practice of everyday life do not derive from an ascribed normative consensus, but emerge from the cooperative interpretive process of the participants themselves, *concrete* forms of life and *universal* structures of the lifeworld become separated. Naturally, there are family resemblances among the plurality of totalities of life forms: they overlap and interlock, but they are not embraced in turn by some supertotality.
>
> (Habermas 1987b: 343)

The lack of reflexivity in Marx's own account of ideology that Mannheim rejected has been remedied in these later Marxist formulations. For Althusser, ideology will not disappear with the advent of socialism, and scientific practice can exist only as a social practice articulated on ideological apparatuses. For the Frankfurt School and early Habermas, critical theory can claim only an emancipatory interest, it cannot claim an epistemological privilege or a transcendent insight. It is only through theory as political practice that the contradictions of ideological forms can be confronted – but this is not to propose that a false account can be replaced by a true one.

The theory of ideology has informed or developed into an analysis of discursive forms or communicative action. Marx's reference to language as the material form of consciousness is finally pursued while an account of consciousness as such is rejected for its idealist implications. As the knowing subject is displaced from the centre of analysis (by Althusser's 'ideology interpellates subjects' and Habermas's 'dialectical relations constitutive of social being') any reduction to the consciousness of an individual subject is rejected as idealist in the same way as reference to an historical or class Subject. The reduction to an idealized subject is recognized as being a travesty of the possibility of dialectical material-ism just as much as is a reduction to an economic base. Such reductions promise an analysis that can reveal truth as such but negate the possibility of social practices having political effect to transform the process of history. Mannheim's own account of social being, while he did make reference to the intentionality of the historical actor, resisted any reduction to either an individual subject or to a group subject (such as by postulating a group mind).

It is the Marxist concept of social practice that enables a fuller account of social being than Mannheim offered. In Marx's critique of political economy it is the social practice of labour that is central to the historical process of the mode of production. But Habermas has argued that an analysis of labour alone is insufficient to understand the social relations that give rise to the social practices that reproduce those relations. Habermas proposes the analysis of communicative action as a social practice that is necessary if the resistance of capitalism to its inherent contradictions is to be understood.

STRUCTURALISM

Mannheim, I have argued, did not adequately establish an empirical category of knowledge. His own empirical work depended on a documentary understanding (both of texts and of action) of the categories of the sociology of knowledge – the perspective of the social group. His failure to establish a consistent and systematic method for identifying either a social group or its perspective led to the criticism of the imputation involved in the empirical sociology of knowledge. The presuppositions taken to be constitutive of a perspective had to be imputed to a theoretically constructed social group.

The content of myths (both 'primitive' and 'contemporary') as studied by Lévi-Strauss and Barthes, can be recognized as knowledge in that they contain presuppositions about the world which constitute for a social group a perspective through which individuals can comprehend the world they live in. The repetition and learning of myths demonstrates how the individual is socialized into particular cultural formations. Myths enable the social group to cope with its material conditions of existence; myths are also a 'solution' to contradictions apparent at the material level of existence (e.g. Barthes's analysis of how the symbolic form of products – the car as goddess, etc. – obscures their commodity form in the capitalist mode of production and the origins of the desire for them).

The development of structuralism in anthropology (Lévi-Strauss) and semiology (Barthes) borrowed a method of analysis from structural linguistics that described structure in terms of the relations of similarity and difference between its constituent parts. In borrowing structural methods however, the application was changed from an attempt to understand the system by which meaning is exchanged (i.e. language) to an attempt to understand the meanings being exchanged. In early structuralism the interpretation of meaning was by reference to the structural features of social systems of meaning (kinship systems, mythical systems); the aim of interpretation was to 'decode' from the content of such systems a more stable and universal level of meaning.

While structuralism failed to establish a theoretical basis for decoding, it has constituted an empirical object by addressing the human, social practice of meaningful exchange – discourse. For Lévi-Strauss, for example, kinship systems and myths are meaningful because participants intend and understand meanings in the utterances of these systems of exchange. The meanings exchanged are not a property of individual participants or their intentions but are constituted from the knowledge system of the members of the society.

The attempt to interpret according to a schema of meta levels of meaning is dropped in favour of a relational approach in which discourse is interpreted according to its social context and location in relation to other discourses. A similar strategy is adopted by Foucault who explores meanings in terms of the tension between discourse as a social practice and the material conditions of existence. The regularities of discourse are those which enable meaning to be exchanged. Thus, 'reason' not only is a category created by discourse, but also defines and constitutes discourse – the mad are exactly those who are unable to participate in meaningful exchange. Foucault retains the material category of the 'body' as the site of discursive effects and describes the relation of particular discourses to the body (e. g. those concerned with reason, medicine, discipline and sexuality).

The Foucauldian analysis follows the discontinuities and transformations between discourses that can illuminate the emergence of categories or presuppositions (such as those surrounding life, labour and language). In *The Order of Things* Foucault engages in a sort of sociology of knowledge by relating the emergence of the human sciences to the collapse of the unitary perspective of religion. The possibility of the human sciences, knowing about the world of human beings in a positive way, comes about with the transformation of presuppositions about 'being'. Foucault argues that the centring of human agency brings about a transformation of the discourses on life, labour and language. But he argues that the centring of 'Man' as an idealized subject, while it transforms discourse, also creates limits for knowledge. It is in his critique of the 'subject' and his analysis of discourse that he tries to go beyond these limits.

While Foucault does not theorize social structure as such, his account shows the effects of discourse on the material form of human being: the body. In his later work the issues of politics become more important in describing the context of social practices that constitute discourse and his category of power/knowledge provides a way of analysing the differential social relations that are effective in determining the regularities of specific discourses. He describes the mechanisms by which discursive relations are also social relations which determine the form of knowledge with his concept of the 'will to truth'.

Derrida's analysis by 'deconstruction' reveals the constitution of knowledge by discursive forms. It is through the devices by which discourse is constructed (the creation of an imbalance between presence and absence, the domination by a logos, the effacing of the play of differance in the sign) that 'truth' and knowledge are produced. Derrida's critique operates devices that reveal the constructive effects of discursive practices (i.e. the analyses of differance, erasure, and the supplement) not merely to criticize the content of knowledge but to demonstrate its determination in its context as discourse. In the work of Derrida, and to some extent Foucault, the techniques of analysis are employed reflexively to reinforce the situationally specific relational character of knowledge. The deconstruction of the metaphysical and the critique of the will to truth, not only undermine other knowledge claims but also are clear that they provide no path to a transcendent analysis.

In these later versions of structuralism reduction is avoided. The status of 'structure' and the 'sign' as stable categories that can be treated as having consistent properties is progressively eroded. But the categories are not dispensed with entirely; the critique of structure produces an analysis of networks of structures characterized by empirically describable forms (the orders of discourse, the metaphysics of presence). The critique of the sign relocates signification in a social and historical context as a chain of signifiers, each sign carrying the trace of its antecedents. Later structuralism resists reifying the sign as existing in abstract and systematic structures (as was the tendency in Lévi-Strauss's analyses and Barthes's semiology). The concept of discourse replaces that of structure so that the forms analysed retain their significance as empirical phenomena with their own historical and social specificity. The analysis of discourse is an analysis of the exchange of meanings; meaning is not merely a function of structure but a product of the interplay of signifiers that occurs in the social practice of discourse.

I have argued that structuralist work can be treated as the sociology of knowledge in the limited sense of describing the relations between presuppositions (meanings) and social relations (the social practice of discourse). In different ways, the later Barthes, Foucault and Derrida analyse the empirical relations that constitute particular discourses with reference to their antecedents, their effects as presuppositions and their context in the discursive practice of exchanging meanings. They do not produce a 'true' or 'final' account but produce a different account (than that which would be produced by participants) that enables the contents of discourse to be recognized as contingent on historical and social context. Continuities that enable contradictory discourses to be understood in the same way are not continuities of time or space (historical sequence, spatial proximity) but continuities of form. It is the regularities of form that enables structuralist analysis to provide an understanding across discourses that are different in content.

KNOWLEDGE AS IDEOLOGY AND DISCOURSE

Following Mannheim, the concept of knowledge cannot refer to a true unitary account of the world; different accounts can be effective as 'true' knowledge in different historical and social contexts. The concept of ideology, both in Mannheim's usage and in the Marxist theory of ideology, refers to the contingency of knowledge on social structure. The problem for the sociology of knowledge is to understand knowledge in its relation to its specific context without attempting to generate a universally 'true' knowledge to which other, different, knowledges can be reduced.

Early accounts of knowledge and ideology treat them as phenomena which occur empirically at the level of consciousness. While Mannheim avoided describing knowledge as consciousness, it is difficult to understand what he means by knowledge without reference to the structure and faculties of the human mind – he does for example refer to the 'collective unconscious' (Mannheim 1936: 30–48). Marx, Engels and Lukács, on the other hand, do equate ideology with a phenomenon effective in the minds of individuals and refer directly to consciousness. There are two problems with treating knowledge or ideology as existing at the level of consciousness or the individual mind. Firstly, it becomes an empirically inaccessible phenomenon that always has to be construed in analysis. Secondly, it separates off knowledge from the material, concrete level of existence laying emphasis on the individual, subjective level of consciousness.

The structuralist category of 'discourse' refers to an empirical phenomenon; the concrete utterances by which human individuals exchange meaning. It is not a function of some other level such as consciousness, universal conditions of existence (i.e. universal truths) or even the material conditions of existence (the economic base). The category of discourse does not refer to meanings produced and construed by individual intention but to the product of the exchange between individuals. As a theoretical category 'discourse' does not do the same work as the category of 'knowledge' or 'ideology' but it does describe an empirical phenomenon where knowledge and ideology are effectively produced.

The links between these three areas have been addressed in the previous substantive chapters which have been, in effect, explorations of the definitions of knowledge, ideology, and discourse that I offered in Chapter 1. As the three categories have been merged, especially in Chapters 8 and 9, they have also been modified and have acquired characteristics that are part of their role in the sociology of knowledge.

KNOWLEDGE AND SOCIAL BEING

The conception of knowledge that has emerged is one that includes both common-sense, everyday knowledge and specialized or high-status knowledge. Different types of knowledge will occur in different social and discursive contexts and will have a different relation to action. But none of these types exists independently of social being.

The 'presuppositions' that Mannheim referred to I have characterized as abstract relations. They are meanings given in social being that order the world for the individual prior to any cognitive attempt by that individual to order the world. As a set of meanings sufficient for the individual to experience the world she lives in as ordered, they constitute a perspective; the perspective enables past, present and future experience to be (largely) understood and enables the possibilities for future actions to be conceived and choices made. By engaging in particular discursive exchanges the individual acquires 'knowledge'. The socialization of a child through parental relationships, educational experience and peer group interaction constitutes a network of discursive 'exchanges of meaning' that enable the human individual to participate in social being. But the process is not limited to 'socialization' for the discursive practices of socialized individuals continually involve the exchange of meanings. Thus the experiences of being a teacher or a parent as well as working and travelling with people, reading books and newspapers, watching television and films, talking in pubs, parties, bingo halls, etc. all involve discourse in which meanings are exchanged and transformed that are effective as knowledge (i.e. as usable to understand experience and to guide action).

The concept of social being refers to the structural and organizational features of the group by which individual human beings are sustained within their biological limits and the material conditions of their existence. The individual's relationship with her material conditions is mediated by her location within the social organization of the group. This mediation through the historical and social context of action is what I have described as 'social practice'. Concretely, social practices are individual actions. But they occur within a social context that makes the actions effective and meaningful both for the individual actor and the other members of the group.

In relating knowledge to social being a contrast is being drawn with an understanding of knowledge as a property of an idealized, individual 'knowing subject'. The decentring of such ideal subjects in later structuralist writing brings the category of social being to the forefront of considerations of knowledge and discourse. There is, however, a danger of losing the individual, of subjugating the agency characteristic of lived experience to the structure of social systems and discourse. For Foucault, the status of lived experience is reasserted through the identification of 'bodies'. This rather unsatisfactory depersonalization of lived experience focuses attention on the objectifying tendency of discourse to treat individuals as instances of an ideal form of subject, but it does not provide an adequate way of theorizing the individual as an agent of discursive or emancipatory action. Feminist theory has recovered the status of lived experience by locating the group identity within a set of common experiences. Because the feminist discourse has an emancipatory dynamic it has, by and large, resisted the obscuring of individual difference within a totalizing category of 'woman'. There has instead been a focus on the plurality of experience and variations in perspective while at the same time a sustaining of the grounds of common experience.

The individual in the social context can perhaps be considered as an agent who expends resources in the field of action, including communicative action. The resources available to agents include knowledge and the agent can be recognized as socially situated or 'positioned' as Giddens puts it:

> Social systems only exist in and through the continuity of social practices, fading away in time. But some of their structural properties are best characterized as 'position–practice' relations. Social positions are constituted structurally as specific intersections of signification, domination and legitimation which relates to the typifications of agents.
>
> (Giddens 1984: 83)

Pierre Bourdieu's conceptualization of the 'habitus' of social being brings together the interplay between agents who are 'positioned' and the symbolic realm of representations that I have termed the 'exchange of meanings':

> So the representations of agents vary with their position (and the interest associated with it) and with their habitus, as a system of models of perception and appreciation, as cognitive and evaluative structures which are achieved through the lasting experience of a social position. The habitus is at once a system of models for the production of practices and a system of models for the perception and appreciation of practices.
>
> (Bourdieu 1990: 131)

The 'habitus' is similar to Mannheim's conceptualization of 'presuppositions' in that it contains the meanings given to social being through which individuals make sense of their world and with which they construct knowledge. The links with agents' position and interest that Bourdieu builds into the social space or set of relations in which the habitus exists, parallel Mannheim's understanding of the social basis of ideology.

Agents will tend to utilize resources either in their own interests or in the interests of a 'collectivity' (Callinicos 1987: 129–30). The concept of agency not only links individuals through their positioning in social structure, but also allows consideration of their joint or shared interests – and indeed their distinct and unshared interests. The interests of agents are not then those of a class or a group but are held by individuals 'by virtue of their membership of particular groups, communities, classes, etc.' (Giddens 1979: 189). And it is through the power and resources of groups of agents that interests are related to knowledge:

> For there is one sectional interest, or 'arena of sectional interests', of dominant groups which is peculiarly universal: an interest in

maintaining the existing order of domination, or major features of it, since such an order of domination *ipso facto* involves an asymmetrical distribution of resources that can be drawn upon to satisfy wants.

(Giddens 1979: 190)

Social being is not a unitary quality of all human beings equally because individuals are 'positioned' as agents with different access to resources and, therefore, knowledge and power to act. The particular presuppositions given to an individual human being are also determined by their social position, for example, in terms of class, gender, geographical and historical situation. Positioning may of course be reinforced or countered by the individual's experience in the context of socialization.

KNOWLEDGE AND POWER

There is a simple sense in which knowledge is power. For example, certain types of knowledge enable certain sorts of action which are beneficial to the actor. This sort of 'powerful' knowledge is easiest to recognize in the struggle against material conditions. Knowledge about how to design and use a plough can enable humans to act in a way which will maximize the effects of their efforts to grow plants that satisfy the need for food. But this model of the powerful effects of knowledge is too simple. Firstly, the application of knowledge to action occurs in social contexts and the effects of power are felt differently by different members of the group. There is a potential division of labour between the designing of the plough, the planning of its use and the actual use of the plough, that Marx saw as crucial in the development of social being. Secondly, and following on from this, knowledge becomes a scarce resource that human beings 'need'. In a society organized around commodity production, knowledge becomes a commodity like the food it can help to produce and the labour which produces it. Thirdly, and again following on, knowledge of the process of production and of the social relations involved can also be powerful. That is to say, knowledge need not be knowledge about how to satisfy material needs in order that it may be powerful. Indeed, just about any knowledge can be powerful provided that it is recognized within a social context as knowledge.

Lukes criticizes the behaviourism, individualism and concentration on conflict of traditional, pluralist theories of power, including the modified version of Bacharach and Baratz (Lukes 1974). These theories adopt the model of power where A gets B to do something which B would not otherwise do. Lukes sociologizes the model of power by considering it in terms of social groups, the effects of inaction and the possibility of conflict being potential rather than observed. But the model remains rigidly based on the interaction of two agents where one acts to affect another. Importantly the powerful agent must intend and know the consequences of their action whereas the subjected agent can be unconscious of their interests and even unknowing of the effects of power (Lukes 1974: 52–6):

> To use the vocabulary of power in the context of social relationships is to speak of human agents, separately or together, in groups or organisations, through action or inaction, significantly affecting the thoughts or actions of others (specifically, in a manner contrary to their interests). In speaking thus, one assumes that although the agents operate within structurally determined limits, they none the less have a certain relative autonomy and could have acted differently. The future, though it is not entirely open, is not entirely closed either (and, indeed, the degree of its openness is itself structurally determined).
>
> (Lukes 1974: 54)

Lukes's concept of power is then based on the tension between the relative autonomy of human agents and the structural determination of the context in which they act. He accepts that the limits of an agent's action are structurally determined but these limits are not just formal limits that constrain action, they also include limits that determine the knowledge and intention that will be necessary for a recognizable exercise of power. The examples that Lukes comments on are to do with political issues – the exercising of power lies in making political decisions such as those about clean air legislation. The advances that his theoretical account of power make are in recognizing the significance of the power to determine the 'agenda' of political debates and to influence such situations by 'inaction'. Lukes has been criticized for his 'voluntarism' and 'moral relativism' (Clegg 1989: 102–3) but his way of understanding the exercise of power makes knowledge a central issue; knowledge can be a legitimation for the exercise of power but power can also legitimize particular forms and contents of knowledge.

Foucault's approach to power is to recognize that it involves a counter force, a resistance rather than being characterized by open conflict; he considers power relations as the 'antagonism of strategies' (Foucault 1982: 211). As we have seen (in Chapter 7) Foucault describes power in relation to discursive formations through the rules of exclusion and inclusion of 'speakers' that regulate the discourse and its potential contents. Power has both an institutional site in the organization of privileged groups – those with the right to speak – and a discursive site in the discursive practices of the 'will to truth'.

The regulation of discourse both maintains existing meanings and limits the possibilities of their exchange. At first it does not appear to be a process of 'power' in Lukes's sense of the term but the privilege accorded to 'reasoned' utterances, those that claim to speak the truth, is dependent on the relatively autonomous agency of participants following particular patterns of action. The regularity of a discursive practice not only confirms a certain form and content of meaning but also confirms and maintains existing differential social relations. The 'will to truth' maintains (1) a status quo of meanings, (2) limits on possible changes in meanings and (3) power relations surrounding individual participation in and practice of discourse.

When Foucault talks of 'resistance' he says it is directed against a form of power:

> This form of power applies itself to immediate everyday life which categorizes the individual, marks him by his own individuality, attaches him to his own identity, imposes a law of truth on him which he must recognize and which others have to recognize in him. It is a form of power which makes individuals subjects. There are two meanings of the word *subject*: subject to someone else by control and dependence, and tied to his own identity by a conscience or self-knowledge. Both meanings suggest a form of power which subjugates and makes subject too.
>
> (Foucault 1982: 212)

For the individual then, to participate in discourse is to enter into power relations. The effects of power transforming individuals into subjects in discursive practice connects with the Althusserian concept of ideology. The aspect of discourse which can be regarded as ideology is the network of power relations that interpellates subjects:

> If power is no longer thought of simply as a negative and repressive force but as the condition of all speech, and if power is conceived as polar rather than monolithic, as an asymmetrical dispersion, then all utterances will be potentially splintered, formally open to contradictory uses. Utterance is in principle dialogic. Both 'ideology' and 'resistance' are *uses* of discourse, and both are 'within' power . . . . Resistance is the possibility of fracturing the ideological from within or of turning it against itself (as in children's language games) or of reappropriating it for counter-hegemonic purposes.
>
> (Frow 1985: 206)

To go further than Foucault, power can be seen as bringing about the very structure of the discourse. To utter, to propose an exchange of meanings is to attempt to exercise power over the meanings extant in the discourse. Put another way it is an attempt to exercise power over knowledge previously accepted as such (for example through the use of modality – see Chapter 8). An utterance not only may involve a new exchange but also may attempt to recover previous meanings already exchanged.

To use 'power' in this context is different from Lukes's application of the term because it is not clear that 'A is getting B' to do anything. Changing meanings does not directly affect people's lives although it may have indirect effects; the exchange of meanings about 'poverty' in a political debate may well have effects on legislation determining the income of people dependent on state benefits. But this is an unusual case. It is more likely that exchanging meanings has a more insidious effect on people's lives. In one of the examples I shall discuss in Chapter 11 the exchange of meanings about sexuality and sexual activity will potentially affect the sexual practices of participants (readers). The connection between power and knowledge is one of mutual support; the claim to know rests on power (i.e. to achieve an utterance) which in turn supports the knowledge claim (i.e. the demonstration of achieving the utterance is also a demonstration of the viability of the knowledge claim) and the effect of the knowledge claim, if it is accepted, is to influence other participants' actions.

The analysis of power relations in discourse relates the content of discourse (the meanings, presuppositions or knowledge) to the social context in which it operates without recourse to a total 'structural determination' theory. The concept of power retains a relative autonomy for the individual agent in discourse while allowing an account of the social practices which limit and constrain that autonomy.

KNOWLEDGE AND ACTION

The relationship between knowledge and action was not one that Mannheim explored. By 'action' I mean those expenditures of energy by humans, that can be construed as meaningful. Knowledge may be an end in itself when the discourse is abstract and closed – theological and sociological debates often seem like this. Even in this case however, knowledge is connected to action in so far as participations in the discourse are actions. It is more often the case that knowledge is connected to action that is not exclusively communicative.

There are four relations between knowledge and action that can be theoretically described. One is discursive action where the action is merely a medium for the transmission of abstractions. Discursive action is bodily in that hands move writing implements and vocal chords are controlled to produce speech. Posture and gesture may also contribute to the process of discourse. However this range of bodily actions are mediators of meaning and as such maintain the abstraction of sets of relations that constitute knowledge. There is a corollary relation with the emphasis reversed where an action is firstly an action, a 'doing', but it also provides a representation of the world that can be interpreted as a set of abstract relations. This form of action/knowledge I shall call 'demonstration'. An individual can communicate, without even intending to, by an exemplary action. The swimmer swims and communicates how swimming is done, demonstrating knowledge of swimming. Demonstration requires an interpreter or 'reader' who by their discursive action of attempting to understand the action as an abstraction sees more than just a body moving through the water.

These two relations of knowledge and action are points on a continuum between discursive action dedicated to communication and bodily action where there is action but no communication. There are two more complementary relations between knowledge and action that turn on the distinction between action and abstraction. On one side action gives rise to knowledge. In the individual this may be biographical experience that is personal but for the group it is history. Past actions are retained as abstractions and may be referred to in discourse. In the process of the discourse they may represent further abstractions – the recalling of loss of life in a war may be taken as a representation of the folly of war. While for individuals experience may be retained as an inarticulate feeling (such as a fear of the dark) for the social process of knowledge, action must be reduced to communicable sets of relations and uttered in discourse. In so far as exchanges of meaning refer to specific past events they constitute history. Action giving rise to knowledge in this way may be of a completely non-discursive type but the process of rendering past action communicable requires inter-pretation in the same way as 'demonstration'.

The final relation between knowledge and action is the reverse of the last; knowledge that gives rise to action. This is where the abstract relations of knowledge are later acted out in the concrete realm of bodily action – the process in which actions are planned. It is in this relation that knowledge is presumed to have its *raison d'être* in those philosophies where knowledge is assumed to improve the quality of action. In the abstract relations of discourse, possible courses of action can be 'tried out' or rehearsed in a very short space of time without producing an effect in the concrete world of bodily action. There is then a different temporality existing within the realm of discourse which enables any action which follows it to be more effective than could otherwise be possible. This means that at the level of theory, possible action can be tried out, that could never be enacted experimentally; that is, without final and irredeemable consequences. Within the realm of discourse possible courses of action can be explored and transformed infinitely and in a much shorter span of time than the same action would take in the concrete world. These four relations between knowledge and action can be summarized diagrammatically, as shown in Figure 2.

In the routine of everyday life, knowledge will not be applied to action through 'planning'. The application of knowledge to action, once the relation has been worked out to the individual's satisfaction, becomes habituated in routine actions. When this happens, knowledge seems to become part of the body, integrated with action and as 'skill' indistinguishable from it.

The term 'action' traditionally involves the notion of intended consequences or their absence. Where intention is absent it is taken to be mere behaviour; either habitual behaviour where intention has lapsed in the frequent repetition of action or instinctive behaviour consequent on the individual's biological functions. This way of characterizing action relates it always to the individual; either as an

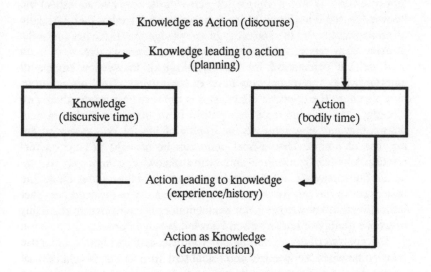

Figure 2 Relations between knowledge and action

intending subject habitually acting on a past intention or a biological individual acting in accord with its biological functions. To overlay the concept of action with the concept of social practice is to describe actions in their social context as learned and recognized as meaningful. This includes biologically determined actions which become framed in social practices. Habitual behaviour is even more obviously a social practice; for example the habits of smoking or wearing make-up involve the individual in a set of social relations regardless of any originating 'intention'. The operation of intention at the level of cognition is itself predicated on social being since the individual must be able to construe the results of possible actions to intend the action they initiate. Such a construal and the cognitive action of choice from among possible actions, depends upon a participation in social being that makes available a perspective to the individual.

CRITIQUE

It might appear that the sociology of knowledge by investigating the social process of knowledge could provide material for improved theories of knowledge which could in turn lead to improved knowledge production and thence to improved human action. The final consequence might be assumed to be an improvement in the quality of human life in general. The problem is of course that the idea of 'improvement' is not a simple 'objective' criterion but an aspect of knowledge that is itself part of the social process. It cannot then be taken as an assumption by the sociology of knowledge that there are instantly or even easily recognizable, 'improving' forms of knowledge.

A critical orientation for the sociology of knowledge begins to emerge; while knowledge may have an 'improving' effect on action it may also have the opposite effect. This is the very basis of the theory of ideology – knowledge may be a political instrument of exclusion and domination and may improve the quality of life for one group at the expense of others. This critical point can be brought to bear on the relation between knowledge and action. Knowledge may give rise to action but it may also inhibit action. This effect of knowledge on action may improve the quality of life or be emancipatory but it need not. The indication that knowledge is not emancipatory is connected to the issue of whose quality of life any given knowledge may improve.

The analysis of power and ideology in discourse can both establish a relation between 'knowledge' and social structure and achieve a critical perspective. As Thompson puts it:

The analysis of ideology is fundamentally concerned with *language*, for language is the principal medium of the meaning (signification) which serves to sustain relations of domination.

(Thompson 1984: 131)

For Foucault this involves the strategy of 'transgression' of the existing limits, for Derrida the strategy is of 'deconstruction'. For critical theorists however critique is not simply directed at theory but at social practice itself. By providing the basis of a 'political praxis, which consciously aims at overthrowing the existing system of institutions' (Habermas 1974: 2), critical theory is concerned not exclusively with theory but also with the effects of theory. In this approach, critique not only analyses power relations but also aims to initiate an exercise of power.

As the sociology of knowledge describes the determinative relations between social context and knowledge, it may reveal the illegitimacy of knowledge claims. However, the critical moment of the sociology of knowledge seems unavoidable. Treating meanings as contingent on their social context involves questioning the implicit claim of utterances to speak the 'truth' in a way that is valid beyond the immediate context. The uttering of a statement does not merely refer to its context but also to the world in general; it is through the relationship between a knowledge claim and the world it claims to know, that knowledge claims have effects on action. If this were not the case then knowledge would be futile and the exchange of meanings meaningless. The effects of discourse are presumed to be in a world beyond the 'abstract relations' of discourse, that is in a world of concrete and material social relations. As Mulkay and Gilberts' analysis of modern scientific discourse indicates (see Chapter 8), strategies that attempt to establish the privilege of one particular knowledge claim over another, involve establishing its immanent nature in contrast to the socially contingent nature of competing claims.

Critique is not merely about the content of discursive exchanges but also involves an orientation of the critical practice to the exchange. Unlike 'resistance' which stays within the discourse to challenge power relations over an institutional site, critical practices attempt to establish new exchanges, new discourses that move beyond the forms of existing ones. In filmic critical practice this involves establishing a different way of exchanging meaning that cuts across existing genres (that might be treated as dialects) to establish a different way of speaking (see Kuhn 1980). Foucault's attempt at a transgressive theorizing seems to aim for something similar; by throwing away all the existing categories of history he can re-use them in a transformed way to begin a new discourse of history. For Derrida, the critique of metaphysics cannot proceed except by doing some violence to the existing categories by which meaning is established.

By attempting to understand different knowledges in terms of their differences, the sociology of knowledge opens up a new discourse that cuts across those it analyses. By interpreting discourses with reference to their discursive form as exchanges of meaning in a specific social context, it articulates the presuppositions that will have been more or less taken for granted by participants. The analysis of the sociology of knowledge, by proposing the social determination of knowledge, undermines discursive claims to universality of meaning. If this analysis includes the relations of power within and without the discourse then the continuity between power and knowledge is explored, further undermining the claims of utterance to be independent of social determination. In these ways the sociology of knowledge is a critical approach that does not engage in the discourses it analyses but offers a critique of the basis for the exchange of meanings within that discourse.

11 Analysing knowledge as ideological discourse

The central claim of this book is that discourse is the form in which knowledge appears as a social phenomenon, as something that can be shared. At the same time, the process of discourse has ideological effects in that as lived relations are rendered into representations in language, those relations are simplified and transformed. Most importantly, the representation of lived relations in language-like processes obscures or smooths over contradictions. If these remained too starkly in accounts, the meaningfulness of those accounts would be seriously undermined; the 'speaking-against' of contradiction would involve a negation of meaning. This process is neither arbitrary nor circumscribable. Although ideological effects are not the intention of speakers (unlike lies, propaganda, economies of truth and so forth), they do involve the perspective of the utterer but cannot be simply derived from class or other interests. 'Perspective' involves the presuppositions given to social being through continuous socialization and may involve the interests of other groups, especially more powerful groups.

While there is no way of getting around the ideological effects of discourse, there are ways of studying it that recognize the perspectival nature of knowledge and relate it to the context of its utterance as discourse. This approach is 'relationist' and involves relating the contents of knowledge to the context in which it emerges. If the contents of knowledge are treated as present in discourse, rather than present in 'thought' as in the traditional sociology of knowledge, then the relations between knowledge and its context can be analysed through studying discourse.

Accounts in discourse are not simply 'accounts of' the world; they are also among those human practices that constitute the world. They cannot be interpreted as simply static reflections on the state of the world but have to be seen as current performances that construe the world, interpellate subjectivity and attribute agency within it.

References to the past not only speak of the past but also construe the present by establishing how it was in relation to how it is.

In Chapters 6 and 7 I have tried to show how structuralist writers began this process of the analysis of knowledge through their studies of various cultural forms. In Chapters 8 and 9 I have looked at more modern analyses of scientific knowledge, of ideological forms in language and culture and the feminist critique of knowledge. These analyses constitute a tradition that can be claimed as engaged in the practice of the sociology of knowledge in the way it was formulated by Mannheim. Within this broad range of analyses addressing the social bases of knowledge, some have attended to the social construction of knowledge, others to the ideological effects of discourse. All have dealt with an empirical object that has taken a form as discourse but there have been many different approaches to analysis and even to the construal of discourse as an empirical object.

THE EXCHANGE OF MEANING

Rather than exploring in any more detail the range of ways of construing, and methods of analysing, discourse, this chapter will expand on the role of a particular discursive process; the exchange of meanings. This process is particularly important for the sociology of knowledge because, firstly, it occurs above the level of interaction or the linguistic structure of discourse, and, secondly, it obscures the contradictions of lived relations.

The structure of discourse is that of a network of differences between meaningful elements (the sign, the statement) that constitute knowledge through the process of exchange. It is the differences at the level of meaning rather than the differences at the material level of language that are constitutive of discourse as the object of analysis. The exchange of meanings involves transforming meaning elements through a series of exchanges in which one replaces another, establishing a pattern of connection through equivalence or similarity. The exchange may also include negative elements which specify a lack of similarity.

Knowledge is both constructed and reproduced in the process of participants exchanging and transforming meanings in discourse. Meanings introduced into exchanges are presupposed by utterers to be shared with hearers/listeners. The process of exchange may transform these presuppositions, thereby changing the stock of knowledge. Or the exchange may confirm the existing relations between meanings, reproducing the same set of presuppositions. Knowledge produced and reproduced in this way may be used to guide future action but it can also be recalled or referred to in accounts of action:

Since reality is a social construct, it can be constructed only through an exchange of meanings. Hence meanings are seen as constitutive of reality. This, at least, is the natural conclusion for the present era, when the exchange of information tends to replace the exchange of goods-and-services as the primary mode of social action.

(Halliday 1978: 191)

Participants in discourse can be presumed to be party to the meanings being exchanged – that is they can be presumed to be sufficiently competent to participate. This does not necessarily mean that they believe a particular set of meanings or regard them as 'true'. What it does mean is that they accept the tenability of *that* exchange of meanings, they accept those issues as meaningful. Participants may cease to accept the exchange of meanings by ceasing to participate; they may stop buying the newspaper, walk out of a political speech, switch off the television or change the topic of conversation. Their refusal to accept may involve a challenge to the power involved in the institutional context of the discourse and lead to 'resistance'; by writing in complaint to the newspaper, haranguing the political speaker, making use of a 'viewer access programme' or being extremely rude to a conversant. These actions are still 'in the discourse' and are discursive practices of resistance, challenging the power relations of the existing discourse.

In an early paper Zellig Harris described a method of analysis that focused on the relative occurrence of elements within a discourse (Harris 1952). One feature of this style of analysis was the identification of equivalence between elements. Harris's very formal analysis articulated the *equivalence* between non-identical words and phrases which constituted a structural analysis of the text. The elements were established by identifying 'stretches' of text that shared the same 'environment' (Harris 1952: 6). I am arguing that equivalence, including the lack of it or a measure of it, between one meaning element and another is established by the formation of an utterance as an exchange of meaning. The approach being developed here is interpretive and some way from Harris's systematic method but not so far from Halliday's concern with language use.

SEQUENCE

A fundamental feature of linguistic communication is its linearity. The communication of meaning takes place over time; one word follows another for both utterer and receiver and one effect of this is that one meaning follows another. Linguistic strategies (e.g. poetic forms, narrative devices) can be effective in partially counteracting this inexorable feature of linguistic communication. Sequence involves previous meanings being replaced by present or current meanings. This process of one meaning being put in the place of another is not done with an erasing effect like recording over the top of something on a magnetic tape. Meanings are displaced with linguistic devices (such as a negation, affirmation or qualification) but always a trace of the displaced meaning is carried forward into the meanings for which they are being exchanged. This is a cumulative effect in that the trace of old meanings is always there but as the new meanings are put in place of old, the oldest fade. Techniques of utterance enable meanings that occurred earlier in or beyond the discourse to be recalled.

Linguistic competence is not merely about uttering meaningful words in context but also about constructing a sequence of words that involve a transformation of the meanings that have already gone before. This is the process that I wish to call the exchange of meaning.

EXCHANGE

I have used the term 'exchange' to describe what happens to meanings in discourse, to evoke the idea that one meaning is put in place of another. This is a consistent feature of discursive action and is the social practice in which participants share their view of the world.

There are two distinct processes in which discourse involves an exchange. At an interactional level, meaningful communication is exchanged between participants through the discursive practices of uttering and listening/hearing. It is this interactional level that has been studied in depth by conversational analysis (see for example Atkinson and Heritage 1984) and by discourse analysts whose approach has its roots in linguistics (e.g. Coulthard 1977; Stubbs 1983). The interactional approach attends to the competencies of participants in achieving and managing performance features of the exchange, such as taking turns and dealing with misunderstandings. Meaning is significant in so far as it determines particular interactional strategies.

The second process of exchange in discourse is between elements of meaning. This occurs in the contents of discourse, not in the interaction. There needs to be an interactional process with utterers and listeners/ readers but the exchange of meanings can take place within an utterance. Its form is that of a statement and interactionally all that is necessary is that there is a 'receiver', a listener/reader, who understands the statement. Statements can also be constructed with exchanges that straddle utterances from different participants (this happens in Extract

One on p. 212). At the level of meaning, the exchange of elements of meaning either can be within a single utterance or can occur across different utterances.

The discourse analysis approach proposed here is concerned with the contents of discourse as they relate to the world of experience and action. The exchange of meaning is a social action but it is a meta-action in that it comments on, whilst also constructing, the world inhabited by subjects.

The approach to discourse as the exchange of meaning elements is concerned with establishing *relations* at two levels. Firstly, at the level of meta-social action, in its reflective mode, discursive action involves 'relating' one abstract thing to another, establishing a relationship between these things by exchanging one meaning for another. Secondly, at the level of performance, discursive action involves, human agents 'relating' things to each other in the sense of telling or recounting. It is at this level that knowledge is transformed into power as it represents the relations between people.

While the equivalence of meaning implied by 'exchange' is appropriate as is the connotation that it is a social practice of reciprocity, the economic meaning of 'exchange' carries inappropriate connotations. This is because in economic contexts exchange refers to replacing objects of value in the possession of agents ('a measured reciprocal payment is what constitutes the essential characteristic of exchange' – Mandel 1968: 49). But meanings are not possessable in the same way as objects and require a relatively negligible expenditure of labour power for their reproduction. Meanings are not reducible to a standard such as monetary value that can be used as a short-hand to describe precisely and arithmetically the process of exchange.

To show how some of these features of the exchange of meaning work, I will present some abstracted texts below and comment on them.

HEALTH AND AGE

During the course of a small group of interviews with older people,[1] respondents were asked about their experience of old age. The questions attempted to find out how the person felt about their age and what it meant to them. The answers involved constructions about the category of 'old age' that built on presupposed meanings – frequently old age was related to poor health. In Extract One Mr Bence, who was 96 at the time of the interview, responds to a question about feeling old by telling the interviewer just how well he is.

Extract one [2]

01	TD:	Well I – one of the things I haven't asked you
02		about is, is whether you feel old (1) how you
03		felt about growing old (.) Do you feel old
04		now?
05	Mr B:	No (2) I haven't got an acre of pain. Except
06		I've just had a, now you talk of it, had a
07		bit of a swelling
08	TD:	Have you
09	Mr B:	Got a crêpe bandage on it (1) I haven't had a,
10		I've never, as I say I've hardly (1) any
11		record of the doctor, on the doctor's notes
12	TD:	Do you think of yourself as old?
13	Mr B:	No (.)
14	TD:	What, what do you think –
15	Mr B:	The only thing is, now, that I wobble (.)
16	TD:	Umm, mm
17	Mr B:	And I've had to stop (.) walking because here
18		the wind has been so heavy and the leaves on
19		the meadow, you know, fall and they're all
20		wet, and this that and the other, and I'm
21		afraid of (.) just (unclear)
22	TD:	Of course, yes. uhh So wh– what do you think
23		of, do you look at other people and think of
24		them as being, old?
25	Mr B:	Well I, I think y– you've struck on the wrong
26		person because I'm exceptional
27	TD:	Yes, but that's all right I'd like to hear what
28		you feel. What do you think about other
29		people, do you think, gosh they look old to
30		me or?
31	Mr B:	To tell you the truth I think everybody is
32		thinking these days that I'm all right Jack and
33		not bothering about anybody else

The category of 'old' or 'old age' has been present throughout the interview as a topic; the interview was with Mr Bence because he was over 75 and he presented his age almost as a credential at the beginning. He was asked to tell how he feels about old age in lines 02–03. He construes what he knows about old age in terms of health; pain and record of contact with the doctor. He consistently excludes himself from knowing about the category of old age because he does not feel old (lines 05, 13, 25–26). At lines 23–24 he is invited to speculate or to construct knowledge of old age not from personal experience but from observation. Again he excuses himself as exceptional, as having no knowledge of old age because of his good health. At lines 31–32 he does respond, offering a perspective, presumably from the situation of old age, which stands as knowledge of old age.

There is then an exchange of meanings that can be represented as a series of equivalences:[3]

(feel old)	≠ no pain, except a bit of swelling
no pain	= hardly any record on doctor's notes
(think of yourself as old)	≠ no [but] now, I wobble
wobble	= had to stop walking
stop walking	= heavy wind/leaves/wet/afraid
(think of others as old)	≠ wrong person/exceptional
(think of others as old)	= everybody not bothering about anybody else

What is interesting here is that many of the equivalences are constructed out of negations and most also involve modifications. To reconstruct an exchange of positive elements would involve exchanging 'old age' with the experience of pain and of frequent contact with the doctor. But the modification of the negative categories of 'no pain' and 'hardly any record on the doctor's notes' are interesting. In lines 05–07 no pain (an 'acre' of pain seems to be a slip for 'iota' of pain – which may or may not be significant) is modified with a 'a bit of swelling'. Later in lines 15 and 17–21 a more substantial modification occurs. Just as old age has been exchanged for 'no pain' (modified) it is also being exchanged for 'wobbling', for vulnerability to heavy winds and wet leaves and for fear (probably of falling). Mr Bence can contribute quite a lot of knowledge about what he feels it is to be old, despite his demurring.

One way of beginning to understand this is to note the presupposition about old age with which Mr Bence began the exchange: that old age is equivalent to poor health. This may be treated as knowledge or as ideology in that it represents a presupposition about what old age is for some people (not necessarily held only by those who have some experience of it). Mr Bence knows of the presupposition and utilizes it in his utterance. His own lived experience contradicts that presupposition so he excludes himself from feeling part of the category. In tackling the contradiction involved in the version of old age as poor health, Mr Bence begins to substitute a new exchange between old age and wobbling and frailty. When pushed he is also able to construct an old age perspective (lines 31–32) which involves a contrast available only to those of sufficient age to have experienced 'those days' when everyone was not thinking 'I'm all right Jack'.

If the presupposition of an equivalence of meanings between age and poor health is ideological it is not because it is a 'falsehood' or 'not true'. It is rather because it obscures the contradictory nature of old age as it is lived.

Mr Bence was not alone in this set of interviews in calling on a presupposition about old age as existing in an exchange relation with health. But many also began to construct a knowledge of old age drawing in other exchanges of meaning – with retirement, boredom, and changing relationships with family. While health as such was often not sustained as an exchange, physical frailty or some lack of ability were frequently used in exchanges for the category of old age.

WHEN TO DO SEX

Morality, especially sexual morality, is a strange form of knowledge. It involves rules which will govern action but the rules are taken to have some basis, either in a religious or other social system in which moral codes are subordinate to other codes. Moral codes both constitute knowledge by acting as an abstract construal of the world used to guide action and yet they are also derived from knowledge: a prior knowledge that describes how the world is that leads to a particular set of rules. The text chosen here to illustrate this process is derived from a book[4] intended as a resource for discussing moral issues with young people, probably in groups in relatively formal settings such as a classroom.

In this first extracted section (not the first section in the original text) a scene is set and a problem articulated – how can we get personal relationships 'right'?

Extract two

Life is a web of intricate relationships; if we get them right the first time the business of living is rendered much less painful for all. At present a great wave of liberality is sweeping through many dusty corridors; sexual relationships are receiving a great deal of welcome illumination. In the midst of this rethinking it is important to remember that although heterosexual relationships are fundamental, the majority of all relationships that are made are not predominantly sexual in nature and are usually well divided between the sexes. Granted it is vital to choose the right husband or wife and establish a sound basis for a mutually benefiting union, but it is also of great importance to the marriage to develop good relationships outside the immediate family circle. Liberality should not be confused with permissiveness.

There are a multitude of exchanges going on in this paragraph that are not directly related to each other:

getting intricate relationships right	= less painful living
wave of liberality	= welcome illumination
personal relationships	= usually well divided between the sexes
right husband or wife	= mutually benefiting union
good extra familial relationships	= important to marriage

What these exchanges are doing is to set out a field of presuppositions that are being drawn into the discourse. At this stage there is nothing like the cumulative sequence of exchanges that will come later in constructing an argument. A powerful feature of Extract Two is the absence of agency; the only subjects directly referred to are 'we' in the first line. This category of subject is particularly broad; if we use the context to explore who 'we' might be, we find it will include everyone who lives life! Every other exchange is asserted as a knowledge claim, a description of the world as it is. The particular structure of the text is not only establishing a field of presuppositions but also 'modalizing' these claims by asserting them authoritatively:

> Modality points to the social construction or contestation of knowledge-systems. Agreement confers the status of 'knowledge', 'fact' on the system, or on aspects of it; lack of agreement casts that status into doubt. Of course, agreement and affinity may have been brought about by the relations of power-difference: that is, the more powerful may have been successful in enforcing their classifications on the less powerful. Once the classification is accepted, a relation of solidarity then exists around that area of the classification.
>
> (Hodge and Kress 1988: 123)

The positive weight and practical orientation given to the assertions is clearly marked by the metaphorical language used; living is a 'business', that can be got 'right', liberality 'sweeps' 'dusty corridors' (which is self evidently what they need), illumination is 'welcome'. These claims are not associated with the author's agency (I believe ... I think ...) and they are not modified modally (it seems that ... it might be argued ...).

The terms of value are unequivocal and forthright; heterosexual relationships are 'fundamental', it is 'vital' to choose the 'right' husband or wife, it is of 'great importance' to the marriage to develop good relationships outside.

What is notable is that the text is unable to presuppose all of these exchanges; it must assert them and introduce them to the reader as new knowledge – at the very least a reformulation of what the reader already vaguely knew. But the textual style presumes agreement, it presumes that these opening remarks will not be contested and any disagreement will come later. Once the assertions have been introduced in this way they can of course be presupposed in exchanges later in the text. The power of the utterance is in its ability to sustain a broad field of knowledge claims without contest. By the end of the paragraph a perspective has been constructed that the reader can be expected to collude in by not confusing liberality with permissiveness.

In Extract Three a more cumulative exchange of meanings is used to construct an argument.

Extract three

Taking a broad view of evolution we can see that our particular system of reproduction has special advantages over, say, amoeboid binary fission. Great grandfather amoeba must have given rise to all the progeny of this animalcule living today, and since the process of reproduction is by splitting of the parent to create two children, there is little new in the present amoebas that was not in the original model. How boring. How unlikely that such a system would enable a species to survive. Further, the splitting comes involuntarily at the behest of organic controls devoid of parental influence. In contrast, we have a system that provides for a proliferation of new and differing models in each successive generation; a system excellently designed for continuous, rapid evolution, and the act of conception is controlled by the participants, if they so wish. To ensure that man did not die out through indolence nature has caused the act to be pleasurable. With our modern techniques of contraception, intercourse does not necessarily result in conception, so to the freedom that nature has given, to decide upon the time and tide of our sexual relationships, has been added the further freedom of choosing whether a child should be conceived as a result of any particular act.

Again the objective style of reporting how the world is, is used to powerful effect. Individual or particular agency is not attributed to the claims and agreement between the reader and the utterer is assumed, maintaining the power of the utterer's perspective. It is assumed that any reader can be included in the 'we' of the first sentence to see the special advantages of 'our system of reproduction'.

There are a number of modalizing features of this exchange. Firstly, there is a casualness and informality in the style ('say' in the first sentence, 'great grandfather amoeba', 'how boring') which contrasts with, and goes some way to counteract, the rather pompous use of technical terms ('amoeboid binary fission', 'animalcule'). The technical jargon signifies the authority of the knowledge while the informality eases the potential distance created from the reader by that authority. Secondly, there is a conspicuous use of a 'rational' argument in which two cases are presented in contrast, in the form of on-the-one-hand and on-the-other-hand. Thirdly, the technical terms provide a reference to systems which are independent of human knowledge; 'evolution', 'systems of reproduction', 'splitting, 'proliferation of new and differing models'. These processes have effects independent of human action and operate whether or not there is any knowledge about them.

human reproduction has advantages over $\neq$ other systems of
reproduction, e.g. binary fission

binary fission	= similarity
" "	= boring
" "	= unlikely that the system will survive
" "	= involuntary
human reproduction	= difference
" "	= rapid evolution
" "	= controlled by participants
" "	= pleasurable
" "	= consequences can be controlled

Into this exchange of meanings which largely describe a world independent of human knowledge and action, is woven a human agent with knowledge that can be related to action including knowledge of 'modern techniques of contraception'. The determinant of the world described in the passage, 'nature', has conferred a determinant capacity on 'us', the possessors of the particular system of evolution and the modern techniques of contraception; the opportunity to apply knowledge to action.

The text is not only passing on knowledge in a digested, uncontested form, but also defining a context for its usage. However, the text presents itself as merely mediating knowledge about natural processes beyond the text. There is a particular distinction achieved in the exchange of meanings in Extract Three which underlies the exchanges that occur in Extract Four, a distinction between the categories human and not human. There is no contest – human is clearly the better category, the one anyone would wish to belong to . . . But there is a further subdivision between human beings who know and act with that knowledge and those who know but fail to act according to what they know.

Extract four

There exists a deep-rooted feeling that man is still a predatory animal when it comes to sexual relationships. The woman is usually cast in the role of the chaste and chased; indeed the word seduction is specifically related to the surrender of a woman's chastity. The reasons for this situation are partly biological, in that there is a seeking drive within the male, but also because the results are visibly evident on the female; she also bears the burden both in fact and metaphor. How different might our attitudes be if at the time of intercourse a decision had to be made as to who should bear the child – the man or the woman. Two people share the responsibility for the conception of any child and these two must respect the rights of each other, and the rights of the possible child, if they are to retain personal integrity. Ignorance is an excuse; negligence or unconcern are attitudes a person must not be allowed to adopt. In any sexual union the man and woman are one and share the responsibility of any neglect or indifference. How would you like to be fathered in the name of neglect, or born through indifference?

It is in this final extract that the crunch comes; the moral message that underlies what has gone before. The effect of the knowledge constructed through the piece and summarized in the extracts leaves no doubt about how the rhetorical question should be answered. The text does not have to tell us what the moral of the tale is, it merely writes in a space for the reader to complete – now that she or he knows. The way this paragraph is modalized at the beginning shows that the utterer is less confident about the exchange of meanings being attempted here – there is room for dispute. It is only a 'feeling', albeit deep-rooted that 'man' is still a 'predatory animal'. But this modalization leaves space for the previously given knowledge to have effects in human action. If 'man' takes heed of what is *now* known about sexuality and human relations (i.e. after reading this text), then the feeling that he is a predatory animal will be proved wrong.

man	= sexually predatory animal
the woman	= chaste and chased
male	= biological seeking drive
female	= visible and metaphorical burden
if decision about burden	= *then* different attitudes
male + female	= shared responsibility for conception
responsibility	= respect for each other's rights and those of a possible child
"	= retention of personal integrity
ignorance	= excuse for failed responsibility
negligence	= must not be allowed as excuse
"	= responsibility shared
fathered/born	= neglect/indifference

Interestingly the animalistic characteristics of humans are distributed unequally with the male having a biological seeking drive and the female bearing the burden of its effects. But transformed by knowledge into human beings, they have to share equally the responsibility for their actions. So, while the processes of sexual action are different for 'male' and 'female' animals, once they become 'people', 'man' and 'woman' lose their differences as they become 'one' and share equally the responsibility for any 'neglect or indifference' about the outcome of the 'sexual union'. The role of knowledge in this moral code is central – ignorance is an excuse for failure to accept the code but reduces the agent to the sub-human state of animal motivation.

The moral code presented here does not rely on a prior religious code but it does rely on a prior system of knowledge that makes authoritative claims about the (sociological) nature of relationships, the (scientific) distinction between the human system of reproduction and some animal systems and finally about the (humanistic) nature of responsibility in human relationships.

The text is a little old-fashioned and would no doubt use different strategies to achieve a similar end today. For example, the casting of women into the role of 'chaste and chased' relies on an outdated currency, indicated by its dependency on the meaning of 'seduction'. Retaining 'sexual predatoriness' for men implies, unsupportably, that women do not also have within them a 'biological' 'seeking drive'. It is also not clear what is metaphorical about the burden of an unwanted child. The ease with which the text can be read as a moral tale rather than simply as knowledge is increased by these features which give it an historical flavour. A text addressing similar issues a decade or so earlier, or more recently, would draw on different presuppositions to exchange.

In the text cited the feature that is stressed as pertinent to deciding when to do sex is the contiguity between sex and procreation. Knowledge plays the role of separating humans from animals; humans can use their knowledge of this link to avoid it through contraception.

In an earlier period the grounding for the moral impact of knowledge would be located less in scientific knowledge and the outcome for human actors and more in religious knowledge and the code by which humans should act in accord with divine law. Actions would be judged because in human terms they would be 'wicked' or 'evil' rather than negligent or indifferent. Responsibility would be to a standard laid down within a religious doctrine of the good life, rather than to other human beings affected by one's actions.

A number of the presuppositions introduced in the text would however be tendentious today – for example, the presumptions that sex is heterosexual activity and even that heterosexual activity is necessarily linked to procreation. A major focus of the morality surrounding sexuality and when to do sex would, twenty-odd years after this text was published, be the transmission of the HIV virus. The threat of AIDS may provide a different exchange of meanings linking when to do sex with a 'mutually benefiting' marriage and to the techniques of contraception. It may also open the way for a reintroduction of religious values including homophobia. The phrase 'safe sex' would reassert a link between the technical and moral features of sexual activity.

DEAFNESS, LANGUAGE AND EDUCATION

Extract Five is taken from a statement on 'Communication and Education' issued in the summer of 1989 by the National Deaf Children's Society (NDCS). The statement is one amongst a number of documents sent to people making enquiries of the NDCS – often parents whose child has been diagnosed as deaf or hearing impaired. The document is in effect a position paper, making clear where the NDCS stands on a long-standing controversy about the use of language in the education of deaf children. The substance of the whole statement covers just over 1,000 words, of which the extract is about a third.

Extract five

Communication and education

01   Deaf children should have access to a range of
02   communication skills that will enable them to

03   make an informed choice about their
04   communication needs in later life.

05   Communication begins at birth. Good
06   communication for deaf children in the early
07   years is extremely important.

08   Communication is a two-way process. It is
09   important that people communicating with each
10   other have a common language or communication
11   may be limited.

12   Communication involves both using language and
13   understanding language. If a language cannot be
14   used or understood by deaf children, parents,
15   teachers and others, communication may be
16   limited.

Language

17   Language is not the same as speech. Language
18   can be non-verbal as well as verbal.

19   English language is the language of the
20   majority of people in Britain. English is the
21   main language of books, television, newspapers,
22   video productions and the school curriculum.
23   All deaf children should have access to the
24   full curriculum. But it should be recognised
25   that the means by which such access occurs may
26   be different for different deaf children. No
27   deaf child should be disadvantaged because of
28   this.

29   British Sign Language should be recognised as
30   the home language of some deaf children in the
31   same way that other minority languages are
32   recognised.

33   Every deaf child should have access to a
34   language environment in school which
35   complements the language environment of the
36   child's home. Children, most especially deaf
37   children, who have a restricted language
38   environment develop restricted language.

Parents and children – making choices

39	Parents and deaf children should be able to
40	make choices about communication which allow
41	the children to fulfil their potential in
42	education and enable members of the family to
43	communicate with each other.

44	No deaf child or their parents should feel
45	themselves to be so restricted in the choices
46	open to them that the child's ability to learn
47	and to communicate are limited.

48	Parents and deaf children should have access to
49	the same range of choice in communication
50	approach and education wherever they live. A
51	child brought up with one approach or in one
52	kind of school should not be disadvantaged if
53	the family has to move to another area.

54	Deaf children's communication needs can change
55	as they grow older. Wherever possible deaf
56	children themselves should be involved in the
57	choice of approach to communication and
58	education and their views listened to and
59	respected.

What is immediately striking is that this utterance is clear and unequivocal. The repeated use of similar and simply formed constructions gives the piece a clarity of purpose not characteristic of everyday exchanges. The 'statement' describes a state of affairs not a series of events or actions. It does not attempt to 'argue-the-case'; there is no sense of an alternative view of the world present in the text. Most of the sentences are 'relational' (Kress and Hodge 1979: 8) in that they establish a relationship between two things. There are two main modalities incorporating the verb 'to be' in operation – 'is' and 'should be'.

Clearly the principal subjects of the statement are 'deaf children' and in the final section of the extract 'parents and deaf children'. But they are not active agents – they do not *do* things in any of the sentences. Where verbs construct action forms these are to make deaf children *potential* actors. They should have 'access' (lines 01, 23, 25, 33, 48), that will 'enable' (lines 02, 42), be able to 'use' and 'understand' language (line 14), make 'choices' (lines 03, 40, 49, 57), be able to 'fulfil potential' (line 41), be 'involved' (line 56), be 'listened to' (line 58) and be 'respected' (line 59). They should also not be 'limited' (line 11), 'disadvantaged' (lines 27, 52), or 'restricted' (lines 37, 45).

In many of these points there is an exchange of meaning between 'deaf children' (and sometimes their parents) and a state of affairs that should exist. The power of the 'should' is that if things were not as they are, we would be able to see access and choice relating to abilities to use and understand language as part of the presupposed meaning of what it is to be deaf. The point of the statement is that the presupposition is the opposite: the meaning of being a deaf child is that these potential actions are not available. The modality of the 'should' draws on knowledge of how things are and asserts that things 'should' be different. It is not clear who the agents are who would be responsible for realizing the different state of affairs – in the absence of a specified agent those who wield power in society are implicated; government, professionals, administrators.

But why? Why should things be different? There are a set of statements in the text which deal with a more general state of affairs than the situation of deaf children. Between lines 05 and 22 a number of exchanges are made about communication and language that link it with the general state of human being. In line 05 communication is exchanged with the whole life course of human being (beginning at birth, not just with formal education, not just for the period of life when language is used). In lines 06–07 deaf children are specifically included in this process. Lines 19–22 state the dominance of English within the culture.

The problem with making sense of the text is that it is obvious – who would deny that communication is important, a two-way process, must involve a shared language, involves non-verbal as well as verbal language and that English is the dominant language in Britain? These are things that it would be reasonable to expect a casual reader to presuppose. However, someone who had been involved in multi-racial education might recognize the potential for difficulties; which language is the one to encourage a child to communicate in, from birth, in school? The text introduces this problem in line 29 by mentioning an alternative language, British Sign Language. But still it may not be obvious to the reader coming to a discourse about deafness for the first time that British Sign Language is a distinct language, as different from English in lexicon and structure as Gaelic and even more different in that it uses the visual channel exclusively and there is no spoken or written form.

What the statement does not make clear is that it arises out of many years of extreme disagreement on this topic. The presuppositions that a casual reader is likely to bring to the text are unlikely to make sense of the polemic that the utterance is engaged in. The exchanges which may seem to state the obvious do not reveal the contention which lies behind them.

For example, in lines 17 and 18 the exchange might be read as follows:

language ≠ speech
language = verbal + non-verbal

In the first exchange it is clear that speech does not fill the whole of the category language because the category also includes written language. In the second exchange the role of non-verbal communication in language is more tendentious, however, language 'can be' non-verbal in the sense that gesture and facial expression can supplement and reinforce the linguistic force and meaning of speech.

But these two exchanges refer back to an area of disagreement of much greater significance. It was not until the 1960s that linguists recognized the signing systems of deaf people as languages by demonstrating that they had the same range and diversity of expression as any language (Stokoe 1960; Friedman 1977). The tradition of linguistics had treated spoken language as the prime form of language, one which could be re-presented in written form. Until very recently it has been very difficult for deaf people to gain acceptance of sign as language (in Britain the sign system known as British Sign Language). Sign languages were seen as crude gestural systems, not capable of the subtlety of expression of spoken languages.

The NDCS statement circumvents this debate very carefully, avoiding reference to it, and avoiding room for contradiction *within the text*. Communication is set up in the first section as the priority; it is related to human beings, to deaf children and to interaction in a series of exchanges (lines 05–11). In lines 12–16 communication is exchanged with language but is not wholly equivalent with it. In lines 17–22 language is related to speech and English.

communication	≠	language
language	≠	speech
English language	=	dominant cultural language

A comparison with another position statement will begin to reveal the importance of the role of the NDCS statement in obscuring what had become a literal contradiction:

Helping deaf children to understand what is said to them and to talk themselves is always a job that takes a lot of time. You need faith that in the end many deaf children can talk and can become as normal as

possible . . . . It's up to you. Will your deaf child fit into the world of hearing people, or will he grow up as a lonely person who can't understand and talk to other people? Of course he'll grow up to live a full and happy life, because you *can* help your deaf baby to talk.
(Williams 1972: 12 – quoted in Dant and Gregory, forthcoming)

While the form is not that of a position statement in quite the same way as the NDCS extract, it was published by another organization working in the same area, the National College of Teachers of the Deaf (NCTD), addresses the same issues and was also used in advice to parents of deaf children. The difference between the organizations is not so significant as the passing of time between the two statements. In the early 1970s there was a consensus amongst professionals (doctors, specialists, educationists) that spoken English was the mode of communication to be promoted with deaf children. This was because it was the dominant language of the culture and because sign language was seen as a sub-form of language, not as effective as a means of communication.

The belief in the importance of teaching deaf children to use spoken English (often referred to as 'oralism') was very significant in determining what choices were available to deaf children and their parents in terms of advice and education. The NDCS statement is a position statement at a point when the discourse of advice is changing the presuppositions it calls on. The statement as a consequence has to be careful to avoid being too confrontational about the presuppositions that are being rejected by their absence.

The quote from the NCTD is interesting in the orientation of power in the constructions. It is the parent who is to do something, who can change states of affairs. This is partly because the utterance is directed to the parents of deaf children as advice – the orientation to the reader is different in the NDCS statement. But the reference to language and the role of communication is quite different; it is the parent's responsibility to follow a particular path of integrating the child into hearing society. There is no discussion of choice here, or enabling. The meaning of deafness in children is instead exchanged with being helped to understand speech. The process itself is exchanged with being a job, one that requires a lot of time and, in addition, faith. Communication as a category is here fully dealt with as speech, talk, hearing. These are not dealt with as aspects of language or as modes of communication comparable with others. There is a clear exchange in the second sentence:

```
deaf children  +  faith  = ability to talk
    "      "    +    "    = be as normal as possible
```

Here normality is to be created through applying knowledge to action whereas in the NDCS statement knowledge leads to the support and acceptance of difference.

CONCLUSION

In the nature of the examples chosen they are not very good at showing features of whole discourses; it is not possible to explore how repertoires operate in brief extracts. However, the use of poor health as a repertoire for talking about old age worked for the respondent in the interview in Extract One. In uttering moral prescriptions about when to do sex there may be repertoires relating sexual activity to certain types of outcome (religious judgement, procreation, life-threatening disease). These are empirical questions that are unanswerable with the material presented here. To show the effects of relexicalization, a number of succeeding utterances would need to be studied. Of course none of these examples can do any more than illustrate the analytical approach; none goes far enough or involves sufficient data to count as empirical inquiry.

What the examples have attempted to show is that the content of discourse involves utterances that exchange meanings. Presuppositions which are effective as knowledge to the participants are exchanged to redefine and redescribe the world, so altering what is known. In relation to health and ageing the development of knowledge was in relation to particular individuals. None the less, in describing their state, their subjectivity had to be exchanged with categories including health and age about which presuppositions could be made. The moral code about when to do sex involved playing off knowledge about the difference between animal reproduction and human sexual reproduction. The possession of knowledge about the effects of sexual activity and its consequences for human lives, brought with it, in this account, responsibility for those consequences. For the statement on communication and education for deaf children, a series of exchanges about the nature of communication and language set up a discursive environment, using knowledge that could be presupposed. It provided a context for a series of exchanges about how the cultural environment should be for deaf children and their parents.

In each of these examples knowledge was presupposed and then transformed through exchanging meanings, one with another. This process obscured contradictions between the complexity of the lived experience of people and the relative simplicity of the abstract statements in discourse. What an analysis of the exchange of meanings begins to show are the strategies used to construct knowledge about the world using statements about categories. The statements involve elements of meaning that are utilized and transformed through a series of exchanges. The way power is exerted to achieve knowledge effects becomes visible once the issue of the truth of a statement or group of statements is suspended and interpretation looks to discursive and social context for the origins of presuppositions and impacts of meaning.

NOTES

1 These interviews were conducted in the course of the Care for Elderly People at Home project funded by the Gloucester Health Authority and the Nuffield Provincial Hospitals Trust (see Dant *et al.* 1989).
2 In the transcription, a pause is indicated with a full stop in parentheses e.g. (.) and numbers in parentheses indicate the duration of longer pauses in seconds e.g. (1).
3 In the lists of exchanges taken from the interviews the meanings proposed by the interviewer are put in brackets to distinguish them from those originating with the respondent.
4 Taken from *Living With People* by Paul L. Buett, pages 10–15, published in London by Longman, General Studies Series (1968).

12 A future for the sociology of knowledge as discourse analysis?

The sociology of knowledge produces knowledge but it has dispensed with the usual motivations of other ways of producing knowledge. The search for 'truth' has been put to one side in favour of the less universal or enduring claims of relational knowledge, and the method of the sociology of knowledge attempts a broader view than that of a sectional groups' interests. So why should it be mobilized as a perspective and to what uses can the knowledge produced be put?

This book has argued that knowledge as a social process cannot be considered apart from other processes – ideology and discourse – that are in effect different aspects (one political, the other material) of the same process. The sociology of knowledge is the study of knowledge as a social process. Its findings contribute to the understanding of social processes: those characteristic features of human co-existence.

Within sociology, the sociology of knowledge has the role of placing knowledge in a specific relation to other concepts used in describing social processes; power, social structure, the individual agent, socialization, culture and language. It renders knowledge amenable to analysis and not something separate or above other social processes to which sociologists attend. The problem with knowledge as a sociological category is that it is in a double relation to analysis as both object and product of the activity of analysis. This leads to an unnerving requirement of reflexivity because the analyst has to recognize that whatever is said about knowledge as object may also apply to the knowledge produced by the analysis.

The sociology of knowledge is not a path to the truth and its critique neither transcends what it analyses nor modifies it to produce 'better' knowledge. It can however address and illuminate the relations of power obscured by the social processes surrounding knowledge because it suspends epistemological claims which attempt to separate knowledge production from other social processes. The relations of power become apparent through the analysis of discourse in terms of its social context, searching for the ways that knowledge claims are intertwined with social practices and social being.

This view of knowledge is, quite specifically, to take a sociological perspective. Knowledge can be considered from other perspectives – in religion and philosophy as a grasp of the pure state of being, in science as an account of the material state of the world, in information technology as a set of human skills that may be copied by machines. In everyday life, knowledge is a multi-faceted resource that the individual draws on to proceed with living. The sociology of knowledge can tolerate a much more flexible view of knowledge than these other perspectives, and indeed, it is the flexibility of knowledge in social processes that is the main problem facing empirical researchers.

As a sociological perspective then, the sociology of knowledge is not in competition with these other perspectives and is of limited relevance to them. Relationism is incompatible with essentialist views of the pure state of being and would not help the practice of the scientist or the information technologist (although the latter might use it to understand the knowledge that was to be stored in machines). For those who respond to the sociology of knowledge from within a perspective dominated by transcendent or epistemological criteria, the sociology of knowledge may feel like an irritatingly unconstructive criticism. But this is no reason for rejecting its role within a sociological perspective.

THE LIMITS OF HUMANISM

For both Mannheim and Foucault, the collapse of religion as a unifying and overarching system of knowledge is an important event in the development of the human sciences. With the loss of god's perspective as a unitary and unifying view of reality, accounted for and elaborated by the institutional structures of religions, comes the possibility of competing accounts and a knowing subject more amenable to empirical analysis. The arrival of humanism may for Foucault and others herald its end; the centring of the spirit of human essence is more vulnerable to supersession and critique than the centring of a transcendent spirit. Of course Foucault wishes to go beyond the limits of humanism:

> What I am afraid of about humanism is that it presents a certain form of our ethics as a universal model for any kind of freedom. I think that there are more secrets, more possible freedoms, and more inventions

in our future than we can imagine in humanism as it is dogmatically represented on every side of the political rainbow: the Left, the Center, the Right.

(interview in L. Martin *et al.* 1988: 15)

It is however a seriously limited view of history that considers humanism as the extant form of rationality whose limits have to be exceeded, because not everyone gave up on god's perspective. The white, western cultures of the northern hemisphere may have become increasingly secular during the twentieth century, with their focus on the needs of 'Man' (that is, the needs of some men) rather than the will of god to orient values, drive political decisions and give meaning to many individual lives. But within these cultures, religions have survived and adapted. They have retained an enormous cultural influence both through involvement in key institutions (the education and political systems, the services of the welfare state) and through continued statements within a cultural discourse on 'morality'. Even those who do not demonstrate faith or hold the central beliefs of a religion continue to recognize religious teachings on the relation between knowledge and action. The right of theologians and religious leaders to comment on how people should act and live, continues to be treated with respect.

The influence of religion as a system of knowledge has reasserted itself in the west and often in its more fundamentalist forms (for example 'born-again' Christianity). But in the rest of the world it is less clear that it ever ceased to be a dominant mode of knowledge. What is striking about religious knowledge, especially in its fundamentalist forms, is that it pre-empts the sociology of knowledge. Because all knowledge is deemed to derive from god, the claim that it is socially determined is difficult to incorporate. The transcendent nature of religious understanding means that from its perspective, studying the social context of knowledge is futile. The foundations of knowledge are, in fundamentalist versions at least, not open to debate or critique and the only relevance of social context is as a source of bias or misinformation. But the transcendent nature of religious knowledge does not prevent it from having something to say about non-religious life – secular or political activity. The all-embracing view of the major religions includes the whole of life as a religious activity. Once it is accepted that the body is a shrine, there is no escaping the purview of religion.

The process of globalization means that cultural imperialism works in both directions; not only are the ideas of the western world exported to the rest of the globe but also with immigration and the importing of cultural goods (recipes, clothes, religious practices, rugs, ornaments, 'roots' music, dance, etc.) the rest of the world begins to affect western culture. The shifts in global politics mean that the cultural continuity between peoples in different places is as likely, if not more likely, to be through knowledge of Islam, Judaism, Protestantism or Roman Catholicism than through the critical human sciences of Marx and Freud. The modernization of the means by which people, goods and ideas can be moved about the globe seriously challenges the hegemony of a culture based on the demise of the unifying world view of religion.

Even if the sociology of knowledge is founded on the emergence of the humanist sciences and the collapse of a religious perspective, it needs to readdress the role of religion as a mode by which people continue to know and live in the world.

A REFLEXIVE MOMENT

This book is not only a commentary on the process of knowledge but also a discursive utterance with its own knowledge claims. As a text it presupposes knowledge and is itself analysable as an exchange of meanings that have been uttered in a particular social context, constructed within lines of power. The presuppositions involve not only a shared vocabulary but also a shared interest in the topic. The issues of knowledge, discourse and ideology are taken to be of interest to readers, so they organize the book, form the title and are referred to frequently.

Much of the book involves exegesis of other writers' work and this locates the current text in a number of ways. It inserts this exchange of meanings in a specific relation to particular discourses within the field of social inquiry. Major works within the sociology of knowledge are, for example, referenced and cited so that the current text is clearly a 'knowing' utterance within that discourse. The references, the accounts of what other authors have said and in particular the quotations, are used as meanings to exchange in the present text, sometimes with each other, sometimes with what are apparently the author's interpretations. Not only does the exchange of meanings occur at the level of specific ideas or concepts but also at the level of an exchange between the themes of knowledge, ideology and discourse which provides the text as whole with structure. The exegetical style of much of the book and the use of references not only serves to organize the text but also to situate it in a social context. The book itself is not only an utterance but also clearly a move for 'recognition' for the author as a legitimate participant in a particular discourse. The sociology of knowledge begins to sound less disinterested when put like this; there are interests behind sounding 'academic' or disinterested.

A more worrying feature of the argument as it has been presented is that knowledge has in practice been treated as articulated in language – discourse has been dealt with only as it appears as language. Other forms of language-like communication mentioned in the Introduction (music, dance, two-and three-dimensional design, etc.) have been largely ignored. They were of course much too difficult to deal with in the space available. They might have provided a starting point for a debate about the storing, communication and application of knowledge in non-linguistic forms but knowledge has been left still sounding like ideas and thoughts represented in spoken and written language.

AN OVERVIEW

In this book I have tried to argue that the sociology of knowledge has been too summarily dismissed. Those reasons for dismissing it in the 1940s and 1950s are no longer so compelling. The threat of 'relativism', the implications of an historicist tendency, the significance of the claims for a 'free-floating' intelligentsia were all exaggerated in the attempt to defend positivist and functionalist orthodoxy. The desire for a unified system of knowledge and the attempt for a unitary theory in the social sciences has been abandoned by most people. The modernist attempt to secure the content and the method of knowledge production has been put aside in favour of a post-modernist attempt to find ways of knowing that work in the here and now. This trend towards 'anti-foundationalism', as Hekman (1986) calls it, could be seen as a product of the work undertaken by those writers who have been discussed in the book. Or it could be seen as an historical trend, not the product of their 'thought' but of the world they inhabit, its changing social and material relations.

The later view involves adopting the sociology of knowledge thesis, but whichever way this change is viewed the bogies of the sociology of knowledge no longer seem so frightening. At one time relationism could be grasped only as the thin end of the wedge of relativism – and a very destructive wedge it was thought to be. Mannheim's attempt to grasp the role of knowledge in changing social processes was perceived as no different from the sort of teleological historicism that Marx had inverted in Hegel's philosophy. The repeated but qualified comment of Alfred Weber's about the relatively unattached intelligentsia was treated as a founding principle of the sociology of knowledge which did not lay claim to a systematic epistemology.

The debate about the concepts of the sociology of knowledge and how vulnerable they are to criticism can be mounted within the sociology of knowledge. However, a related debate on Marx's account of ideology within a tradition of critical and political theory, transformed the concept to become much closer to Mannheim's usage of the term. The categorial distinction between ideology as false knowledge and science as true knowledge became unsustainable. Instead ideology emerged as a relational concept situating human beings in their social and material context. Ideology could then be seen not as a hurdle to true knowledge but as the means by which human, social beings orient themselves to each other and to the material world in which they live. It may enshrine contradictions about the relations between human beings but these are necessary to their co-existence when they have different relations to the means of production. There is no short cut to achieving 'true', non-contradictory knowledge because while the contradictions inherent in certain relations may be clarified, others enter and others remain. Knowledge cannot be effective as knowledge unless it involves contradictions.

Structuralism has tackled the apparent contradictions between the contents of myth/ideology/knowledge and the concrete world of the social group using them. Rather than seeing myth as an inadequate system of knowledge to be superseded, the structuralists took seriously the significance of the relation between myths and the existence of their users. Myths, like ideology, are not 'true' in a representational sense but they do provide an interpretation of the world that enables human beings to live in it. In them, knowledge can be seen not as revelation of the world beyond human beings but as a set of expressed relations that enable human societies to make sense of their world.

The relations are expressed at an abstract level, that of the sign, which is amenable to adaptation and transformation. Saussurean linguistics was founded on the arbitrariness of the link between the material form of a sign, its signifier, and its form as meaning, its signified. The structuralist writers attended not simply to structures of the materiality of signs (as linguistics had) but also to structures of meaning. An object of analysis emerged as 'discourse', the empirical performances in which the meaning of signs are constructed and transformed. In the field of discourse described by the later structuralists, knowledge can be seen as a social process; it is through the utterances of humans, co-ordinated and directed to similar matters, that knowledge is constructed. It has an historical dimension in that the contents of discourse always take account of what went before. Discourse is related to social practice and experience but not in a direct and seamless way. It is not 'truth' but the mode of describing the world that enables groups of people to share living in it.

The structuralist writers defined an object of study and explored some methods for analysing it but there have been other developments contributing to the analysis of knowledge and ideology as discourse. Within the sociology of science the relativism and reflexivity of Mannheim's sociology of knowledge has been rediscovered and techniques of analysing scientific knowledge as discourse have been developed. These undermine the claims to a special, true form of knowledge called 'science'. Just like other forms of knowledge, science can be shown to be socially constructed and its particular form to be related to the interests of those uttering it. The experience of studying scientific and other cultural practices sociologically has led to a focus on the content of linguistic utterances as the form in which knowledge has social effects – 'ideas', 'thought' or knowledge all have to be mediated through language.

Recent developments in the study of linguistics (although foreshadowed by the work of Voloshinov) have explored the role of social context on discourse and the role of language in bringing about ideological effects. These, together with an approach to culture which recognizes its role as ideology, contribute to a climate in which the project of the sociology of knowledge seems not only much more interesting but also much more do-able. The techniques explored in semiotic, cultural and discourse analysis all address aspects of knowledge in social process. The relationism that underlies these styles of cultural analysis, where there is no fixed system against which to judge all others, can accept that knowledge is perspectival and has to be studied in that way.

The emergence of a debate about women's knowledge has reintroduced many of the debates that surround the sociology of knowledge – the competition between perspectives, the attempt to found knowledge epistemologically, the relation between knowledge as pure abstraction and knowledge as experience. Within the debate on women's knowledge there is less desire for a unitary solution than for political progress and in this climate, the analysis of knowledge as based in the experience of different social groups becomes possible.

In Chapter 10 I have tried to pull together the separate threads of knowledge, ideology and discourse and to articulate the links – although their demarcation in earlier chapters was to some extent a textual device for handling such a broad range of material. But the task of bringing the three strands together brought out gaps in the theoretical apparatus that needed to be noted if not plugged – social being, imputation, agency, action, power and critique. The effects of translating the emerging theoretical perspective into an empirical technique was explored in

Chapter 11 and the exchange of meanings was introduced as a way of empirically analysing the process of knowledge, ideology and discourse.

A FUTURE

Empirical research in the sociology of knowledge is not applied in the sense that it cannot be directed to a specific purpose which would constrain and narrow its perspective. But this does not mean that the analyses of the sociology of knowledge cannot be useful. By providing a critique of the institutional structure of knowledge production, the sociology of knowledge can encourage a plurality of knowledge claims, limiting the aspirations of one set of claims to dominate. It is bound to make enemies and while it may also make friends, the enemies are more likely to be in positions of power – this may ensure that the sociology of knowledge is not promoted outside of the discipline and does not attract substantial research funds.

Even within sociology, the sociology of knowledge is often seen as an arcane and specialist field. It has survived within the discipline by retreating from the forefront and taking an historical and overviewing role. However, I have argued that much of the social theory that currently informs sociology is actually very concerned with knowledge and has in effect incorporated a sociology of knowledge perspective. Empirical and theoretical analyses have been produced from within the theory of ideology perspective and from within structuralism that can be seen as contributing to and developing the sociology of knowledge programme established by Mannheim. Recent work in the sociology of science, in cultural analysis and in studies of women's perspectives has incorporated an analysis of knowledge in social process and has begun to apply a relationist perspective. Clearly, there is a need to extend this incorporation of empirical studies within the sociology of knowledge to include studies of religion, art, skill, movement, and music.

The modern concern with discourse is particularly important to the sociology of knowledge – these other areas of culture need to be considered in so far as they constitute and contribute to discourse. Sociologists have always studied discourse (interviews and accounts, written texts, notes of observations) but have often sought the essence of the text and treated knowledge as something lying behind it, imperfectly represented. The approach to discourse as not representative of anything but itself, involves recognizing that knowledge is socially constructed as discourse. Discourse does not mediate transcendent essence, the essence of 'Man' or even of human being. It is the material form of a level of social interaction that, like the labour process, has a dynamic and social context much greater than the immediate situation. For this reason discourse is an appropriate object for sociological analysis; it is a form of social practice through which social cohesion and continuity is maintained. It is in the flow of discourse, the continuous exchange of meanings, that we as people, not only as sociologists, find our knowledge.

Bibliography

Abercrombie, N. (1980) *Class, Structure and Knowledge*, Oxford: Basil Blackwell.

Abercrombie, N., Hill, S. and Turner, B. (1980) *The Dominant Ideology Thesis*, London: George Allen & Unwin.

Adorno, T.W. (1967) *Prisms*, London: Neville Spearman.

Althusser, L. (1969) *For Marx*, London: Allen Lane.

Althusser, L. (1971) *Lenin and Philosophy and Other Essays*, London: New Left Books.

Althusser, L. (1976) *Essays in Self Criticism*, London: New Left Books.

Althusser, L. and Balibar, E. (1970) *Reading Capital*, London: New Left Books.

Ashcroft, R. (1981) 'Political theory and political action in Mannheim's thought', *Comparative Studies in Society and History* 23, 1: 23–50.

Ashmore, M. (1989) *The Reflexive Thesis: Wrighting Sociology of Scientific Knowledge*, Chicago and London: University of Chicago Press.

Ashmore, M., Mulkay, M. and Pinch, T. (1989) *Health and Efficiency: a Sociology of Health Economics*, Milton Keynes: Open University Press.

Atkinson, J.M. and Heritage, J. (1984) *Structures of Social Action: Studies in Conversation Analysis*, Cambridge: Cambridge University Press.

Bacon, F. (1985) *The Essays*, ed. J. Pitcher, Harmondsworth: Penguin.

Barnes, B. (1976) *Interests and the Growth of Knowledge*, London: Routledge & Kegan Paul.

Barrett, M. (1982) 'Feminism and the definition of cultural politics', in R. Brunt and C. Rowan (eds) *Feminism, Culture and Politics*, London: Lawrence & Wishart.

Barrett, M. and McIntosh, M. (1982) 'The "family wage"', in E. Whitelegg, M. Arnot, E. Bartels, V. Beechey, L. Birke, D. Leonard, S. Ruehl and M.A. Speakman (eds) *The Changing Experience of Women*, Oxford: Martin Robertson.

Barrett, M., Corrigan, P., Kuhn, A. and Wolff, J. (eds) (1979) *Ideology and Cultural Production*, London: Croom Helm.

Barth, H. (1977) *Truth and Ideology*, Berkeley, California: University of California Press.

Barthes, R. (1969) *Elements of Semiology*, London: Jonathan Cape.

Barthes, R. (1973) *Mythologies*, London: Paladin.

Barthes, R. (1975) *S/Z*, London: Jonathan Cape.

Barthes, R. (1988) *The Semiotic Challenge*, Oxford: Basil Blackwell.

Berger, P. (1970) 'Identity as a problem in the sociology of knowledge', in J.E. Curtis and J.W. Petras (eds) *The Sociology of Knowledge: A Reader*, New York: Praeger.

Berger, P. and Luckmann, T. (1971) *Social Construction of Reality*, Harmondsworth: Penguin.

Bernstein, B. (1974) *Class, Codes and Control: Volume 1: Theoretical Studies Towards a Sociology of Language*, London: Routledge & Kegan Paul.

Billig, M., Condor, S., Edwards, D., Gane, M., Middleton, D. and Radley, A. (1988) *Ideological Dilemmas: A Social Psychology of Everyday Thinking*, London: Sage.

Bloor, D. (1976) *Knowledge and Social Imagery*, London: Routledge & Kegan Paul.

Bouchier, D. (1977) 'Radical ideologies and the sociology of knowledge', *Sociology* 11: 25–46.

Boudon, R. (1971) *The Uses of Structuralism*, London: Heinemann.

Bourdieu, P. (1990) *In Other Words: Essays Towards a Reflexive Sociology*, Cambridge: Polity Press.

Brittan, A. (1989) *Masculinity and Power*, Oxford: Basil Blackwell.

Brown, B. and Cousins, M. (1980) 'The linguistic fault: the case of Foucault's archaeology', *Economy and Society* 9, 3: 251-78.

Brown, P. and Jordanova, L. (1982) 'Oppressive dichotomies: the nature/culture debate', in E. Whitelegg, M. Arnot, E. Bartels, V. Beechey, L. Birke, D. Leonard, S. Ruehl and M.A. Speakman (eds) *The Changing Experience of Women*, Oxford: Martin Robertson.

Bryant, C. (1985) *Positivism in Social Theory and Research*, London: Macmillan.

Buett, P.L. (1968) *Living with People*, General Studies Series, London: Longman.

Burton, F. and Carlen, P. (1979) *Official Discourse: On Discourse Analysis, Government Publications, Ideology and the State*, London: Routledge & Kegan Paul.

Callinicos, A. (1976) *Althusser's Marxism*, London: Pluto Press.

Callinicos, A. (1983) *Marxism and Philosophy*, Oxford: Clarendon Press.

Callinicos, A. (1987) *Making History: Agency, Structure and Change in Social Theory*, Cambridge: Polity Press.

CCCS (1976) *Resistance through Rituals*, London: Hutchinson.

CCCS (1977) *On Ideology*, London: Hutchinson.

CCCS (1980) *Culture, Media, Language*, London: Hutchinson.

Charles, N. and Kerr, M. (1988) *Women, Food and Families*, Manchester: Manchester University Press.

Child, A. (1941a) 'The problem of imputation in the sociology of knowledge', *Ethics* 51: 200–215.

Child, A. (1941b) 'The theoretical possibility of the sociology of knowledge', *Ethics* 51: 392–441.

Child, A. (1942) 'The existential determination of truth', *Ethics* 52: 153–185.

Child, A. (1944) 'The problem of imputation resolved', *Ethics* 54: 96–109.

Child, A. (1947) 'The problem of truth in the sociology of knowledge', *Ethics* 58: 18–34.

Clarke, S., Seidler, V.J., McDonnel, K., Robins, K. and Lovell, T. (1980) *One Dimensional Marxism*, London: Allison & Busby.

Clegg, S.R. (1989) *Frameworks of Power*, London: Sage.

Collins, H.M. (1981) 'What is TRASP?: the radical programme as a methodological imperative', *Philosophy of Social Science* 11: 215–24.

Collins, H. (1982) 'Special relativism – the natural attitude', *Social Studies of Science* 12: 139–43.

Collins, H. (1985) *Changing Order: Replication and Induction in Scientific Practice*, London: Sage.

Connerton, P. (ed.) (1976) *Critical Theory*, Harmondsworth: Penguin.

Corrigan, P. (1976) 'Doing nothing', in CCCS, *Resistance through Rituals*, London: Hutchinson.

Coser, L.A. (1971) Review of 'The Sociology of Knowledge: A Reader', by J.E. Curtis and J.W. Petras (eds) in *Social Forces* 49: 641.

Coulthard, M. (1977) *An Introduction to Discourse Analysis*, London: Longman.

Cousins, M. (1978) 'The logic of deconstruction', *Oxford Literary Review* 3, 2: 70–7.

Coward, R. (1984) *Female Desire*, St Albans: Paladin.

Curtis, J.E. and Petras, J.W. (1970) *The Sociology of Knowledge: A Reader*, New York: Praeger.

Dant, T. and Gregory, S. (forthcoming) *The Social Construction of Deafness*, Unit 8 in 'Social Issues in Deafness' (D251), Milton Keynes: Open University (Course Unit).

Dant, T., Carley, M., Gearing, B., and Johnson, M. (1989) *Co-ordinating Care: The Final Report of the Caring for Elderly People at Home Project*, Milton Keynes: Open University (mimeo).

De Gré, G. (1970) 'The sociology of knowledge and the problem of truth', in J.E. Curtis and J.W. Petras (eds) *The Sociology of Knowledge: A Reader*, New York: Praeger.

Derrida, J. (1973) *Speech and Phenomena*, Evanston, Illinois: Northwestern University Press.

Derrida, J. (1976) *Of Grammatology*, London: Johns Hopkins University Press.

Derrida, J. (1978) *Writing and Difference*, London: Routledge & Kegan Paul.

Derrida, J. (1981) *Dissemination*, London: Athlone Press.

van Dijk, T.A. (1988) 'Social cognition, social power and social discourse', *Text* 8, 1–2: 129–57.

Dreyfus, H. and Rabinow, P. (1982) *Michel Foucault: Beyond Structuralism and Hermeneutics*, Chicago: University of Chicago Press.

Eco, U. (1977) *A Theory of Semiotics*, London: Macmillan Press.

Eriksson, B. (1975) *Problems of an Empirical Sociology of Knowledge*, Stockholm: Almqvist & Wiksell.

Foucault, M. (1967) *Madness and Civilization*, London: Tavistock.

Foucault, M. (1970) *The Order of Things: An Archaeology of the Human Sciences*, London: Tavistock.

Foucault, M. (1971) 'Orders of discourse', *Social Science Information* X, 2: 7–30.

Foucault, M. (1972) *The Archaeology of Knowledge*, London: Tavistock.

Foucault, M. (1977) *Language, Counter-Memory and Practice*, ed. D. Bouchard, Harmondsworth: Penguin.

Foucault, M. (1979a) *The History of Sexuality, Volume 1: An Introduction*, London: Allen Lane.

Foucault, M. (1979b) *Discipline and Punish: The Birth of the Prison*, Harmondsworth: Penguin.

Foucault, M. (1980) *Power/Knowledge: Selected Interviews and Other Writings 1972–1977*, ed. C. Gordon, Brighton: Harvester Press.

Foucault, M. (1982) 'The subject and power', afterword to H. Dreyfus and P. Rabinow, *Michel Foucault: Beyond Structuralism and Hermeneutics*, Chicago: University of Chicago Press.

Fowler R., Hodge, R., Kress, G., and Trew, T. (1979) *Language and Control*, London: Routledge & Kegan Paul.

Fraser, N. (1989) *Unruly Practices: Power, Discourse and Gender in Contemporary Social Theory*, Cambridge: Polity Press.

Friedman, L. (1977) 'Formational properties of American sign language', in L. Friedman (ed.) *On the Other Hand: New Perspectives in American Sign Language*, New York: Academic Books.

Frisby, D. (1983) *The Alienated Mind*, London: Heinemann.

Frow, J. (1985) 'Discourse and power', *Economy and Society* 14, 2: 193–214.

Gandy, R. (1973) '"Structure" in mathematics', in D. Robey (ed.) *Structuralism*, Oxford: Clarendon Press.

Geras, N. (1977) 'Althusser's Marxism: an assessment', in New Left Review (eds) *Western Marxism, A Critical Reader*, London: New Left Books.

Giddens, A. (1979) *Central Problems in Social Theory: Action, Structure and Contradiction in Social Analysis*, London: Macmillan.

Giddens, A. (1982) 'Labour and interaction', in J.B. Thompson and D. Held (eds) *Habermas: Critical Debates*, London: Macmillan.

Giddens, A. (1984) *The Constitution of Society: Outline of the Theory of Structuration*, Cambridge: Polity Press.

Giglioli, P.P. (ed.) (1972) *Language in Social Context*, Harmondsworth: Penguin.

Gilbert, G.N. and Mulkay, M.J. (1981) 'Contexts of scientific discourse: social accounting in experimental papers', in K. Knorr, R. Krohn and R. Whitley (eds) *The Social Process of Investigation*, Dordrecht: Reidel.

Gilbert, G.N. and Mulkay, M.J. (1982) 'Warranting scientific belief', *Social Studies of Science* 12: 383–408.

Gilbert, G.N. and Mulkay, M.J. (1984) *Opening Pandora's Box: A Sociological Analysis of Scientists' Discourse*, Cambridge: Cambridge University Press.

Goff, T.W. (1980) *Marx and Mead: Contributions to a Sociology of Knowledge*, London: Routledge & Kegan Paul.

Goldmann, L. (1964) *The Hidden God*, London: Routledge & Kegan Paul.

Goldmann, L. (1969) *The Human Sciences and Philosophy*, London: Jonathan Cape.

Goldmann, L. (1977) *Cultural Creation in Modern Society*, Oxford: Basil Blackwell.

Graham, H. (1984) 'Surveying through stories', in C. Bell and H. Roberts (eds) *Social Researching: Politics, Problems, Practice*, London: Routledge & Kegan Paul.

Graham, H. and Oakley, A. (1982) 'Competing ideologies of reproduction: medical and maternal perspectives on pregnancy', in E. Whitelegg, M. Arnot, E. Bartels, V. Beechey, L. Birke, D. Leonard, S. Ruehl and M.A. Speakman (eds) *The Changing Experience of Women*, Oxford: Martin Robertson.

Grant, J. (1987) 'I feel therefore I am: a critique of female experience as the basis for a feminist epistemology', in M.J. Falco (ed.) *Feminism and Epistemology: Approaches to Research in Women and Politics*, New York: Haworth Press.

Grunwald, E. (1970) 'The sociology of knowledge and epistemology', in J.E. Curtis and J.W. Petras (eds) *The Sociology of Knowledge: A Reader*, New York: Praeger.

Gupta, D. (1982) 'Paradigms and discourses: new frontiers in the sociology of knowledge', *Sociological Bulletin* 31, 1: 1–23.

Gurvitch, G. (1971) *The Social Frameworks of Knowledge*, Oxford: Basil Blackwell.

Habermas, J. (1970a) 'On systematically distorted communication', *Inquiry* 13: 205–18.

Habermas, J. (1970b) 'Toward a theory of communicative competence', *Inquiry* 13: 360–375.

Habermas, J. (1971) *Toward a Rational Society,* London: Heinemann.

Habermas, J. (1972) *Knowledge and Human Interests*, London: Heinemann.

Habermas, J. (1974) *Theory and Practice*, London: Heinemann.

Habermas, J. (1976) *Legitimation Crisis*, London: Heinemann.

Habermas, J. (1979) *Communication, Evolution and Society*, London: Heinemann.

Habermas, J. (1984) *The Theory of Communicative Action Volume One: Reason and the Rationalization of Society*, Boston, Massachusetts: Beacon Press.

Habermas, J. (1987a) *The Theory of Communicative Action Volume Two: Lifeworld and System: A Critique of Functionalist Reason*, Cambridge: Polity Press.

Habermas, J. (1987b) *The Philosophical Discourse of Modernity: Twelve Lectures*, Cambridge: Polity.

Hall, S. (1977) 'Culture, the media and the "Ideological Effect"', in J. Curran, M. Gurevitch and J. Woollacott (eds) *Mass Communications and Society*, Milton Keynes: Open University Press.

Halliday, M.A. K. (1978) *Language as Social Semiotic: The Interpretation of Language and Meaning*, London: Edward Arnold.

Hamilton, P. (1974) *Knowledge and Social Structure*, London: Routledge & Kegan Paul.

Harris, Z. (1952) 'Discourse analysis', *Language* 28: 1–30.

Hartung, F. (1952) 'Problems of the sociology of knowledge', *Philosophy of Science* 19: 17–32.

Hebdige, D. (1988) *Hiding in the Light: On Images and Things*, London and New York: Routledge.

Hekman, S. (1986) *Hermeneutics and the Sociology of Knowledge*, Cambridge: Polity Press.

Hekman, S. (1987) 'The feminization of epistemology: gender and the social sciences', in M.J. Falco (ed.) *Feminism and Epistemology: Approaches to Research in Women and Politics*, New York: Haworth Press.

Hinshaw, V.G. (1973) 'The epistemological relevance of Mannheim's sociology of knowledge', in G. Remmling (ed.) *Towards the Sociology of Knowledge*, London: Routledge & Kegan Paul.

Hirst, P.Q. (1976) 'Althusser and the theory of ideology', *Economy and Society* 5: 385–412.

Hirst, P.Q. (1979) *On Law and Ideology*, London: Macmillan.

Hjelmslev, L. (1953) *Prolegomena to a Theory of Language*, Bloomington, Indiana: Indiana University Press.

Hodge, R. and Kress, G. (1988) *Social Semiotics*, London: Polity Press.

Hollis, M. (1982) 'The social destruction of reality', in M. Hollis and S. Lukes (eds) *Rationality and Relativism*, Oxford: Basil Blackwell.

Holzner, B. (1972) *Reality Construction in Society*, Cambridge, Massachusetts: Schenkman.

Horkheimer, M. (1972) *Critical Theory: Selected Essays*, New York: Seabury Press.

Horowitz, I.L. (1961) *Philosophy, Science and the Sociology of knowledge*, Westport, Connecticut: Greenwood Press.

Horton, R. and Finnegan, R. (eds) (1973) *Modes of Thought: Essays on Thinking in Western and Non-Western Societies*, London: Faber & Faber.

House, J.D. (1977) 'In defence of Karl Mannheim: the sociology of knowledge, epistemology, and methodology', *Sociological Analysis and Theory* 7: 207–25.

Jay, M. (1974) 'The Frankfurt School's critique of Karl Mannheim and the sociology of knowledge', *Telos* 20: 72–89.

Keller, E. Fox (1989) 'Holding the center of feminist theory', *Women's Studies International Forum* 12, 3: 313–18.

Kettler, D. (1967) 'Sociology of knowledge and moral philosophy', *Political Science Quarterly* 82: 399–426.

Kettler, D. (1975) 'Political theory, ideology, sociology: the question of Karl Mannheim', *Cultural Hermeneutics* 3, 1: 70–80.

Kettler, D., Meja, V., and Stehr, N. (1984) *Karl Mannheim*, London: Tavistock.

Knorr-Cetina, K. (1981) *The Manufacture of Knowledge; An Essay on the Constructivist and Contextual Nature of Science*, Oxford: Pergamon Press.

Knorr-Cetina, K.D. and Mulkay M.J. (eds) (1983) *Science Observed: Contemporary Analytical Perspectives*, London: Sage.

Kress, G. and Hodge, R. (1979) *Language and Ideology*, London: Routledge & Kegan Paul.

Kristeva, J. (1973) 'The semiotic activity', *Screen* 14, 1/2: 25–39.

Kuhn, A. (1980) *Women's Pictures*, London: Routledge & Kegan Paul.

Lacan, J. (1968) *Speech and Language in Psychoanalysis*, London: Johns Hopkins University Press.

Lacan, J. (1970) 'Of structure as an inmixing of an otherness prerequisite to any subject whatever', in R. Macksey and E. Donato (eds) *The Languages of Criticism and the Sciences of Man*, London: Johns Hopkins University Press.

Lacan, J. (1977) *Ecrits*, London: Tavistock.

Laclau, E. (1977) *Politics and Ideology in Marxist Theory*, London: New Left Books.

Langholz Leymore, V. (1975) *Hidden Myth: Structure and Symbolism in Advertising*, London: Heinemann.

Larrain, J. (1979) *The Concept of Ideology*, London: Hutchinson.

Latour, B. and Woolgar, S. (1979) *Laboratory Life: The Social Construction of Scientific Facts*, London: Sage.

Lemert, C. and Gillan, G. (1982) *Michel Foucault: Social Theory as Transgression*, New York: Columbia University Press.

Lévi-Strauss, C. (1966) *The Savage Mind*, London: Weidenfeld & Nicolson.

Lévi-Strauss, C. (1968) *Structural Anthropology*, Harmondsworth: Penguin.

Lévi-Strauss, C. (1970) *The Elementary Structures of Kinship*, London: Tavistock.

Lichtheim, G. (1967) *The Concept of Ideology and Other Essays*, New York: Random House.

Loader, C. (1985) *The Intellectual Development of Karl Mannheim: Culture, Politics and Planning*, Cambridge: Cambridge University Press.

Longing, H. (1989) 'Feminist critiques of rationality: critques of science or philosophy of science?', *Women's Studies International Forum* 12, 3: 261–69.

Lukács, G. (1971) *History and Class Consciousness*, London: Merlin Press.
Lukes, S. (1974) *Power: A Radical View*, London: Macmillan.
Lyotard, J.-F. (1984) *The Postmodern Condition: A Report on Knowledge*, Manchester: Manchester University Press.
Macksey, R. and Donato, E. (eds) (1970) *The Languages of Criticism and the Sciences of Man*, London: Johns Hopkins University Press.
Mcdonagh, R. (1977) 'Ideology as false consciousness: Lukács', in CCCS (eds) *On Ideology*, London: Hutchinson.
McRobbie, A. (1982) '*Jackie*: an ideology of adolescent femininity', in B. Waites, T. Bennett and G. Martin (eds) *Popular Culture: Past and Present*, London: Croom Helm.
Mandel, E. (1968) *Marxist Economic Theory*, London: Merlin Press.
Mannheim, K. (1922) *Über das Eigenart Kultursoziologischer Erkenntnis*, unpublished manuscript, trans. and quoted in Frisby 1983.
Mannheim, K. (1936) *Ideology and Utopia*, London: Routledge & Kegan Paul.
Mannheim, K. (1940) *Man and Society in an Age of Reconstruction*, London: Routledge & Kegan Paul.
Mannheim, K. (1943) *Diagnoses of Our Time*, London: Routledge & Kegan Paul.
Mannheim, K. (1952) *Essays on the Sociology of Knowledge*, London: Routledge & Kegan Paul.
Mannheim, K. (1982) *Structures of Thinking*, London: Routledge & Kegan Paul.
Mannheim, K. (1985) *Conservatism*, London: Routledge & Kegan Paul.
Maquet, J. (1973) *The Sociology of Knowledge*, Westport, Connecticut: Greenwood Press.
Marcuse, H. (1972) *One Dimensional Man*, London: Abacus.
Martin, L., Gutman, H. and Hutton, P. (eds) (1988) *Technologies of the Self: A Seminar with Michel Foucault*, London: Tavistock.
Martin, R. (1977) *The Sociology of Power*, London: Routledge & Kegan Paul.
Marx, K. (1973) *Grundrisse: Foundations of the Critique of Political Economy*, Harmondsworth: Penguin.
Marx, K. and Engels, F. (1968) *Selected Works*, London: Lawrence & Wishart.
Marx, K. and Engels, F. (1974) *The German Ideology* (students' edition), London: Lawrence & Wishart.
Meja, V. (1975) 'The sociology of knowledge and the critique of ideology', *Cultural Hermeneutics* 3, 1: 57–68.
Mepham, J. (1979) 'The theory of ideology in Capital', in J. Mepham and D.-H. Reuben (eds) *Issues in Marxist Philosophy Vol. III*, Brighton: Harvester Press.
Merton, R.K. (1957) *Social Theory and Social Structure*, Second edn, New York: Free Press.
Mills, C. Wright (1940) 'Methodological consequences of the sociology of knowledge', *American Journal of Sociology* 46: 316–30.
Mukarovsky, J. (1977) 'Art as a semiotic fact' in J. Burbank and P. Steiner, *Structure, Sign and Function*, London: Yale University Press.
Mulkay, M.J. (1979) *Science and the Sociology of Knowledge*, London: George Allen & Unwin.
Mulkay, M.J. (1985) *The Word and the World: Explorations in the Form of Sociological Analysis*, London: George Allen & Unwin.
Mulkay, M.J. and Gilbert, G.N. (1981) 'Putting philosophy to work: Karl Popper's influence on scientific practice', *Philosophy of the Social Sciences* 11: 389–407.

244 *Knowledge, ideology and discourse*

Mulkay, M.J. and Gilbert, G.N. (1982a) 'Accounting for error: how scientists construct their social world when they account for correct and incorrect belief', *Sociology* 16: 165–83.

Mulkay, M.J. and Gilbert, G.N., (1982b) 'Joking apart: some recommendations concerning the analysis of scientific culture', *Social Studies of Science* 12: 585–613.

Mulkay, M.J. and Gilbert, G.N. (1982c) 'What is the ultimate question? Some remarks in defence of the analysis of scientific discourse', *Social Studies of Science* 12: 309–19.

Mulkay, M.J., Potter, J. and Yearley, S. (1983) 'Why an analysis of scientific discourse is needed', in K. Knorr-Cetina and M.J. Mulkay (eds) *Science Observed: Contemporary Analytical Perspectives*, London: Sage.

NDCS (1989) *Communication and Education*, pamphlet, London: National Deaf Children's Society.

Neisser, H. (1965) *On the Sociology of Knowledge*, New York: James H. Heineman.

Oakley, A. (1981) 'Interviewing women: a contradiction in terms', in H. Roberts (ed.) *Doing Feminist Research*, London: Routledge & Kegan Paul.

Parsons, T. (1967) *Sociological Theory and Modern Society*, New York: Free Press.

Pateman, T. (1980) *Language, Truth and Politics: Towards a Radical Theory for Communication*, Lewes: Jean Stroud.

Pêcheux, M. (1982) *Language, Semantics and Ideology: Stating the Obvious*, London: Macmillan.

Piaget, J. (1971) *Structuralism*, London: Routledge & Kegan Paul.

Popper, K. (1957) *The Poverty of Historicism*, London: Routledge & Kegan Paul.

Popper, K. (1966) *The Open Society and its Enemies: II Hegel and Marx*, London: Routledge & Kegan Paul.

Popper, K. (1979) *Objective Knowledge*, Oxford: Clarendon Press.

Potter, J. (1984) 'Flexibility, testability; Kuhnian values in psychological discourse concerning theory choice', *Philosophy of the Social Sciences* 14: 303–30.

Potter, J. and Wetherall, M. (1987) *Discourse and Social Psychology: Beyond Attitudes and Behaviour*, London: Sage.

Potter, J., Stringer, P. and Wetherall, M. (1984) *Social Texts and Contexts: Literature and Psychology*, London: Routledge & Kegan Paul.

Rasmussen, D.M. (1975) 'The symbolism of Marx: from alienation to fetishism', *Cultural Hermeneutics* 3, 1: 41–55.

Remmling, G. (1973) *Towards the Sociology of Knowledge*, London: Routledge & Kegan Paul.

de Saussure, F. (1974) *Course in General Linguistics*, London: Fontana.

von Schelting, A. (1936) Review of 'Ideologie und Utopie', *American Sociological Review* 1: 664–74.

Scott, A. (1988) 'Imputing beliefs: a controversy in the sociology of knowledge', *Sociological Review* 36, 1: 31–56.

Shmueli, E. (1977) 'Objectivity and presuppositions: a re-evaluation of Karl Mannheim's sociology of knowledge', *Social Science and Social Research* 62, 1: 99–112.

Shotter, J. (1989) 'Social accountability and the social construction of "You"', in J. Shotter and K. Gergen, *Texts of Identity*, London: Sage.

Silverman, D. (1987) *Communication and Medical Practice: Social Relations in the Clinic*, London: Sage.

Silverman, D. and Torode, B. (1980) *The Material Word*, London: Routledge & Kegan Paul.

Simmonds, A.P. (1975) 'Mannheim's sociology of knowledge as a hermeneutic method', *Cultural Hermeneutics* 3, 1: 81–103.

Simmonds, A.P. (1978) *Karl Mannheim's Sociology of Knowledge*, Oxford: Clarendon Press.

Simmons, A. and Stehr, N. (1981) 'Language and the growth of knowledge in sociology', *Social Science Information* 20, 4/5: 703–41.

Smith, D. (1987) 'Women's perspective as a radical critique of sociology', in S. Harding (ed.) *Feminism and Methodology*, Milton Keynes: Open University Press, and Bloomington and Indianapolis: Indiana University Press.

Smith, D. (1988) *The Everyday World as Problematic: A Feminist Sociology*, Milton Keynes: Open University Press.

Sperber, D. (1979) 'Claude Lévi-Strauss', in J. Sturrock (ed.) *Structuralism and Since*, Oxford: Oxford University Press.

Spivak, G.C. (1976) Translator's preface to J. Derrida, *Of Grammatology*, London: Johns Hopkins University Press.

Stark, W. (1958) *The Sociology of Knowledge*, London: Routledge & Kegan Paul.

Stehr, N. (1981) 'The magic triangle: in defence of a general sociology of knowledge', *Philosophy of the Social Sciences* 11: 225–9.

Stehr, N. and Meja, V. (eds) (1984) *Society and Knowledge*, London: Transaction Books.

Stern, G. (1930) 'Über die sog. "Seinsverbundenheit" des Bewusstseins', *Archiv für Socialwissenschaft* 64: 492–509, trans. and quoted in Frisby 1983.

Stokoe, W. (1960) 'Sign language and structure: an outline of the visual communication system of the American deaf', *Studies in Linguistics: Occasional Papers 8*, Buffalo, NY: University of Buffalo.

Stubbs, M. (1983) *Discourse Analysis*, Oxford: Basil Blackwell.

Sturrock, J. (ed.) (1979) *Structuralism and Since*, Oxford: Oxford University Press.

Sumner, C. (1979) *Reading Ideologies*, London: Academic Press.

Sydie, R.A. (1987) *Natural Women, Cultured Men: A Feminist Perspective on Sociological Theory*, Milton Keynes: Open University Press.

Therborn, G. (1980) *The Ideology of Power and the Power of Ideology*, London: Verso/New Left Books.

Therborn, G. (1984) 'New questions of subjectivity', *New Left Review*, 143: 97–107.

Thompson, J.B. (1984) *Studies in the Theory of Ideology*, Cambridge: Polity Press.

Ungerson, C. (1985) *Policy is Personal: Sex Gender and Informal Care*, London: Tavistock.

Voloshinov, V.N. (1973) *Marxism and the Philosophy of Language*, London: Seminar Press.

Wagner, H. (1952) 'Mannheim's historicism', *Social Research* 19: 300–21.

Wetherell, M. and Potter, J. (1989) 'Narrative characters and accounting for violence', in J. Shotter and K. Gergen (eds) *Texts of Identity*, London: Sage.

Wilden, A. (1972) *System and Structure*, London: Tavistock.

Williams, K.H. (1972) *You CAN Help Your Deaf Baby*, London: National College of Teachers of the Deaf.

Williams, R. (1981) *Culture*, Glasgow: Fontana.

Williamson, J. (1978) *Decoding Advertisements*, London: Marion Boyars.

Williamson, J. (1985) *Consuming Passions: The Dynamics of Popular Culture*, London: Marion Boyars.

Willis, P.E. (1978) *Profane culture*, London: Routledge & Kegan Paul.

Woolgar, S. (1981) 'Interests and explanation in the social study of science', *Social Studies of Science* 11, 3: 365–94.

Woolgar, S. (ed.) (1988) *Knowledge and Reflexivity: New Frontiers in the Sociology of Knowledge*, London and Beverly Hills: Sage.

Znaniecki, F. (1970) 'Sociology and theory of knowledge', in J.E. Curtis and J.W. Petras (eds) *The Sociology of Knowledge: A Reader*, New York: Praeger.

Name index

Subject index

action 58–9, 70, 90, 119, 159, 160, 174, 179, 195, 198, 201, 208, 214, 234; actionals 160; communicative 76, 89, 91–3, 95–8, 190; and discourse 133; discursive 84, 202; and emancipation 89; and experience 87; and knowledge 201–4; individual actions 83; purposive-rational 93; scientists' 143, 148, 150, 152
actions as signs 108
agency 8, 49, 52, 122, 151, 159, 161, 193, 196–7, 234; and consensus 97; economic agents 82; interpreting agents 110; and power 198–201; textual 151–3
anthropology 101, 105, 106, 118, 192; cultural 103; structural 102–3
anti-foundationalism 178, 190, 232
archaeological method 125, 130

base/superstructure 47, 67–8, 77–8
binary oppositions 103, 138, 170

the church 12–13, 31, 82
class 20, 31, 47, 60, 66, 69–70, 73, 81–2, 156, 182, 187, 197; consciousness 68–73, 76, 96; domination 81–2, 86; interests 66, 189; message 172; subjects 189; system 76
contradictions 66, 72, 74, 77, 78, 82, 87, 89, 163, 169, 172, 174, 182, 184, 189–92, 207, 224, 233; of capital 92; in the conditions of existence 88; in myths 106

critical rationalism 37, 54
critical theory 48–9, 69, 72, 76, 85, 87–9, 189, 205
critique 5, 34, 55, 67, 72, 76, 85–6, 91, 94, 98, 188, 192, 204–7, 234; and deconstruction 137–8; of epistemology 187; feminist critique 172–3, 175, 177; gendered 124; of metaphysics of presence 135, 206; of political economy 191; of rationality 179; and resistance 133; of the sign 101, 136, 138; and transgression 125; of the will to truth 193
culture: consumption culture 86; cultural artefacts 108; cultural codes 115; cultural forms 118, 208; cultural ISA 81; cultural norms 185; human cultures 102; as ideology 165–8; and the lifeworld 97; mass culture 85; the sociology of 23, 105; as the store of knowledge 190; subcultures 167–8; transition from nature to 107

deafness 220–6
decentring of the subject 123, 124
deconstruction 135–6, 193, 205
dialectic 87, 189; dialectical relations of the subject 89–91; of the sign 154; with the 'other' 123
dilemmas 163
discourse 6–8, 25, 31, 45, 68, 83, 95, 101, 115, 117–18, 129–30, 140, 155–7, 161, 167, 180, 182, 185, 192–5, 199, 205, 207–9, 215, 225,